Culture, Mind, and Society

The Book Series of the Society for Psychological Anthropology

The Society for Psychological Anthropology—a section of the American Anthropology Association—and Palgrave Macmillan dedicated to publishing innovative research in culture and psychology that illuminates the workings of the human mind within the social, cultural, and political contexts that shape thought, emotion, and experience. As anthropologists seek to bridge gaps between ideation and emotion or agency and structure and as psychologists, psychiatrists, and medical anthropologists search for ways to engage with cultural meaning and difference, this interdisciplinary terrain is more active than ever.

Series Editor

Alexander Laban Hinton, Department of Anthropology, Rutgers University, Newark

Editorial Board

Linda Garro, Department of Anthropology, University of California, Los Angeles

Catherine Lutz, Department of Anthropology, University of North Carolina, Chapel Hill

Peggy Miller, Departments of Psychology and Speech Communication, University of Illinois, Urbana-Champaign

Robert Paul, Department of Anthropology, Emory University

Bradd Shore, Department of Anthropology, Emory University

Carol Worthman, Department of Anthropology, Emory University

Titles in the Series

Adrie Kusserow, *American Individualisms: Child Rearing and Social Class in Three Neighborhoods*

Naomi Quinn, editor, *Finding Culture in Talk: A Collection of Methods*

Anna Mansson McGinty, *Becoming Muslim: Western Women's Conversion to Islam*

Roy D'Andrade, *A Study of Personal and Cultural Values: American, Japanese, and Vietnamese*

Steven M. Parish, *Subjectivity and Suffering in American Culture: Possible Selves*

Elizabeth A. Throop, *Psychotherapy, American Culture, and Social Policy: Immoral Individualism*

Victoria Katherine Burbank, *An Ethnography of Stress: The Social Determinants of Health in Aboriginal Australia*

Karl G. Heider, *The Cultural Context of Emotion: Folk Psychology in West Sumatra*

Jeannette Marie Mageo, *Dreaming Culture: Meanings, Models, and Power in U.S. American Dreams*

Dreaming Culture

MEANINGS, MODELS, AND POWER IN U.S. AMERICAN DREAMS

Jeannette Marie Mageo

First published in 2011 by
PALGRAVE MACMILLAN®
in the United States—a division of St. Martin's Press LLC,
175 Fifth Avenue, New York, NY 10010.

Where this book is distributed in the UK, Europe and the rest of the world,
this is by Palgrave Macmillan, a division of Macmillan Publishers Limited,
registered in England, company number 785998, of Houndmills,
Basingstoke, Hampshire RG21 6XS.

Palgrave Macmillan is the global academic imprint of the above companies
and has companies and representatives throughout the world.

Palgrave® and Macmillan® are registered trademarks in the United States,
the United Kingdom, Europe and other countries.

ISBN: 978–0–230–33735–0

Library of Congress Cataloging-in-Publication Data

Mageo, Jeannette Marie.
    Dreaming culture : meanings, models, and power in U.S. American
dreams / Jeannette Marie Mageo.
        p. cm.—(Culture, mind and society)
        ISBN 978–0–230–33735–0 (hardback)
        1. Dreams—United States—Psychological aspects. 2. Dream
interpretation—United States. I. Title.

BF 1078.M26 2011
154.6'30973—dc22   2011015474

A catalogue record of the book is available from the British Library.

Design by Newgen Imaging Systems (P) Ltd., Chennai, India.

First edition: November 2011

10 9 8 7 6 5 4 3 2 1

Printed in the United States of America.

Previous Publications

Dreaming and the Self: New Perspectives on Subjectivity, Identity, and Emotion. 2003.

Power and the Self. Edited volume. 2002.

Cultural Memory: Reconfiguring History and Identity in the Postcolonial Pacific. Edited volume. 2001.

Theorizing Self in Samoa: Emotions, Genders, and Sexualities. 1998.

Spirits in Culture, History, and Mind. Coedited with Alan Howard. 1996.

Contents

List of Tables   ix

Acknowledgments   xi

1   Introduction: Dreaming Cultural Models   1
2   Narrative Spectrums and Dreaming the
    U.S. American Family   23
3   Cultural Complexes and Boyfriend/Girlfriend Dreams   59
4   Holographic Dreaming and "Moving On" in the U.S.A.   93
5   U.S. Traveling Self-Models   123
6   Dreams as Cultural Remembering   161

Appendix A: Dreamers   173

Appendix B: Glossary   175

Appendix C: Instructions   177

Notes   181

References Cited   189

Index   209

Tables

1	Exercises, Analyses, and Models	14
2	Dream Data	15
3	Intertexts and Family Models	29
4	Boyfriend/Girlfriends and Choice-as-agency	61
5	Missing Pieces and Moving On	98
6	Recurrent Car Dream Features	127
7	Car Dreams Features and Variants	135
8	Models and Schemas Summary	169

Acknowledgments

I thank Stanley P. Smith for reading this manuscript many times and for his many useful editorial suggestions. I thank my former research assistant, Kristina Cantin, for helping me reflect on the implications of my model of dreaming for well-being, for bringing numerous additional sources to my attention, for her careful computations in Chapter 5, and for her editorial suggestions. I thank Ingrid E. Josephs for her inspiring commentary on my 2002 Cultural and Psychology article on intertextuality and the dream. I thank Janet Keller for securing me excellent comments on an early article-version of Chapter 5 and my 2006 Publishing and Professional Communication class for their comments on an early version of this chapter. I thank Thomas Csordas for suggesting that I saw dreams as a transitional realm in his comments on my paper, "Dream Stages," delivered at the tenth biennial meetings of the Society for Psychological Anthropology (2007) at Manhattan Beach, California. I also thank Alex Hinton who sheparded this book through the review process. Lastly, I thank the many undergraduate students who contributed dreams and analyses to my study.

Chapter 1

Introduction:
Dreaming Cultural Models

Dreams seem the most private territory of experience. More often than not, emerging from a warm, sleepy drowse, we see them as ephemeral traces just at the horizon of our inner eye, which may vanish inward at the ringing of a clock or a phone that recalls us to normal wakefulness. Yet as subjective and fleeting as they appear, dreams have a vital public aspect: they are a space in which we practice, consider, question, and adapt cultural models.

This theory of the dream, developed and illustrated throughout this book, permits me to do something new: to write an ethnography based primarily on dream data. Why might one want to write a "dream ethnography"? By revealing cultural models, along with their tensions, ambiguities, and contradictions, as well as people's ambivalent and complicated relations with them, dreams offer unique insight into cultural psychologies. Assessing models through dreams, moreover, is at least a methodological addition to and possibly a methodological advance in our ability to discover cultural models and their complex meanings for individuals. This assertion raises a second question. If dreams are a "royal road" into cultural psychology, a space where one hears the fractious dialogues among discrepant voices that always surround a cultural model, why do so many contemporary ethnographies neglect them? There are problems with collecting reliable dream data that have discouraged psychological anthropologists, problems to which this book poses solutions, but first, let me define my terms.

Definitions of schemas and models vary,[1] but here I take a model to be a complex set of ideas about a domain of experience, composed of shared, interrelated schemas, while schemas are simple mental representations that one can hold in short-term memory (see D'Andrade 1995:151–181). Thus, "I am independent," is a common self-schema in the United States: a shared mental representation of the self that the person can easily remember and discuss. Americans also have a cultural model of the self as a free individual; this is a complex idea that includes many lower-order schemas: for example, a person should be self-directed, each person is unique, the true self is within, merit trumps social status, and so forth. While people can tell you about their schemas, often they are less articulate about models. One might conceive of models as master plans for how to live in a particular culture; there are models for all cultural domains, from navigation to popular games (Shore 1996, D'Andrade 1995). While all models probably have implications for cultural psychology, my focus here is on models that pertain to it directly, such as models of relationships, agency, gender, sex, and self.

Psychologists distinguish between rapid-eye-movement (REM) dreams and non-REM dreams. REM dreams are those that we are most likely to remember and are the dreams of which I speak in this volume. REM dreams, in my view, are most often about disturbing instances when people's models fail to help them; this is why dreamers experience negative feelings much more frequently than positive ones.[2] Models falter for predictable reasons.

First, models can be representationlly deficient. Building on Bruner's work (Bruner et al. 1956:12), Levy says that categories in many cultures underrepresent some emotions: they are "hypocognized" (1973:324). When Tahitians, for example, experience something akin to what English speakers would call "sadness," they can only say they are "disturbed" (Levy 1984:219). Levy tells of a Tahitian young man who is sad after his woman and child leave for another island; because he has no category for this emotion, he concludes that he is ill (1973:324). According to Levy, people relegate undercoded emotions to the body, art, and dreams (1984:219, 225; 1973:324). Dreams, I hold, are not about emotions per se, but about all experiences that do not fit cultural models—experiences that affect us physically and emotionally, in part, because we lack the means to order and articulate them.[3]

Second, rather than genuinely forwarding individuals' interests, models may resemble, to differing degrees, what Marcuse (1955) calls performance principles. Performance principles are particular to a culture and direct people into performances that support an existing socioeconomic order and its concomitant power relations. When people wrongly take such an order for immediate "reality" and subscribe to the mistaken belief that these performances further their eventual fulfillment, they create a gulf between hope and experience that can only result in baffling disappointments.

Third, different forces affect models and hence they evolve at dissimilar rates, resulting in emergent contradictions between them (cf. Nuckolls 1998, Keller 1992). During a period starting around 1970, for example, a contradiction between U.S. husband and wife models developed: wives came to expect they might have careers and make a financial contribution to the family. Husbands' expectations, however, did not necessarily expand to include contributing to childcare and housekeeping (Kleinberg 1999, Evans 1997, Kimmel 1996). The rise in U.S. divorce during this period, leveling in the 1980s and 1990s, reflects a legal and socioeconomic revolution, but also this emergent contradiction. Since the late 1990s, U.S. divorce rates have declined, suggesting increasing consonance between these two interrelated models.[4]

The case of U.S. marriage testifies that, when model problems become extreme, they are the focus of discussion, argument, and political movements. Yet, our minds and hearts attempt to keep pace with change to avert ruptures in the social fabric or to repair them as soon as possible. There are at least three reasons why this "keeping pace" should occur in dreams.

First, during the day we must get on with the business of living, and the subtler ways in which models fail to help us solve problems may escape notice. Indeed, Grenell (2008:224–225) shows that in daily life people often cope by shunting contradictory feelings aside, but in dreams they connect conflicting aspects of their personality at the root of these feelings.[5] Dreams, I shall argue, are not just about individual conflicts but are also about shared conflicts rooted in models; when dreamers strive to resolve them, therefore, they encounter more than their personal shortcomings.

Second, in waking life we are likely to resist awareness of the instability of our cultural worlds. Strauss and Quinn (1997:5) tell us that cultural models must be relatively stable to get us "through the day": models are like words in that, if they change too abruptly, too randomly, we could neither communicate nor negotiate social life. Relatively stable cultural models are integral to what Giddens (1991) calls "ontological security": people's basic sense of safety in the world (cf. Kinnvall 2004). Yet, if models do not keep abreast of people's ever-changing worlds, they cannot use them to make cognitive and affective sense of their lives. Dreams provide a space where we can update models without ruffling the surface of daily existence.

Third, as a sanctuary for imaginative thinking, dreams provide special access to what Winnicott (1951) says play represents for infants and children—a "transitional realm."[6] In transitional realms,

infants recognize reality by playing with its disconcerting dimensions, recreating these in their own terms much like Freud's little
nephew did in the famous Fort/Da game ([1920]1964). Removed
and insulated from daily struggles, there we can remember all those
places we were not, relive them, just as in fantasy we so often relive
times we fell short, saying or doing the wrong thing, striving to give
these episodes better conclusions. Dreams, then, are an experimental
realm, the backstage of culture where models morph in preparation
for reentering the public stage.[7] There, all of us create metaphors for
those problems with models we have encountered during the day,
metaphors that summon from memory similar problems from our
past.

The role of dreams in learning is foremost in many psychologists' investigations: as Stickgold observes, practice does not make
perfect; practice plus dreaming makes perfect (Stickgold and Walker
2004, Walker 2005, Nishida et al. 2008). Non-REM dreams typically use iterations of a scene or routine where a dreamer (partially)
learned an activity, skiing for example, to practice and master that
activity; REM dreams use remote memories and associations to
reassess and even reinvent it (Stickgold et al. 2001, Stickgold and
Walker 2004, Barrett and McNamara 2007). Yet, our ways of being
in the world derive not merely from learned activities but also from
cultural models. Surely, then, these too are what we practice and
reinvent in dreams.

Quinn argues that in talk models take metaphorical form (1987,
1996, 2005). The dream "speaks" in metaphor.[8] We can discover
models in dreams, then, through the metaphors dreamers borrow
from their public worlds. Dreamers use remote memories available
to them in REM dreaming that in some way resemble a problem with
a model the dreamer has encountered in daily life. Distant memories remain with us because of their affective charge. They mean
something to us, like Proust's madeleine, although unlike Proust
often we can't say what they meant, but these shards of experience
become metaphors for these inaccessible meanings, metaphors that
the dream takes up and melds with those public metaphors that con-
vey models. In this way, dream symbols combine public meanings
and our most private and embodied responses to assay and address
problems with models.

REM dreams traffic in pastiches of loosely related and visually
condensed memories that make for bizarre imagery. States (1993,
2000) argues persuasively that dreams' meanings lie in this imagery.
Indeed, such imagery is a popular symbol of the dream itself—as in

the melting clocks of Dali's series of paintings, *Dream Approaches*. In fact, dreams are not consistently bizarre (Domhoff 2007, Stickgold et al. 2001). Why, then, does such imagery evoke the dream for so many?

Domhoff and Schneider (2008) recommend a sample of at least 250 dreams to accurately reflect similarities and differences in a larger data set with an error rate of only 1 percent–3 percent. In a random sample of 250 dreams from my data, 18 percent featured solely pleasure or neutral affect (absence of displeasure); 76 percent featured at least one scene of displeasure; 20 percent started with displeasure but shifted to a scene of neutral affect or pleasure. Of those that shifted, 89 percent contained bizarre imagery. When dreams contained bizarre imagery followed by a shift to neutral or positive affect, dreamers consistently reported hopeful feelings about the problem they thought the dream represented in waking life.[9] The chapters to follow contend this is because bizarre images blend remote memories and associations with metaphors that represent models to depict and address dreamers' problems with these models.

Although bizarre elements are more frequent in home-reported dreams than in dreams from a laboratory setting, they are not more bizarre than other stories with which people are familiar in their culture or than the background flow of their own imaginative thinking (Domhoff 2007:16). All imaginative thinking, whether it occurs when one is awake or is asleep, can work to resolve problems of meaning via unrealistic (in the sense of practically unlikely) associations. Yet, Lacan (1968, 1977a) argues that, while imaginative thought is the first type of cognition to emerge in childhood, it soon shifts to the background of consciousness, yielding to verbal thinking about the practical and urgent realities of daily life. In REM dreams, however, imaginal thinking comes back into focus and takes center stage.

Psychologists and anthropologists agree that dreams are highly creative, prospective as well as retrospective, and that dreamers aim at solving life problems through evolving new ways of thinking and feeling.[10] Inasmuch as these problems are traceable to models, however, dreamers solve more than their own problems: they solve those of their group. Anthropologists and historians further show that individuals who share remarkable dreams with others in their society may generate changes in rituals, institutions, and religious beliefs.[11] My point is that all dreamers work on changing those models from which specific rituals, institutions, and beliefs derive.

Individuals' innovations, moreover, take root in other's lives because in dreams they too have grappled with the problems these innovations address.

Much in sympathy with my views, Stephen (2003) argues that dreams change the individual's "emotion schemas," and Hollan argues that dreams change "self-schemas" (2003a; 2003b:122).[12] In both cases, they believe these schemas come from culture. What I am saying is that dreamers both deconstruct and remake, not only the self and its emotions, but also models, because they are what humans weave into those webs of significance, enlisting Weber's famous phrase, in which cultural meaning systems consist—webs that are frayed by personal and collective history and by encounters with the new.

Psychological anthropologists often infer cultural models from discourses and practices,[13] that is from relatively conscious processing. Waking consciousness is likely to reflect norms, ideologies, and epistemes, but to underrepresent the full range of people's reactions (Levy 1973, Foucault 1977, Spiro 2003). We need new avenues for collecting data about shared models that reach beyond normal awareness. In dream reports and associations, meanings are often initially opaque to the dreamer and, therefore, have the potential to slip by censorship. As dreams traffic in images, they may have the potential to subvert linguistic modes of thinking as well.

More recently, researchers have investigated models as patterns of sharing or diversity among a population through free listing, surveys, and Cultural Consensus analysis.[14] These approaches do not identify which cultural models in a population are dysfunctional or emotionally troubling for individuals, nor do they reveal why a model is troubling (Garro 2000). Dreams, these most idiosyncratic stories, are often attempts to think about just this: why does a model prove unsatisfactory or even vaguely disquieting?

I am not suggesting that dreams *only* concern our inarticulate discomforts with models. Indeed, dreams open windows on many kinds of inarticulate experience. Western psychologists show, for example, that dreams may anticipate the onset or resolution of an illness.[15] Then why not also, in just as an immediate way, would they not shed light on those model inadequacies that subtly trouble our daily lives?

Models and Narratives

Like a contemporary experimental psychologist, then, my interest in dreaming is as a cognitive process, albeit one triggered by affect.

What is the nature of this process? Many regard dreams as narrative thinking in sleep.[16] States (1992) calls dreams protonarratives because they lack what Aristotle in the *Poetics* defined as a play's constituent parts: a beginning, a middle, and an end. Dreams are all middle. Yet, stories, dreams among them, have more elemental parts: images and their associated motifs, which together I call "figures." An image in a dream is any object, human or nonhuman. Motifs are action themes—for example hunting or fixing dinner. Figures combine images and motifs; so, a racing car is a figure. Characters in action or of whom a listener might expect/anticipate action, are in this sense "figures." So are objects that forward the dream plot: the role they play, the "part" they "act," one might say, serves as their associated motif. Thus, in Chapter 4, a refrigerator door that displays a lesson for the dreamer is a figure. *Dreamers ponder, update, and challenge models by merging images, motifs, and figures that symbolize these models as they occur in public stories circulating in a culture with personal memories.* Here I am suggesting something close to what Obeyesekere (1981:77) would call "objectification," but he defines objectification as the projection and externalization of private emotion in a public idiom. Dreams are not externalizations and, I believe, emotion is too narrow a term for what they express.[17]

If dreams, as Freud ([1900]1964) believed, are about fulfilling wishes and they are about models, then it seems likely they are about models as ways to fulfill desire. I would expand this proposition: dreams, indeed all narratives, iterate a model or combination of models, flagging them as ways to fulfill desires *and* they may represent models as *failing* to fulfill desires. I further suggest that if what Bourdieu (1992) calls "practices" supply models' "how to," narratives supply their "why to."[18] In other words, it is one thing to offer people a way to accomplish something; it is another to persuade them that they should *want* to accomplish it. Narratives, dreams among them, have the power to represent models as the means of "living happily ever after," but also to suggest that they are ways of "living happily ever after" that do not or no longer work. Let us begin with an example of the simpler case, a traditional Samoan tale that represents a model as a way to happiness titled "Scabby Oven Cover."

A dying father instructs two older sisters to serve the youngest girl, contravening the Samoan age-grade system (Moyle 1981:196–207). Instead, they make her their servant and force her to live in the cookhouse, the place of lowest status, naming her Scabby Oven

Cover. A handsome young chief appears who marries Scabby Oven Cover, bestowing an exalted status upon her. Her envious sisters become her servants. We recognize this tale as a Cinderella story—a story type one finds in many cultures (Bettelheim 1976:236).

In Samoa, traditional female mating models offered a strategy that might be loosely termed hypergamous. Hypergamy means to marry up. I say loosely, because when Christian missionaries arrived circa 1830 there was no indigenous term for marriage (Schultz [1911] n.d.:22). Rather than marrying up, girls were to beget up; doing so, entailed a union with a high-status partner that produced an offspring who was a "genealogical step forward," meaning the child would increase family or even village status (Hjarnø 1979/1980:91–93). Extended families (rather than the mating pair and their children) comprised the basic social unit; relations among families revolved around contested claims to titles that determined status and land ownership. Exalted genealogies justified title claims. Lower-ranking families could advance through children sired by highborn men because these children had rights in their paternal family's estate. If a girl from such a family bore an intelligent and charming son who served his father's family well, he might gain a minor title in that family. If he entered a ritualized union with the virgin daughter of a ranking family, his descendants had yet better prospects. "Wedding" titled males was a female mating model and a good strategy to further practical Samoan ends (Mageo 1998, 2008a). Scabby Oven Cover portrays hypergamy as a dream come true and as a solution to many of the frustrations that coming-of-age Samoan girls were likely to experience.

A second example: Holland and Eisenhart (1990) document gendered strategies among female college students in the southern United States during the 1980s that might likewise be termed hypergamous. Many women in their study sought success by attracting a male who was wealthy or who promised to be because the United States was and indeed still is a capitalist society organized at least in part around money. In the Ozzie and Harriet era of the 1950s and 1960s, people talked about mating in ways that anticipated Holland's and Eisenhart's findings. Men spoke of pursuing women because they were beautiful, particularly blondes, who therefore "had more fun"; women spoke of seeking a man who was "tall, dark, and handsome," but also a "good provider."[19] Bleaching one's hair blond was a common practice for women during this period, promoted by Clairol television commercials that assured them "only your hairdresser knows for sure." One also found this mating model, along with its attendant ploys, in films of the period like *How to Marry a Millionaire* (Fox 1953), and in the syndicated television serial by the same name broadcast nationwide from 1958–1960. Narratives appear in many places, from political speeches to children's songs, but particularly in our mediated U.S. world, their most prominent and highly circulated form is popular entertainment.

While pre-Christian Samoan mating models aimed at marrying titles, U.S. capitalist models aimed at "marrying money." One might call "poor girl gets prince" the female variant of the classic U.S. American "poor boy gets rich" story. This Cinderella model was congruent with other long-standing social structures. Historians trace a split between a public world of commerce negotiated by men and a private world of family relations and emotions sustained by women to nineteenth-century Europe and to the emergence of the bourgeoisie during and after the Industrial Revolution (Davidoff and Hall 1987, McClintock 1995).

Models, as cultural templates for perception and action, operate as performance principles to the extent that they support power relations in the guise of offering fulfillment. Cinderella models in various societies, for example, in effect reward successful men with pretty women. A young woman who has internalized such a model may welcome a wealthy wooer whom, realistically considered, she finds somewhat unattractive, or disagreeable, inattentive, unkind, and so forth, in this way cutting off, as it were, feelings out of line with the model. The Grimm's version of Cinderella ([1819]1977:83–89) offers a grim physical metaphor for this sacrifice: one of Cinderella's sisters cuts off her toes and the other sister her heels to fit the slender slipper. Tales that celebrate a model often include a grisly cautionary note, but it applies to others, not to the character with whom the listener identifies.

After the rise of second-wave feminism in the 1960s and 1970s, televised versions of the "poor girl gets prince" strategy for success were less blatant, but into the 1990s Hollywood continued to produce Cinderella stories in which female hypergamy was a dream come true. Thus in *Pretty Woman* (Touchstone Pictures, 1990), Vivian Ward, beautiful (at first in a blond wig), but reduced to the oldest profession by socioeconomic circumstances, beds Edward Lewis, a handsome, older, rich male. Although the road to happiness (and wealth) in *Pretty Woman* is bumpy and indirect (it leads first to a rejection of short-term economic gains), Edward turns out to be a prince and a dream come true. He fulfills Vivian's secret adolescent desire for rescue.

Consider the difference, however, between *How to Marry a Millionaire* and *Pretty Woman*. The first film's protagonists are merely broke; the protagonist of *Pretty Woman* is a whore. By the 1990s, the "let's make a deal" character of this "rags to riches" strategy became starkly apparent, probably because women were then in a better position to acquire money through their own labor. I compiled the data for this book between 2004 and 2006. Up through this period, Hollywood continued to produce the Cinderella story in new forms, forms that grappled with this model's increasing moral ambiguity. In the very popular *Sex and the City* (Warner Brothers, 2008), for example, Carrie Bradshaw has respectable and gainful employment. Her visibly older and much wealthier boyfriend, Big, wants to provide her regal digs: a New York penthouse with the closet as big as a bedroom. She asks if they will share ownership. They decide to marry to resolve otherwise ambiguous property relations, but then hurt one another. True to her Cinderella heritage, Carrie loves expensive shoes and leaves a pair behind in the palatial closet; these shoes become the fortuitous occasion for Carrie's and Big's reunion.

Americans' feelings about hypergamy have changed, and definitions of a Cinderella have shifted: now accomplishment as well as beauty may distinguish her, and the size of her shoes is less important than that of her dress. Yet, the capitalist version of hypergamy that characterizes this model is still recognizable. When people in a culture begin to sense the inadequacy of a model, or become aware of contradictions between the effects its promises and those it delivers, they come to share ambivalent feelings about it. What Americans call "chick flicks" often represent mixed feelings about this evolving cultural model.[20] Such models are also likely to become the subject of dreams, as the Cinderella model is for many of the dreamers this book surveys.

New Methods for Approaching Dreams

Let us now turn to the methodological problems with dream collection and analysis, which I suggested at the opening of the chapter explain why contemporary ethnographies often neglect dreams. I do not mean to say that dreams are absent from the playbook of psychological anthropologists. Indeed, they commonly prefer three approaches. First, anthropologists have often documented dream practices, performances, rituals, and associated beliefs, along with ideas about closely related cultural domains such as religion. Second, those inspired by ethnopsychology seek to discover indigenous categories for understanding psychological phenomena such as emotion, the self, and the dream. Third, anthropologists who believe in a person-centered approach, draw larger cultural implications by analyzing a corpus of dreams by a single individual or a small number of individuals with whom they have a close and sometimes a therapeutic relationship. Some contemporary anthropologists combine these approaches to document emic understandings of the dream and their implications for self-construction (see, for example, Tedlock 2001, Hollan 2003, Groark 2009, 2010).

Together these methods are a valuable alternative to those prior studies that imposed Western frameworks and categories on indigenous material. Yet, we need sizeable collections of dreams reports themselves, along with dreamers' associations to them, to assess psychological tensions associated with models within a culture and these models' attendant directions of change. Five problems stand in the way and thus provide explanation of why this royal road to the cultural unconscious is so lightly and infrequently tread by anthropologists.

First, Crapanzano (2003) rightly contends, the "dream" itself is a metadiscursive category that presumes universality. In fact, many non-Western cultures do not distinguish dreams from visions. When asked whether her visionary experience happened in sleep or when awake, for example, one of Bourguignon's Haitian informants at first could not answer: these distinctions were not indigenous (2003). Even to say that the dream is one kind of imaginal thinking makes experiences "psychological" that people in many cultures consider "spiritual," in the sense of having commerce with spirits. The term "spirits" too profits by deconstruction: it makes distinctions between humans and other categories of the person that are not universally recognized (Howard and Mageo 1996). Our categories are inevitably cultural and from a social position, yet this recognition should not silence us. We can still talk about "dreaming" and "imagining" without precluding the possibility that there are other ways for seeing these kinds of experience.

Second, the cultural institutions surrounding dreaming shape the way people experience dreams, how they report dreams, and even the manner in which people act in dreams. Shamans in a number of cultures, for example, use lucid dreaming in initiations, in healing, and to injure enemies (Tedlock 1987, Kracke 2003). While conventions of dreaming and dream telling vary widely, dreams from a culture feature many similar images, motifs, and figures, which I will show reveal salient and problematic models. Just as there are different ways of understanding the nature of dreams, so there are different ways of dreaming and of using dreams, but here again we can admit the validity of other ways without abandoning a cognitive anthropological perspective.

Third, studying transference, psychoanalysts have taught us that dream reporting is always a message about the relationship between the dreamer and the person(s) to whom she tells it. Anthropologists have found the same effect in relationships with informants (Crapanzano 1981, 1992, 2003; see also Tedlock 2001, Kracke 2003). This is true, this is helpful, but additional messages in dream reports do not invalidate attempts to interpret the dream in relation to the dreamer's life history and associations or in comparison to other dreamers in a culture or between cultures. It simply means we should be sensitive to these messages and to how interpersonal and cultural contexts shape what dreamers remember and recount.

Transference underlines the fact that the report is not the dream experience. Yet, words are never the experience, for language only points.[21] Dream reports are like other kinds of chronicled experience. Reporters try to get down "the facts," although they render them from a position within a cultural world. Their conscious and unconscious agendas, as well as those of their interlocutors, inevitably affect them. Yet, we do not think historians should abstain from reading a period's journals and other transcripts because these are not wholly objective or because reading is not the same as actually living through an experience. Historians, we think, should read widely with the hope of distilling powerful explications from a plethora of reports. So also, common features of a cultural psychology emerge when one reads a large number of dream reports and interpretations from a place and a period.

These first three problems are conceptual; the remaining two are practical and require practical solutions. Many psychological anthropologists, influenced by psychoanalysis, believe that only through an in-depth, long-term relationship with a dreamer can a researcher discover anything beyond, in Spiro's words (2003:171–172), "materials that are conscious, that are culturally normative, and that are not emotionally painful (i.e., that do not arouse shame or guilt)." This condition would seem to militate against collecting a large number of dreams. In the chapters to follow, I present and illustrate new projective methods that I gave my subjects, methods that allowed them to reach material that was often emotionally painful and that violated social norms. Ethnographers may question whether they can teach indigenes new ways of approaching dreams, yet the projective techniques these methods involve, such as role-playing dream images and associating dream images and actions to other stories, resemble practices people in a range of cultures use to work with dreams (see, for example, Tedlock 1981, Degarrod, 1989, Graham 1995).

Last, a researcher's system of interpretation always affects the dream. Thus, people in psychoanalysis have dreams with Oedipal characters and those in Jungian analysis tend to have archetypal dreams (Kracke 2003). This does not mean that the dream is merely a reflection of the analyst's expectations or, in the case of indigenous systems of interpretation, of the dreamer's cultural consociates. Rather, the dreaming mind, in Kracke's terms, can use different "grammars" of dreaming, just as the waking mind can use different languages. While languages and interpretive systems shape what we say or dream, they can account for them only to a degree. Yet, if interpretative systems inevitably influence dreaming, it makes more sense to invite our subjects to become collaborators than to pretend our interventions are without effect (cf. Bonime and Bonime 1987:82, Edgar 2004:12–41).

I issued such an invitation to my subjects by giving them a set of useful ideas about dreaming and culture in how-to form. These ideas enabled them to circumvent resistances in associating to dreams and to add appreciably to the process of interpretation. James Clifford (personal communication) suggested to me that I provided a toolkit—a camera, if you will, to make a psychological version of home movies. A camera changes one's world and one's experience but also allows the person as a moviemaker to intimately document that world. The situation was not one, as in the classic positivist paradigm, in which a naive subject provides "pure" data and an authoritative researcher does the theorizing. I offered dreamers various theories and we worked together to produce meaningful data—data I could not have collected without their help, help they could not have given without the methods I provided. The subsequent chapters offer instructions for and illustration of these methods. They also introduce forms of meta-analysis that researchers can use to discover how dreamers are working on cultural models (Table 1).

I call these meta-analyses because they build on analytic work done by the dreamers themselves. At the back of the book, I also provide a summary table comparing the dreams each chapter presents along the lines prescribed by the relevant form of meta-

Table 1 Exercises, Analyses, and Models

	Projective Exercises	Forms of Analysis	Major models
Chapter 2	The Intertextual method	Narrative Analysis	Close Family Devoted Mom Supportive Dad Good Kid Cinderella Femininity Supermasculinity
Chapter 3	Dream Play	Dramatic Analysis	Choice-as-agency Pinup Sexuality Girlfriend/ Boyfriend
Chapter 4	The Selfscape method	Holographic Analysis	Moving on-as-Progress
Chapter 5	Dream Play	Figurative Analysis	Traveling Self Free Individual Intersubjective Person

analysis. These projective methods and meta-analyses together, cannot replace former anthropological approaches to dreams, but they can contribute to their power and validity.

The Data

This book developed from dream accounts and interpretations that I collected during four semesters in an undergraduate class on psychological anthropology, entitled "The Self and Culture," which I taught at Washington State University (WSU). In all, 114 undergraduates participated (62 women and 52 men). Of the 995 dreams they contributed, 400 came from men and 595 from women; student dream analyses accompanied 217 of these reports (Table 2).[22]

Students wrote short dream papers during the semester and kept dream journals to provide them with material. I recommended that: while falling asleep, they suggest to themselves that they would remember a dream; as they awoke, they scan their minds for dreams or dream fragments; they keep a pad and pen beside their bed to record dreams immediately upon waking. No doubt, some followed

Table 2 Dream Data

Year	Participants	M	F	Total Dreams	M Dreams	F Dreams
2004	36	19	17	411	221	190
2005	38	18	20	232	87	145
2006	40	15	25	352	92	260
Totals	114	52	62	995	400	595

these instructions more closely than others did. They wrote a final paper about two dreams with whatever projective method they favored. At the end of each semester, in my absence, students filled out a form indicating their willingness to have their final papers and dream journals included in the study (IRB No. 5921). They deposited these forms in an envelope that I did not open until after I submitted their grades. To ensure confidentiality, I have changed names and obscured places of residence when I thought that a number of other pieces of personal data, together with natal residence, might give clues to the person's or their family's identity.

"The Self and Culture" fulfills a general education requirement that students can meet through a considerable range of courses intended to provide a liberal education. This class endeavored to give students a comparative view of being a person. To that end, students read ethnographic studies of the self or of dreaming in various societies and wrote short assignments that brought these perspectives to bear on their dreams. At the beginning of the course, I briefly introduced students to the idea that some cultures have more "egocentric" and some more "sociocentric" self-models. After that, I used the terms egocentric and sociocentric as simple adjectives to describe degrees of difference between cultures. Some student readings employed the term "cultural schema," but not "cultural model." No dreamer in the 2004–2006 data set used the term "cultural model" in a paper. A few times in their analyses, a student used the term "self-model" but only to denote their personal psychology, either in association with an adjective like "a positive self-model" or as tantamount to a personal emotion or quality, for example "not liking to be alone," "discomfort with who I am," or "being unlikable."

Dreamers did not find cultural models in their dreams; they found their personal histories. Although I encouraged them to speculate about the relationship of this history to their culture, they usually did so by generalizing what they had found about themselves. Scarlet (Chapter 5), for example, discovers her need to "fix" others in her dream analysis and opines: "As Americans we long to fix things. Not just physical things like our cars, houses, or appliances. We long to fix each other." I don't mean to say that student analyses, either of themselves or their culture, lacked insight. As a teacher, I cannot resist a little pride at how insightful many of these analyses were. I only mean that students' insights were not about cultural models.

"The Self and Culture" is a 400-level class—a class intended for, although not restricted to, seniors. The imminent entry of many students into "real life" raised prototypical U.S. American life-stage issues in their dreams such as losing friends and transiting to novel circumstances and responsibilities. This class also dovetailed with that U.S. personal project, particularly salient in adolescence and young adulthood: "finding oneself." Today finding oneself entails finding one's unique perspective on the social world, finding a career, and finding a mate, all evident in students' dreams.

Finding oneself, Giddens (1991) argues, is an important personal project during high modernity. High modernity is an apocalyptic era: individuals live with risks that surpass those of the past such as weapons of mass destruction, ecological catastrophe, and global economic collapse; distant happenings invade intimate space, creating interpersonal alienation and inner fragmentation (Giddens 1991:4). The self then becomes a reflexive project "which consists in the sustaining of coherent, yet continuously revised, biographical narratives" (Giddens 1991:4–5). Undergraduates in my classes seemed intensely interested in using the anxious narratives of dreams to reflect on themselves. As their professor, I presided over this identity project.

Students shared a premise with psychoanalysts—that finding themselves necessitated sorting out mixed feelings about family and friends, terms that for them referred to a primary social matrix that was either the setting of their childhood and youth, or that they wished had been. "Family and friends" was a model of a child/adolescent world with relatively stable relationships, one in contrast to the national landscape of ethnic, racial, and cultural strife and often of shifting, uncertain connections. Indeed, U.S. Americans often speak proudly of being friends with someone since childhood or adolescence. At universities like WSU, students from every location try to make enduring friendships among a diverse array of people on their way to somewhere else. The United States is, I will argue in Chapter 5, a traveling culture—to invoke Clifford's famous phrase (1992:101–103). For many young Americans, universities are important depots in their wayfaring lives.

If my dream analyses do not move deeper into students' individual psychologies, it is because my intent is not to fathom individual psychology per se, but cultural psychology, which I argue is accessible at least in part through metaphors common to many dreamers as well as to other narratives in a culture. I hope to demonstrate that even in circumstances in which researchers cannot gather all the information about individuals they might like (after they have returned from the field, for example), a fruitful cultural reading of their dreams is still possible if the researcher has used the projective methods for collecting data I propose.

Dream Selection

When I collected this data, the WSU undergraduate population consisted of approximately 15,000 students from Washington counties, approximately 1,500 students from other states mostly in the West, a few from U.S. territories, several hundred from other countries predominately in Asia, and a roughly equal number of males and females. I excluded students from my sample whose home address was a foreign country and who were merely schooling in the United States.

Of the 14 dreams I analyze in depth, women contributed 8 and men 6, maintaining a ratio similar to that between male and female participants in the study (Table 2). To develop each chapter, I made sets of final papers that used a single projective method and let a topical focus emerge from these methodological sets, narrowing my focus to papers that shared this topic. When more than three or four papers fit these criteria, I selected those papers with more autobiographical material. Chapter 5 attempts a comprehensive analysis of all dreams collected in which a single figure (cars traveling) plays a significant role and then uses this analysis to consider three dreams in depth.

I tried to conduct follow-up interviews with the students whose dreams I feature. By the time I learned who wanted to participate and could conduct interviews, several students had moved elsewhere. Some interviews, therefore, I conducted in person and others by phone. Some individuals, while willing to contribute their final paper and dream journal, did not want to talk further about their dreams. During interviews, I refrained from asking leading questions, confining myself to requests for further biographical material and associations to the dream.

I often asked students about their "ethnicity." By far the most common response was race: for example, they might identify as

"African American," "Asian American," "Caucasian," or "white,"
which have no specific ethnic dimensions. For WSU students,
apparently, race trumps and often subsumes ethnicity as a marker
of difference. When I was growing up and moving among a number
of white Los Angeles suburbs during the 1950s, my schoolmates
typically spoke of what U.S. Americans now call their ethnicities
as percentages of European nationalities. An acquaintance might
say, for example: "I'm half Irish, a quarter German, and a quarter
Italian." This was so even if one or all of the national groups to
which the person referred were several generations back and parents
or grandparents were actually born in Vermont or South Carolina.
I attribute these nationality-style genealogies to kids' pride in what
Americans then hailed as the "melting pot" character of U.S. society. At that time, people still told Polish jokes: overcoming preju-
dice against some European groups was a relatively recent social
achievement.

Young people with Caucasian Asian heritage were among the few
in this study who used percentage-style genealogies. In Chapter 3, for
example, we will meet Dave who identified as "Korean/German." I
did not have many African Americans or Hispanics in classes: only
three or four in each class of approximately 40 to 65 students. They
did not report mixed origin or heritage. In 2008, Oprah's Martin
Luther King Day special (1/21) featured a story about an African
American woman who had a DNA test that revealed genetically she
was 28 percent white—a mathematically precise version of reporting heritage by percentage. Barack Obama too anticipated a decay
of the "one-drop" rule in the 2008 presidential campaign. Obama
identified as black, but often mentioned that his mother was white
and his father was African, implicitly invoking the percentage-style
genealogy used by my Caucasian Asian students.

A few words about the limitations of this study are in order. Dream
collection was limited to the period in which the students took the
class. In the 14 cases I present, this period was adequate for seeing how problems with a model shaped dreamers' waking concerns,
to see repeated patterns in students' dream journals, and in some
cases to see how these problems and patterns affected the interval
between the dream and a later interview, usually a few months later.
In Madison's case (Chapter 4), for example, the problem she confronts in her dream clearly dictated the unsatisfying career path she
took after graduation and was still on at the time of our interview.
The solution her dream intimates, however, greater risk-taking, was
one that was likely to make a difference in her professional trajectory

over a longer period. How people's dreams change their histories must be left to a longitudinal study.

Urbanites have suggested to me that by the 2004–2006 period young people in New York, or Seattle, or Los Angeles had already moved on from the sex and gender models my students' dreams featured: namely, what I call the Cinderella model of femininity, the Pinup model, and the Supermasculinity model. I can only speak of what recurs in my students' dreams and reports, which the period and provincial locale may in part explain. Students did not merely iterate these models in dreams but questioned, struggled with, and changed them. Women dreamers often explored or experimented with models associated with masculinity in the U.S. social world, although the reverse was less often true. Men's dreams, however, sometimes suggested that U.S. femininity models were dictating their feelings and reactions, to their dismay! In any case, my intent is not to reify these models but to investigate their dream transformations. These transformations, I will argue, proceed through a process of repeating-with-variation. Dreamers do not simply invent new models out of nothing; rather, they replicate existing models while at the same time bringing original and often contesting memories to bear upon them.

Models that appeared in my data would take dissimilar but related forms among varying age and demographic groups in the United States. What I call the Close Family model in Chapter 2, for example, would look different from the perspective of 30-something parents, or late middle-aged grandparents, or people of another socioeconomic class, race, or ethnicity (see for example Kusserow 2004). Indeed, all models that are salient in my data might or might not be so in another U.S. group, while other models would be. Thus, Quinn (1987) documents a U.S. model of Marriage-as-a-Journey that is probably more relevant to young people at Northwest urban campuses where students have often begun what Americans consider "normal" adult life, or to those who have finished college or to young people who do not attend college and wed soon after high school. Neither does this study purport to be an exhaustive account of my students' models. Some significant models may not have emerged in the dream sets (those that featured a shared model *and* that illustrated the usefulness of my methods for providing this data), which formed the basis of each chapter. My aim, rather, is to illustrate ideas about dreams and methods for working with them through a number of models that were emotionally and practically consequential for my students. Yet, this "slice of life" gives significant ethnographic insight into students' interior landscapes and into compelling cultural models that shaped these landscapes.

Students often reported long dreams and made lengthy comments on them. For readability and length, I did not include material I felt was redundant. In any dream analysis, a single word can change nuances in significant ways. I can only ask readers to trust my judgment, while I acknowledge other possible interpretations might use this deleted material. In any case, the methods and forms of analysis I present do not aim at understanding an individual's personal psychology per se, which requires the steady, lengthy commitment that psychotherapists and their clients invest, but at assessing common cultural issues that appeared in their dreams.

Within these limits, I follow Bulkeley's four principles for rigorous, intersubjective dream interpretation (2001b:230): (1) privileging the perspective of the dreamer, (2) attending to dream details (internal coherence), (3) connecting the dream to waking life (external coherence), and, (4) being open to surprise. Indeed, coming to appreciate what these dreams meant about my students' lives usually surprised me: their social circumstances were often more economically and emotionally difficult than I had imagined.

While Bulkeley's principles serve well for individual dream interpretation, I offer two additional principles for *cultural* dream interpretation. First, interpret material in light of socioeconomic relations and historical change within the ethnographic context. Second, collect dreams horizontally, across members of a group, and vertically, over a several-month period. Horizontal collection allows one to discover models, which emerge as common dream elements. Vertical collection allows one to better understand an individual's problems with a model, which are likely to reoccur in a number of dreams.

University Culture

WSU is in the city of Pullman. Pullman is part of a region self-identified as the "Inland Northwest." Long-term local residents take pride in the Inland Northwest's rural character, which many believe includes honesty and friendliness. People often express an appreciation of open spaces, lack of population density and, in Pullman itself, good elementary and secondary schools. Pullman is approximately 73 miles south of Spokane, adjacent to the state line and to the University of Idaho in Moscow just on the other side of that line. Even today, it feels far away from the intensity of city life.

For undergraduates, Pullman is Student Land. During all but a few weeks between the last summer session and fall semester, students make up the preponderance of the local population. In the majority, these are not the part-time students trying to pursue a career while holding down a full-time job or returning to get more education while a spouse pursues a career—student types that are common at Northwest coastal campuses. Rather, they are young people out to have a classic college experience. Not only the Pullman campus itself, but also local businesses cater to their needs and pleasures. Whatever the venue, students are most likely to meet one another. Because of its remote locale, undergraduates must *choose* to come to WSU; most do for these reasons.

The typical undergraduate is from Spokane, the second-largest city in Washington, from midsized towns of Yakima, Ellensburg, and Wenatchee in the middle of the state, or from Seattle and other towns of the Northwest coastal plane. Coastal towns from which my students hailed were often rural by U.S. standards during their childhoods, although connected by a corridor of freeways that made them part of an extended urban system. Today, when these students return home, these towns have often become suburbs of adjoining cities; spacious homesteads are now tracts for housing developments.

If the United States is a child-centered culture (Hays 1996), WSU is a student-centered university: that is the image it promotes— "World Class, Face-to-Face" is its slogan. Throughout the contemporary United States, I believe, student evaluations have heightened this effect. The administrators, who increasingly rule universities, tend to judge classes, programs, and professors on the basis of how they appeal to students. For most students, the result is an environment that is safe and nurturing, albeit expensive. Many WSU students have part-time jobs and are accruing debts that will be with them for years to come. Yet, during the period of my study, this sobering economic circumstance had not yet dampened the Pullman campus bon vivant—a heady sense of youth, play, and possibility set amidst quasi-traditional redbrick buildings, parks, and trees, which very much resembled many Americans' fantasy of going away to college.

This study is a regional report and one from a specific university during a particular period in U.S. social history. Yet, as significant as this time and place is in many of the dreams I consider, my focus is not on documenting campus culture per se, as did Holland and Eisenhart (1990) in their important study of three Southern U.S. universities. I intend, rather, to use these young people's dreams at a critical time in their lives as a lens through which readers can see that we are always dreaming culture.

Chapter 2

Narrative Spectrums and Dreaming the U.S. American Family

Dreams are the extreme subjective end of what I call a "narrative spectrum." Composed of all tales circulating in a culture, narrative spectrums run from highly conventional stories like founding myths that elders or statesmen evoke in public oratory, to written and oral literatures, to theatre, to popular entertainments like film, television, and video games, to gossip and personal histories, and to the more disordered, spontaneous stories we dream. Narrative spectrums also include song lyrics, jokes, and proverbs when they tell stories or refer to them and extend to more visual and embodied arts like Hawaiian dance or some ballets, even paintings, when they borrow images or motifs from stories. Images and motifs, stories' most basic elements, travel back and forth along narrative spectrums. Politics, for example, may borrow and inflect powerful images from personal biographies, or biographies motifs from popular entertainments. Dreamers too borrow images/motifs from other stories.

Like States (2000), I take dreams to be narrative ruminations without communicative intent similar to what Vygotsky calls "inner thought." For Vygotsky (1962:145, 148), inner thoughts are verbal, yet each word condenses many meanings. Dream images and motifs, I will show, evoke and thus condense other tales.[1] The idea that dreams borrow from other stories draws upon Kristeva's (1986) idea of intertextuality and Vygotsky's (1976:57) activity theory. For Kristeva (1986:37, 112), each literary text and the words that compose it evoke and transform other words/texts. While in its original formulation, Kristeva's idea referred to a relation among literary texts, intertextuality came to refer to a limitless field of signs and tropes in which a vast range of human productions were "read" as texts. Looking at dreams, I am neither interested in the narrow circle of literary texts, nor in the broad circle of all cultural "texts," but only in the movement of images and motifs back and forth between dreams and other kinds of narratives. Vygotsky argues that children internalize the social relations in which they develop. Yet, children also internalize what we might call their *narrative environment*. Storytelling in childhood helps kids (re)construct their personal experiences in cultural terms (Miller, Fung, and Mintz, 1996). This incorporative-reconstructive process, I will show, continues in dreams.

I argued in Chapter 1 that metaphors represent cultural models and that in narratives these metaphors take the form of figures and their component images and motifs. By appropriating images and motifs from other stories, this chapter argues, dreamers evoke the models they symbolize. Yet, the images and motifs of dreams also evoke and represent dreamers' personal memories. In effect, then, dream images and motifs combine metaphors circulating in public culture with very personal experience. Many of a dream's meanings, I hold, lie in such combinations, which comprise imaginal thought about dreamers' problems with models and creative responses to them.

The creativity I attribute to dreams, many social scientists ascribe to fantasy generally.[2] Stern (1938:330), for example, says fantasy produces a new reality in inner experience that transforms people and profoundly changes their relation to the world. Josephs (1998:185) argues that people use fantasy to reconstruct their world's meaning. Fantasy is a broad category and for some a synonym for what Lacan (1977a), calls the Imaginary. A distinction must be made, then, between fantasy as the whole of the Imaginary, of which dreaming is a part, and fantasy as that form of imaginal thinking that remains in waking consciousness after verbal thought takes center stage in the process of cognitive development. If one takes the broader definition, then my topic in this chapter is the relation of dreaming as one form of fantasy to other forms. If one takes the narrower definition, then dreams are a more cloistered realm than fantasy—farther away and freer from immediate practical concerns, as well as the constraints of convention and of logical processing (cf. Fosshage 1987:302). Dreaming is that locale where imaginal thinking can unfold in ways it cannot in the margins of waking consciousness to better master models or to encounter those disquieting problems of meaning with which they are associated. There we can do concentrated narrative thinking about a cultural model, pondering problems that are our own but that we also share with others in our communities.

The Intertextual Method and Narrative Analysis

I devised a projective exercise for my students to help them see the relationship between their dreams and other stories, which I call the Intertextual Method. When using this method, a *dreamer* first picks a vivid dream and names one or more stories that the dream evokes for him. These may be children's tales, television shows, movies, novels, myths (like the self-made man in the United States), jokes, ballads, and so on. Following Kristeva, I call such stories the dream's "intertexts." Second, the dreamer associates personal memories to the dream. Third, he identifies major dream images and motifs, asking what these represent in those stories that comprise the dream's intertexts and in personal memory. Fourth, he assumes that the dream is about an unfulfilled wish and an anxiety and guesses what the wish and the anxiety are. Last, he speculates how these wishes and anxieties link to widespread feelings in his society. The Intertextual Method is similar to indigenous ways of interpreting dreams in a number of small-scale cultures (Tedlock 1981, Degarrod, 1989); it is, therefore, likely to appeal to people in such cultures too.[3]

Here, I also offer Narrative Analysis, which *researchers* can use to discover how dream images and motifs draw on other stories to depict problems with cultural models. In Narrative Analysis, a researcher collects dreams that a number of dreamers have explored through the Intertextual Method. She then looks for an emergent topic in this dream set. Narrative Analysis directs her to view this topic broadly, both in her ethnographic data and in other studies of the culture, to determine how the topic suggests a cultural model and then to examine societal and historical problems with the model. She then zooms in on individual dreams.

First, she considers the intertext(s) the subject associates to the dream and then expands this narrative context by relating the dream to further stories that share the dream's images and motifs circulating in the dreamer's culture. Expanding on a subject's insights and autobiographical material, second, the researcher asks how the dream combines motifs and images from the dream's intertexts with incidents from personal history to depict problems with a model and often with an interrelated model. Inasmuch as each model is part of a web of meaning, problems with one model implicate other models. Third, the researcher asks how the dream's portrayal of culturally salient images or motifs comments on or changes these models. Changes may occur in a dream series rather than in a single dream,

so Narrative Analysis works best when dreamers have kept a dream
journal upon which the researcher can draw.

Troubles with U.S. Close Family Models

When I assembled the dreams that my students interpreted using the
Intertextual Method, family emerged as a common topic. The model
of and for family evident in my data I call the "Close Family" model.
In this model, "family" is a small group of closely related relatives
(mom, dad, kids, and sometimes grandparents) who are supposed
to feel close to one another: they are strongly attached, support
one another in all endeavors and challenges, and sympathize with
one another's feelings (see also Schneider 1968). In a world of tran-
sient relations, close families have an enduring commitment to one
another. U.S. Americans usually understand close family as larger
than the couple and as aiming at making kids into happy, successful
individuals. My students fit into families as children and I consider
the Close Family model from their standpoint. The Close Family is
what I call a metamodel: we will soon see that it provides an organizing framework for a set of tightly linked models.[4]

Students' most widespread problem with their close family was,
in their view, a good family had two parents living with and attending to a child, but while they were growing up their fathers were
often physically, financially, or emotionally absent. Absent fathers
go way back in the Western mythology. Oedipus had an absent
father: he did not meet his father, Laius, until he killed him. Slater
(1968) says that absent fathers characterized Greek family life and
mythology generally. At least since the late twentieth century, absent
fathers are prominent figures in U.S. stories too. Take, for example,
a film I discussed in Chapter 1, *Pretty Woman* (Touchstone Pictures,
1990). The male protagonist, Edward Lewis, had a wealthy father
who deserted Edward's mother; she died, we infer, because of his
father's neglect. Edward grows up hating his father and becomes
a high-flying financier. His father is a mid-twentieth-century busi-
nessman who specializes in production. Edward is a millennial capitalist: he doesn't produce but simply trades for profit—capturing
failing companies, breaking them into pieces, and selling off their
parts. The first company he dismembers is his dad's. Edward has
an Oedipus complex with a twist: his problem is not competition
for his mother; he grows up alone with her. Edward is angry at his
father's absence.

In 2000, only 69 percent of U.S. families consisted of mother, father, and minor children, as opposed to 87 percent in 1979 (Fields and Casper 2001:7). During the study period, by some estimates half of U.S. babies were born out of wedlock (McKee and Stone 2007:201–225). As of 2005, when parents divorced, courts gave residential custody to mothers 83.8 percent of the time (Grall 2007). After divorce, most children had less than weekly contact with their dad (Kelly 2006).[5] My students in postdivorce households reported that their father was often financially absent: while he was prosperous, their mother, with whom they resided, in no way shared in that prosperity and was sometimes poor.

Students whose parents had not divorced frequently commented on the relative emotional availability of fathers: "I can talk to my mom about anything, we're close," many said, but "I can't talk to my dad." In other words, moms conformed to the Close Family model; often, dads did not. Students' fathers were usually busier than their mothers and were away from home more to pursue vocations and avocations. As the dreams to follow indicate, an effect of absent fathers is kids' overinvolvement with mothers. This overinvolvement is one of the Close Family model's inherent dangers in part because Americans tend to imagine early life as revolving around a close mother-child bond. Hays (1996) documents contemporary U.S. beliefs in "intensive mothering": people assume that childcare should be primarily by mothers, centered on the child's needs, and is labor-intensive. I call these ideas the Devoted Mom model. A Care schema is definitive of this model: moms are supposed to submerge their own needs, to varying degrees, in order to nurture their children. Motherly devotion and the child's response to it provides a research focus in U.S. studies of human development, for example studies of attachment (Ainsworth 1973, Cassidy and Shaver 1999, Ahnert et al. 2004, Mageo 2011). Of my 14 major dreamers, all but one had moms who were far more devoted to their care than were their dads.

Devoted moms play a fundamental role in encouraging the achievement orientation integral to U.S. values and life ways. Beatrice Whiting (1978) argues that when U.S. kids perform an activity, such as drawing a picture, they solicit attention for the activity: "See my picture." Mom responds: "That's a very good picture." This mother-child engagement becomes the basis for many future relations, for example teacher/student, and is likely to insure adults strive to recreate a situation in which an authority figure rewards them with recognition. Whiting contrasts this childrearing model to the Kikuyu where children interact with peers or other adults as frequently as they do with mother.[6]

The Devoted Mom's counterpart is the Supportive Dad. In this U.S. model, a father supports his family, financially and by providing a safe environment for them more generally.[7] According to Benjamin (1988), the father's role is also to create transitional space—a space in which the child can practice risk-taking in relative safety (Winnicott 1953, 1971). Risk-taking ability is necessary for U.S. kids to "make something of themselves." Like the achievement orientation that Whiting believes U.S. moms cultivate, a willingness to take risks is necessary for success in a high-modern order where life often feels risky (Giddens 1991). The importance of risk-taking and hence of transitional space in contemporary child development may help to explain why Winnicott's idea has been important in U.S. psychological theory.

Close Family is a middle-class (and possibly white) model. Thus, Kusserow (2004) found that in lower-class U.S. homes, mothers simply did not have the time to shower children with attention. Indeed, as an increasing number of U.S. mothers work full time or have careers, devoted moms may become a white middle-class historical memory that fewer and fewer families actually replicate. Strauss (1992b) shows, moreover, many lower-class dads' responsibility as breadwinners precludes taking the risks with their time and other resources that can produce individual achievement, making it less likely that they would foster such risk-taking in their kids.

I do not mean to eulogize devoted moms or supportive dads, but to argue that models *usually* conspire to create a workable social reality for a particular cultural subgroup in which the models develop. We will see, however, that models circulate beyond their originating subgroups. Neither do I mean to imply that two opposite-sexed parents are necessary to kids, but simply to outline my students' expectations, problems, and disappointments. My personal position on family, which I do not argue in this book, is that kids thrive best in a large extended family that provides many different bonding opportunities. This kind of family is unlikely in a capitalist society like the United States where the labor market depends on small mobile reproductive units, although some of my dreamers favor a family model that resembles mine.

Let us turn, then, to three students, Clark, Lois, and Kent, who dreamt about problems with the Close Family model and who used the Intertextual Method (Table 3). True to the study's location in the Northwest United States, I begin with a Bigfoot dream.

Table 3   Intertexts and Family Models

	Clark	Lois	Kent
Intertext	Harry and the Hendersons	Sleeping Beauty	Leave it to Beaver
	Sasquatch Mountain	Cinderella	Viva la Bam
Images	Big footprint	Dragon	Pushpins
	GMC, Road	Cliff	Carpet
	Forest	Crossroads	Bare feet
Motifs	Hunting	Dragon-slaying	Making dinner
	Fixing	Jumping	Cleaning up
Wish	To prove manhood	To have options	To protect the family
Anxiety	Not being in control	Choosing	Hurting the family
Genre	Family Comedy	Cliffhanger	Family Soap
	Horror Movie	Fairytale	"Reality" Show
Models	Close Family	Close Family	Close Family
	Supportive Dad	Devoted Mom	Good Kid
	Supermasculinity	Cinderella	Bad Boy masculinity
	Good Kid	Free Individual	Free Individual
			Choice-as-agency
Schemas	Extraordinary Powers	Risk-taking	Extraordinary Powers
	Detachment	Detachment	Detachment
	Problem-solving	Protection	Impulse
	Risk-taking		Gratification

Clark

Clark was 24 and from a small town near Seattle, but far enough from the city that the place had a rural feeling. In answer to my ethnicity question, he called himself "Caucasian."

> I dreamt I was hunting Big Foot on Ranger Mountain Road. I was driving the old family GMC.... [T]he GMC was...a hot wheels toy that I could hold in my hand and fix if it were broken. After I fixed the GMC I could put it on its wheels and climb into it and drive away. Hunting Big Foot was my job working for Les Schwab Tires, but

this Les Schwab Tire Center was located at my Mom's house....Her house wasn't actually there because Les Schwab had taken its place. To get onto Ranger Mountain Road, there were a series of "wups" that I had to...jump over in the GMC. I was hunting with my Dad's rifle....The time of year was...late October, the weather was pouring down rain, it was very cold and the sky was very dark....The road itself was...dirt and gravel...very narrow and covered with potholes and deep ruts....There was also white fog that...seemed to be creeping closer and closer to the road as I drove on. All of a sudden the road came to an end and the dark woods enclosed...me. I tried to back up but...I couldn't tell where I was going and the road was so small that there was no place to turn around...I got out of the truck and started looking for prints or any signs left by the Sasquatch. I remember seeing a man-like footprint in the soft dirt entering the woods...the sheer size [was]...at least two times as big as my size 12's....I slung my gun on my shoulder and started following the tracks right into the dark and foggy forest.

Name that Text. "The legend of Bigfoot," Clark wrote, "is almost everyplace on earth. The Sasquatch is believed to originate from Asia 300,000 years ago. Sightings of Bigfoot have been reported by Asia, Africa, Europe, and North America." Sasquatch, however, is a Salish word and originally a Northwest American Indian legend. Clark had seen two Bigfoot movies, both staged in the Pacific Northwest. *Harry and the Henderson's* (Universal and Amblin 1987) was "about a family hitting Bigfoot with their car on a mountain road, eventually befriending him after nursing him back to health. This movie took place...very close to where I grew up which also happened to be a heavily wooded area." Harry becomes one of the Hendersons. The movie renders a comically deformed portrait of a close family, which falls apart at first because of Harry and then becomes closer because of him. An obsessed hunter pursues Harry and he has to return to the forest. "*Sasquatch* was the other movie...a horror film where the Bigfoot killed and ate humans who were lost in the woods." The film's title is actually *Sasquatch Mountain* (Curb Entertainment 2006). Putting Clark's two movies together, we will see, is like a question about Bigfoot: Is he a monster who needs to be alone for others' sake or a misunderstood "endangered species" who has to be protected from (some of) us? Is he the hunter or the hunted?

Images and Motifs. "My father and I even saw what looked like an actual Bigfoot print in the soft soil close to a riverbank deep in the woods," Clark wrote—one like he finds at the end of the dream. Although virtually the last dream image, this "man-like" footprint is defining: it symbolizes Bigfoot through his absence. Clark's father was also absent. His parents divorced. When he is at home, Clark lives with his mom. Clark thought Bigfoot stood for his father: "I don't know how to deal with my father and in the dream I don't know how to capture Bigfoot." We will see that for Clark Bigfoot's print also evokes a U.S. masculinity model, one sported by his father.

"The dream represented Bigfoot as an unobtainable being," Clark continued, "which I had to capture...to prove...my manhood." Bigfoot personifies what I call the Supermasculinity model.[8] Supermasculinity stories in the United States are as popular as Cinderella stories. One finds this model in movies from John Wayne and Clint Eastwood Westerns to Spiderman and beyond. Superman, in his many comic book, TV, and movie avatars, is the longest running instance of this model; during the study collection period, Superman appeared weekly in the series, *Smallville*.

One obvious schema integral to the Supermasculinity model is "Extraordinary Powers," which make for dominance. Indeed, dominance, meaning control over whatever opposes the person (most significantly other people) is another schema critical to this model. Extraordinary Powers come from a multitude of sources. In Superman's case, these powers are extraterrestrial. The creation of the Superman series in the 1950s reflected a budding popular interest in space exploration along with the increased role technology had come to play in society, which people imagined would make exploration feasible. In Kent's dream, presented later in this chapter, these powers come from money: this is the Mogul version of Supermasculinity. For Monroe (Chapter 3), extraordinary powers come from machines: following Haraway (1991), this is the Cyborg version. Bigfoot represents the Tarzan version in which the person's extraordinary powers trace back to kinship with animals: Tarzan is brought up by apes and Bigfoot looks like one. I say "person" rather than "man," because, as we will soon see, women too use masculinity models. Indeed, experimenting with models that others in one's culture ascribe to people of a different gender or race or class or age is one way in waking life and in dream life individuals challenge and change models. Dreams provide a safe space for such experimentation, one without social repercussions, although also a space where dreamers think and feel through these repercussions.

"Supermen" use their extraordinary powers to rescue others, and this is another of the model's constituent schemas. Yet, they often have monstrous counterparts who use their power for evil and resemble Bigfoot in *Sasquatch Mountain*. When there is trouble with a model, we will see in this chapter, its photographic negative is likely to evoke it in dreams: by representing its opposite or underside, this image summons the model from memory.

In the dream report, but not the dream analysis, Clark spelled Bigfoot's name as "Big foot." Not only is Sasquatch defined by the size of his feet, in one of Clark's movies, Bigfoot's name is "Harry," a pun: in legend, Bigfoot is shaggy with dark brown or reddish hair. In psychoanalytic body-part symbolism, feet and hair stand for (phallic) sexuality (Berg 1951). In recent decades, psychoanalysts have largely abandoned an interest in bodily symbols in dreams and social life generally. Indeed, this symbolism has often been used to caricature psychoanalytic interpretation. In this book, I argue for a renewed interest in it.

Bodily symbols partake of what we might call, following Piaget (1985), a sensorimotor logic in which body parts become primary vehicles of meaning. During the sensorimotor period, the body itself is a vehicle of thought. An infant, for example, might discover that a mobile above her crib moves when she shakes her legs; shaking then comes to signify "mobile." Just as Lacan (1968, 1977a) argues that the Imaginary simply moves to the background of consciousness with the onset of linguistic reasoning, I suggest that sensorimotor thinking moves behind the scenes, but remains evident in dream images. Two of the most emotionally charged social realities developing infants and toddlers confront are gender and sexuality. Genital images, by which I mean images that resemble or evoke the genitals, therefore, become sensorimotor metaphors for thinking about a wide variety of experiences. In Clark's case, feet and, we will see, hair too are sensorimotor metaphors for virility, but also for his masculinity model and for perceptions about this model he cannot articulate.

Clark saw his dream's major motif as "hunting Bigfoot in the dark and creepy forest." Watching the trees go past in the dream reminded Clark of sitting in the passenger seat of his dad's car when they went hunting in the semidarkness of early morning. Hunting was a way Clark and his dad bonded: although Clark has a younger brother, he and his dad always went alone. Clark keeps pictures of him and his dad taken after a hunt with a large animal that his dad shot. When they hunted together, his dad "would constantly tell me stories of Bigfoot and tell me to watch out for him and sniff the air for Bigfoot's terrible odor," a trait that in 1840 the Protestant missionary, Reverend Elkanah Walker, found in Spokane Indian lore about hairy giants that roamed the woods.[9]

Although in the contemporary urban United States hunting is seldom an important masculine activity, it still was among indigenous Northwesterners when Clark was growing up. Thus, when I first joined my Inland Northwest academic department in 1993, most of the men hunted together, dinning at one another's homes afterward to feast upon their kill. Hunting/killing a large dangerous animal, furthermore, is a practice through which legendary U.S. men from Daniel Boon to Teddy Roosevelt enacted the Extraordinary Powers schema and symbolically appropriated those of their prey—just as Hal in Shakespeare's *Henry IV* appropriates his rivals' reputations. Motifs that arise repeatedly in stories representing a model often represent its schemas.[10]

Hunting with his dad lasted until Clark killed his first deer; Clark felt sorry for the deer and he didn't want to go anymore. He identified with the prey, not as a predator. In Chapter 4, we will meet George. George's dad too wants him to go hunting; like Clark, George resists. This resistance suggests that the masculinity model with which hunting is associated is problematic for these young men and hence vulnerable to transformation. Yet, in Clark's dream he carries his dad's rifle and the dream genre is "monster-slayer" of a Northwest variety. Like monsters in fairytales, Bigfoot in *Sasquatch Mountain* eats those lost in the darkening woods.

During the semester, Clark enlisted this prey/predator motif in a fishing dream. He was in a red canyon where he felt "so small in comparison to the monstrous walls and wide river" and held a pole he used as a boy fishing with his father. The canyon walls suggest the same monster theme as the Sasquatch dream. "I felt even smaller when I realized what type of boat I was in; a small one-man wooden rowboat." A giant fish pulls Clark down the river. Here the small boat is reminiscent of the tiny toy car that Clark holds in the Sasquatch dream and the enormous fish echoes Bigfoot's print, twice the size of Clark's own. The fish turns and shoots at Clark "like a torpedo fired from a submarine sent to sink me.... When he jumped, he pulled the line out of the reel and the line burned right through my thumb...this caused deep dark red blood to come gushing...down my hand and forearm." Clark forgets about steering his boat, then realizes he is floating toward a waterfall. In North American fish stories, men tell about "the big one that got away": in doing so they brag about their skill as predators. In this Torpedo Fish dream, the prey becomes the predator, while injured Clark's life is threatened.

The family GMC is another important image in Clark's Bigfoot dream and evokes a second cultural model that I call the Car self-model, considered at length in Chapter 5. I use "car" as an inclusive category for all autos that individuals drive themselves. So, a truck like Clark's GMC is a "car," but a bus is not. Based on his psychoanalytic work in Los Angeles, Hollan sees the car as a North American self-symbol, one that suggests:

> [L]ife and people should run smoothly and without interruption; that when life and people do breakdown, they should be repairable; that life is a journey involving constant movement and progress, and that one is in trouble if one is stopped too long by the side of the road; that big, strong, fast, powerful cars are better than small, weak, slow, broken down cars; that it's better to be the driver of a car than a passive passenger; that it's better to own a car than not; that one's car is one's castle and its boundaries are sacred (2003a:70).

The phrase, "one's car is one's castle," derives from the classic U.S. adage: "A man's home is his castle," meaning that home is a small kingdom where he is lord. Today, rather than being kings on a diminutive scale, North American men are members of a domestic democracy where women and, to a lesser extent, children agitate for equal say. If men are no longer lords of their "castles," they are still lords of their cars. During the period in which Clark had this dream, a male identification with motor vehicles was merchandized nightly in ubiquitous commercials for ever-larger and more-expensive cars and trucks that most often featured men in the role of proud owners and drivers.

The Car self-model is male-identified but it is not a gender model. In other words, while associated with males in popular culture (ads, car chases in movies, etc.), the car does not configure only a model of how males should be but a model of how people should be: "going somewhere." Yet, this model, we will see, resembles Supermasculinity in many respects and shares many of its schemas.

Clark's dream GMC, the "Jimmy," first appears as a Hot Wheels toy: it is juvenile, an attribute underlined by its name. Americans often add a "y" to a name to make a nickname for kids: James or Jim may become Jimmy. Clark feels himself to be juvenile: "no matter how hard I try to be self reliant, I always end up leaning on my mother...to feel better or solve problems financially or with relationships." Monster dreams, like the Torpedo Fish dream, are characteristic of children (van de Castle 1994:314–318), probably because they feel their worlds are bigger than they are and out of control—just as Clark does.

The Jimmy is also an old truck and, at 24, Clark feels himself to be old. "I am at the age now where my hair is starting to thin, my metabolism has started to slow and I am not as physically able anymore because of the car accident and surgeries." Clark had a major car accident. His girlfriend insisted on going shopping in nearby Moscow during a heavy snowstorm; he insisted on driving her. What happened to him would have happened to her, he says, if he hadn't gone. He prefers it that way. Clark has a Rescue schema, yet rescues by sacrificing himself, which leaves him impaired.

Fixing the Jimmy is the next dream motif, as well as another activity that Clark and his father shared. "I never got the hang of being a mechanic, but I love cars and when I was little I used to collect Hot Wheels and pretend to be like my father and fix them." At 17, Clark got a job at Les Schwab: "When I was working there, many of the problems I had with my father...started." In the dream, his job at Les Schwab is to hunt Bigfoot, combining hunting and fixing. For U.S. men fixing represents an ability to solve problems (Tannen 1990). Problem solving, we will see in Chapter 3, is another Supermasculinity schema, by which I mean one of those schemas that, all together, define this cultural model. Like hunting, fixing is an activity through which U.S. men often attempt to establish dominance. Fixing dovetails nicely with the technologically enhanced power configured by cars and trucks. Yet, Clark feels he cannot fix his family: he cannot create a close family out of his immediate relatives.

> I cannot bring my family together and I cannot take away the pain that I know everyone is experiencing. I...feel guilty about not being able to fix this problem....I have grown up believing that one should be able to control his life and that one can accomplish anything if enough effort is applied.

In the dream, however, Clark does fix the Jimmy. Like his ability to overcome the "wups" and his willingness to hunt Bigfoot, this dream fact contradicts the feeling of inadequacy expressed above, yet the dream symbolizes this feeling too: it represents the full range of Clark's experience.

What are the "wups"? Do they pun on getting "wupped," a colloquial U.S. term for being beaten up or losing a contest? Clark said they were "obstacles I have had to...put behind me...hurdles...such as my car accident, the neck surgery...my parents divorce and becoming the man of the family and inheriting the responsibility of protecting them." In his study of American kinship, Schneider (1968:36) says that the phrase "the man of the family" suggests that men are "naturally best able to take authority and responsibility for the family"—"pants" (or prints) that Clark feels unable to fill. Clark's dad had affairs. The subsequent divorce left Clark's dad prosperous and his mom in economic difficulty. She got the family house with acreage that she can't keep up by herself. The previous summer, despite his neck injury, Clark chopped five cords of wood for her so that she could be warm in winter. Is this why in the dream Les Schwab is located at the site of his mom's house? This house is a symbol of what Clark cannot fix (or maintain) by himself. Clark is a Good Kid: a Good Kid, we will see later in the chapter, is a model of sons or daughters who help parents and also meet or surpass parents' high hopes. But too much help is asked of Clark, making it less likely that he will fulfill anyone's hopes including his own.

The dirt and gravel road, scored "with ruts and potholes," Clark said also signified "the hardships and difficulties I have had." The road is an important image in U.S. mythology. We ride down Route 61, Dylan's metaphor for modernity, and get our kicks on Route 66. "My way or the highway" is one classic cliché ultimatum that American fathers deliver to wayward sons. Chapter 5 argues that Americans have a Traveling self-model symbolized by the motif of traveling and images of the car and the road—a model that depicts the self as transcendent of social contexts and quintessentially in transit. Since the European Enlightenment, Westerners have seen the self as aimed beyond birth context and its attendant status. This movement is fundamental to Americans' belief that merit, not birth, "makes the man."

Moving beyond birth context seems impossible to Clark given his mom's needs. Clark even feels guilty going to school on the other side of the state because she cannot maintain her house and property without him. His girlfriend recently graduated and moved to Oregon. Clark was supposed to graduate the year before the dream but put it off because she wanted him to live with her, which would mean being even farther from his mom.

The dream road ends in a forest that reminded Clark of his mom's backyard, which "leads into the forest of Ranger Mountain, I...used the forest as an escape....I would build forts and sometimes even camp out over night." So, memories evoked by the dream also allude to an earlier self that Clark seems to have forgotten: as a child he lived in the forest like Bigfoot. This memory hints at the possibility of a positive and successful masculinity. Escape is one way to achieve detachment and detachment is a Supermasculinity schema. In movies, for example, Supermen often fly: they detached from earth and what goes on there. They are also often "cool" meaning detached versus anxiously overengaged, which permits both risk-taking and the objectivity necessary for problem solving. Yet the dream forest, unlike Clark's childhood forest, is anything but an escape.

"[T]he forest seemed to creep up on and surround me...it seemed to represent my path of life stopping and...when the forest rushed me I felt all of my anxieties, problems and insecurities...overwhelming me." Here Clark dissociates agency and attributes it to the forest. What moves in the dream forest (besides Bigfoot) is the white fog, an image that Clark related to a dream earlier in the semester of "a giant skunk that won't stop spraying." Like the fog that creeps ever closer, "the skunk fumes surrounded me, and totally engulfed me....[T]he skunk spray was foggy, thick, it clouded the air and surrounded me even when I got in the house." Clark also associated the skunk with "my mom's house and her dog." Clark and his dad, remember, would sniff the air (like dogs?) for Bigfoot's "terrible odor." Clark associated this dream skunk with a comic figure from childhood cartoons, Pepe LePue, who was "suave...with the lady skunks, but he smelled so bad....[H]e tried to overcome his problems...by being a smooth-talking charismatic skunk."

Ingham (2007:149) shows that heightened disgust reactions, for example to a smell, may reflect persistent incestuous attachment. Clark's chain of associations (the fog; the spray; his mom; the suave, smooth-talking smelly skunk) seems to confirm this idea. I suggest that his issue is not incest per se; rather, incest is a bodily symbol of overengagement between Clark and his mother resulting from his father's absence.

Wishes and Anxieties. "The hunt for Bigfoot represents my quest to gain my father's approval," Clark wrote. He believed that the dream wish was: "I will be able to get over my fears, become a man and gain respect from my father." Chodorow (1974, 1978) argues that when fathers are relatively uninvolved with sons' bodily care, sons develop a "negative gender identity" in which they define manhood as being different from mom and, later, from women generally; this oppositional masculinity is less secure than gender based on a positive identification with a person intimately known. Clark's identity as a man is doubly oppositional. Not only does Clark define himself against his mom as "the man of the family," because he blames his dad for his family's disintegration, he also defines himself in opposition to him, all the while he wants his approval.

People use models and their associated schemas to create identities. Yet, models may not be conscious: they are often implicit and taken to be the way things are. We will later see, however, that people often consciously identify with the figures that symbolize models and that these figures play powerful roles in their emotional lives. As we saw in the introduction, schemas are more likely to be conscious: they are relatively simple ideas that one can hold in short-term memory; their associated motifs, moreover, provide means to enact identity. Clark's absent dad implicitly offers him two schemas: the Extraordinary Powers schema and the Problem-solving schema. His dad enacts these schemas through hunting and fixing respectively—activities combined in Clark's dream job at Les Schwab. Yet, in Clark's experience his dad's way of being a man solved nothing but landed the family in catastrophe, which makes identifying with him about as easy as catching Bigfoot. *Sasquatch Mountain*, remember, was one of the movies the dream evoked for Clark—a movie in which this man-beast eats people lost in the woods. Eating is symbolic of identification, as in the saying, "You are what you eat." To identify as "like" dad, as Clark tries to do, threatens him with being eaten alive—his nascent identity subsumed. Clark felt his dream anxiety was, "knowing that I am not capable of controlling my life."

> My family has basically crumbled and fallen apart, I have difficulty driving my car because I fear...I will get hurt again, and I have no career path...even though I graduate next semester....In waking life, I have also become insecure due to many cultural beliefs that the human body should be flawless and virtually perfect.

Clark's doubly oppositional masculine identity seems to have broken his body, interrupted his life progress, and made any viable masculinity feel "unobtainable." His Bigfoot dream first attempts to resolve his insecurities through memories of good times with his dad, yet the dead end road at the end of the dream (where Clark can neither back up nor turn around) suggests that his dad's model leads only into the dark. Later in the semester, however, Clark arrived at his own version of masculinity in a dream where he sights an overturned red canoe.

> I instantly shed my clothes and jumped in to check for a person underneath the canoe, but the river current was strong, it swept me downstream. I finally managed to get to shore and then saw a kid stuck up in [a] tree. I climbed the tree and talked to the kid and he said

he'd been there for eight days....I brought him back to the trail....I jumped backed in the river, but placed myself in front of the canoe so I wouldn't have to fight the river. I saved the kid under the canoe who said he'd been there for five days and brought him back to his brother. The...two boys turned into two African-American women.

Clark's Bigfoot dream is an Oedipal tale: Clark tries to capture (kill?) a symbol of his dad. This Red Canoe dream, in contrast, opens as what I call a "Band of Brothers" tale, a tale-type Freud tells in *Totem and Taboo* ([1913]1962). Freud believed that the original human family consisted of a dominant male, his several wives, and their children. As male children matured, the father cast them out until one day these boys banded together and killed their father. *Totem and Taboo* is a fraternal variant of Oedipus. After murder, the sons ate their father, a symbolic incorporation of his authority. At first, the brothers had sex with their mothers and sisters, but soon realized that the result was social chaos, so they decided to abide by the same mother/sister avoidances formally enforced by their father—the incest taboo—which Lacan (1977a), calls the Law of the Father.

Totem and Taboo, I suggest, represents Freud's incipient realization that there is a progression of related tales in the development of Western-style masculinities. The first major tale-type in this series is what I call a Knight tale. These tales focus on a son figure and his Oedipal relation with an older or bigger man or monster. Clark's Bigfoot dream features a monster-slaying motif proper to Knight tales, although it is only the opening scene of such a tale.[11] There is a second type where the accent falls on fraternity. In some Fraternal tales, brothers band together against an Oedipal father (a father who's got "the girl"). Think of *Oceans 11*. Other Fraternal tales are about battles among brothers—evenly matched male opponents. Think of Sherlock and Moriarty. At some point along this narrative range, however, the emphasis shifts to rescuing a brother figure. Think of *Saving Private Ryan*. There is also a third major tale-type in this progression, the Damsel in Distress (Bettelheim 1976:111–115). In these tales, the emphasis is on rescuing someone toward whom you might feel conjugal love.

Clark's self-sacrificing stance vis-à-vis his mother and girlfriend are midway between injury and agency in the service of rescue. In the Red Canoe dream, however, Clark rescues two brothers without injury. In recent years, Clark has rescued his real brother from dangerous circumstances. By morphing the two victims into African American women, the dream retrospectively rewrites itself as a

Damsels-in-Distress tale, which symbolizes (given that Clark is heterosexual) an adult orientation to sexuality and to agency. Clark's dreams are a space where he tries to practice and adapt a U.S. masculinity model in a way that promises closer family relations.

Lois

Lois was 20, "white," and born in the larger Seattle area. During the semester, she had a dream, recurrent since childhood. Recurrent dreams point to intractable problems with a cultural model beyond which the dreamer cannot move.

> I am standing on a cliff. When I look down there is nothing, and when I turn around there is a purple and green dragon. The dragon is huge and unfriendly. I am me in the dream, but at the same time I am watching this situation, with me in it, from somewhere else. This is the whole dream, my options are to try and pass by the dragon or climb down the cliff.

Yet, in the dream Lois never takes either option but only stands between the dragon and the brink and also watches herself from afar.

Name that Text. The U.S. genre evoked by the dream scene is the Cliffhanger—a term for a thrilling adventure movie, full of risk and suspense. For Lois, this dream evoked a fairytale: "The dragon looks exactly like the dragon found in the movie *Sleeping Beauty*," Lois wrote, "which I used to watch as a child." Lois refers here to Disney's animated adaptation of Sleeping Beauty (1997). "[T]his is also my mother's favorite movie. In the movie the witch, Maleficent, turns into the dragon at the end of the story. My mother's favorite villain to this day is still Maleficent, and she has a costume of her that she wears every Halloween."

Sleeping Beauty is a coming-of-age tale. In Grimm's Brothers' nineteenth-century version ([1819]1977:175–177), a Wise Woman curses an infant princess because she is not invited to her birth celebration. The curse is that on her fifteenth birthday she will prick her finger on a spindle and die. Twelve other Wise Women are invited; one uses her gift to dilute the curse: the princess will only sleep. The king and queen have spindles banned from the kingdom but on the eve of her fifteenth birthday, the princess opens the door to a secret room where an old woman spins and the princess pricks her finger.

Here Beauty's curse is "the curse": her blood symbolizes menses, sexual maturity—which has often been a curse for women in patriarchal worlds. Latency follows, symbolized by sleep, and for a hundred years (symbolic of a very long time) until Prince Charming hacks his way through the thorns that grow up around the castle and kisses the princess.

This narrative sequence is noteworthy: in classical psychoanalytic understandings, latency is supposed to precede puberty: as boys and girls become young men and women, they awake as sexual beings. In Grimm's Sleeping Beauty, although the girl is sexually mature, she has no sexuality, nor any adult life, except in response to a superhero prince. Freud ([1931]1964) might relate this sequence to his hypothesized reorientation of the girl from agentive clitoral sexuality to responsive vaginal sexuality. Since Masters and Johnson (1965a, 1965b, 1966), however, no one takes Freud's hypothesis seriously. Feminists infer, rather, that in advancing this hypothesis, Freud was influenced by a socioeconomic system that denied women sexual agency.

Sleeping Beauty is a European folk tale collected as part of the nineteenth-century romantic/folkloric movement. Its selection from other European folktales may reflect its correspondence to Victorian models of feminine sexuality. At first its importance in late twenty-first century collections made for U.S. kids and by the major producer of U.S. children's fantasy, Walt Disney Corporation, is surprising. The original folktale seems dated—but is it? To answer this question we must look to how Disney alters the nineteenth-century version.

In Disney's animated film, three good fairies spirit the infant Beauty away to the countryside to escape the evil Maleficent's curse. Their lives are wholly devoted to Beauty; they give up their powers—represented by their wings and wands—for her sake. Maleficent, in contrast, is out for herself and is as curvy as the good fairies are amorphously plump. Disney's mothering fairies reflect the Devoted Mom model. Lois had a devoted mom: after the divorce, she did not work but dedicated herself to bringing up her children. Such devotion can be a curse as well as a blessing. This is why, I believe, in Lois's dream an apparent opposite—the female dragon out of Disney's tale—represents her devoted mom. The underside of the Devoted Mom is an engulfing mom: like a dragon, she eats her children in the sense of disallowing their independent lives. Just as Clark's dream, Lois's dream evokes a monster-slayer motif, although his monster is male while hers is female.

In psychoanalytic terms, a woman dragon—a winged snakelike creature—would be a phallic mother. Many feminist scholars have argued that in cultural worlds where men have more power than women do the phallus signifies power. A phallic woman then symbolizes a powerful woman, which is probably why Lois's mom loved to dress up as Maleficent. Maleficent is also a witch. Klein (1988) explains witches in fairytales. At first for infants, the mother is a giver of love in physical and emotional form. As a child gets larger and begins to develop teeth, it bites and mother draws back; this takes place just as a child is getting hungrier. The result is rage, along with a desire for unlimited nursing, tantamount to eating the mother up. Children cannot face their hostility toward their most loved person; instead, they project their emotions and split their mother into a good mother and a bad mother. Good Mother is the giver. Bad Mother is the witch who wants to destroy the child— indeed who would eat the child.

The classic fairytale, Hansel and Gretel, illustrates the split mother and her relation to eating (Bettelheim 1976:159–165). In Grimm's version ([1819]1977:56–61), Hansel's and Gretel's step-mother (a correlative of the witch within the family circle) urges their father to abandon them in the woods because he cannot afford to feed them. After living in a state of semistarvation for several days, the children find and begin to eat a house of cake, bread, and sugar that belongs to a witch. The witch captures the children. Her plan is to roast and eat them. Eating, remember, symbolizes identification. Klein's witch-mother represents a difference-obliterating identification. Yet, in the end, Gretel roasts the witch by pushing her into the oven in which she was going to bake Hansel, symbolically transforming her into food. The witch is the second most common female figure in U.S. children stories, the most common being the mother (Heim 1995), which suggests that mother/child boundary erosion is a strong fear for U.S. kids.

Klein did not hold that the fantasies she discovered were gender specific, but the Western witch tales that Disney produces for children often have female protagonists, Snow White or The Littlest Mermaid for example, which suggests that they pertain especially to girls' emotions and needs. Oedipus illustrates a son-centered psychology. In Freud's theory, Electra (the jealous matricidal daughter) is an afterthought and a way to universalize the Oedipus tale by suggesting that it applies, in slightly altered form, to women too. While Electra is evident in dreams presented throughout this book, and paramount for Betsy in Chapter 4, the stories/fantasies that Klein explores better describe the psychological problems and developmental scenarios these dreams depict for most of my female subjects.[12] Boundary issues may in part explain why U.S. young women are prone to eating disorders such as anorexia and bulimia. In eating disorders, young women attempt to control their own body and thereby to secure inviolate boundaries (Gremillion 2003).

Why should boundary erosion be a more pivotal psychological theme for young women than for young men? Chodorow (1974, 1978) argues that, because of gender likeness, mother-daughter relations can result in boundary confusion: a sense that the other is not a separate person. Boundary confusion, I suggest, is likely to amplify a child's fear of the difference-obliterating identification with the mother Klein describes. The Close Family model, which intensifies mother-daughter association, further heightens the possibility of identification. Then, as a girl emerges into young womanhood, a mother may be overprotective and fail to acknowledge her daughter as a separate being. In Disney's *Sleeping Beauty,* the good fairies keep Beauty around the house rather than allowing her own adventures. When Lois was a teenager, her mom likewise insisted she always get home early despite her consistently high grades.

Lois's dream of her mother as a dragon/witch suggests that, in the context of a father-absent household, U.S. mothers may sometimes threaten a consuming confusion of boundaries that stands in the way of girls becoming separate individuals who undertake their own adventures—climbing down the cliff in Lois's dream. Lois's developmental experiences make it difficult for her to develop an ability to choose for herself, the difficulty on which her recurrent dream founders. And yet, Lois's memory of her mother as Maleficent in a sense contradicts the problem posed by the dragon. For Lois's mom and evidently for her as well, Maleficent represents a not-so-scary and entertaining game played on one of the nation's favorite holidays, a day when many children court fear for fun. As an image, therefore, Maleficent combines a problem with the Close Family model with a memory that suggests this problem is not entirely real and that also hints at a way out: risk-taking.

Images and Motifs. Lois identified the major dream motif as "coming to a crossroads....[T]he image of the dragon and the cliff are choices that I had to make once in my life, and am now facing again." The curious thing is that, while a crossroads implies choices and attendant action, here there is no action—either jumping down the cliff or slaying the dragon. What are these choices?

Lois's parents first divorced when she was two. Lois and her sister visited their father on weekends and kept some possessions at each parent's house. When Lois was five, they remarried. When she was seven, they divorced again. Lois had to choose with whom she was going to live. It was then she first had this dream. She was "a mommy's girl" and stayed with her mother, but it was a difficult decision. Her dad was well off, while her mother's income was modest and she lived in a small house. While their mom planned their time, their dad "let us decide what we wanted to do." Everything was spontaneous—a surprise. Her dad "shot from the hip, whatever he and his buddies were up to, the kids came along. It was always different." Lois thought that the dream cliff symbolized her dad; in turn, he was "symbolic of... living life on the edge."

Benjamin (1988) argues that fathers represent a larger world to the child along with the power, freedom, and excitement of that world, as he does for Lois. As an anthropologist, I question the cross-cultural consistency of these associations. In a number of pre-colonial Native North American and Polynesian cultures, for example, women held powerful positions in the public world.[13] I do not question these associations, however, in the United States when Lois grew up.

While a devouring dragon represents Lois's (overly) devoted mom, so also a sheer drop symbolizes her (insufficiently) supportive dad. A cliff (like a footprint) suggests something that is not there: where a road might continue there is nothing. Lois's cliff symbolizes her father as an absent transitional space where one jumps into the unknown. It seems likely that Lois learned about risk-taking in her freewheeling times with her spontaneous, permissive dad but, bidding for her attachment, he may have failed to encourage the detachment that makes freedom feel safe. Detachment and risk-taking are related practices: to the extent people detach, they feel they have little to lose and can undertake actions that might otherwise feel scary. It is precisely such detachment Lois's dream tries to supply. Lois's dream frame symbolizes detachment: she is watching the situation and herself in it from somewhere else. In suggesting detachment, Lois's dream points a way out of the situation and toward an ability to take risks.

Wishes and Anxieties. "Every time I have the dream," Lois wrote, "I never try to climb down the cliff or pass by the dragon. The dream is constantly one... scene," a scene, she believed, reflecting her wish "to have other options." People often understand wishing for "options" in the United States as wishing for freedom of choice. Yet, choice is also what Lois fears. "The dream anxiety is that I must choose. I remember being a child and feeling as though I constantly had to choose who to spend more time with, my mom or my dad.... The anxiety has grown over time, like I have." Lois's problem with the Close Family model is: it stands in the way of constituting her identity as someone who can choose.

In families, kids learn many cultural models. To the extent that their close kin do not "live up" to their culture's family model, kids may have trouble developing other models first learned in the family: in Clark's case a Supermasculinity model and in Lois's case what I call the U.S. Choice-as-agency model. Chapter 3 will argue that Americans tend to imagine agency as options but, as in Lois's case, options often bring with them angst and paralysis rather than the expanded horizons they seem to promise. Risk-taking is one of the constituent schemas of the U.S. Choice-as-agency model. Choice evokes angst/paralysis for Lois and a number of other dreamers in this volume because it is risky: one may choose wrongly and then there is no one else to blame. What Lois's family has not helped her do, she is working on in her dreams. Thus, Lois thought that the dream wish was also "to find a path of my own." Americans find such a path by executing choices: "two roads diverged in a yellow wood," as the iconic American poet, Robert Frost, puts it.

Lois thought that her dream was "resurfacing" because the holidays were approaching. Ceremonial occasions are times when people try to enact ideal versions of cultural models—ritual enactments, one might say, they cannot pull off on a daily basis. In the United States, Thanksgiving and Christmas are times when most people enact the Close Family model and, therefore, when an individual's problems with this model becomes painfully obvious. Lois had to decide how much time to spend at each parent's house; she felt this choice made it impossible to demonstrate adequate love and commitment to them both. This anxiety, she believed, followed from a more general need "to please others." The need to choose, then, is one Lois also faces with everyone. The solution, she thought, was drawing "a line" between "one's own needs and the wants of...peers." Here Lois suggests detachment from others is what she needs to make choices: the dream frame anticipates her conscious insight.

One finds an absent-father theme and a jumping motif in the popular American movie series *Tomb Raider* (Paramount 2001), popular during the study period. While originally a British-released video game (Core Designs 1996), Paramount rightly gauged the (revised) story's resonance with the U.S. public. In the first movie, Laura

Croft's father is dead, yet the plot revolves around a magic time-canceling device he planned for her to find. Like Clark's Bigfoot, then, Laura's father is absent and yet also a major presence in the story. One could look at the device he spirits into Laura's world as a transitional space. Transitional spaces are outside the constraints of normal existence; the most important of these is time. Hence time-canceling is an apt symbol for the special character of these spaces. Laura's mother is also dead but this is not so salient an issue, I suggest, because Laura personifies the Free Individual model. In this model, the self is inherently separate and different from others (detached in a word), which is hard to enact in the presence of a boundary-confusing mother figure.

Laura Croft's story and Lois's dreams "think" about how contemporary young women can internalize transitional space on their own. Laura's trapeze-like flights through open space punctuate the film and symbolize her willingness to take risks as well as her detachment (from earth, as a symbol of daily concerns).[14] Motifs, like flying, can configure more than one schema. Flying, as a willingness to jump into open space, is a motif that often represents risk-taking, but we saw above that it can also represent detachment. Detachment and risk-taking, and many more schemas we will encounter throughout this book, resemble what Shore (1996) calls a Foundational schema. For Shore, this means that a schema recurs in various cultural domains. For me, a Foundational schema is constitutive to a number of cultural models. To say that a schema is integral to a model, then, does not mean it is associated *only* with this model.

I argued in Chapter 1 that dreams too offer a transitional space and for Lois they were a place to practice risk-taking and detachment. Later in the semester, Lois dreamt: "I was falling next to a tall building with long glass windows.... My heart rate was elevated because of my fear of heights and falling off high objects." She associates the feeling of falling with "having no control of what is happening around you" and with September 11 and "stories I heard about people being in the buildings after the planes struck them. The people jumped...because the conditions...were so bad that jumping to their inevitable deaths seemed like the best option." She thought that this dream symbolized her wish to be in control of her "destiny": "I'm looking for control in my own life." This dream suggests Lois has escaped her mother's control in favor of (cliff) jumping, but if jumping is going her father's way rather than her mother's, it still doesn't feel like a choice.

Rather than merely delineating a situation where she has no options, in a sense, Lois's Crossroad dream recommends both options. The first is slaying the dragon, which represents, in Lois's words, "drawing a line in the sand," meaning overcoming the boundary confusion associated Devoted Moms; the second, descending the cliff, is taking the leap of faith that "living one's own life" in the U.S. demands. Her difficulty is not merely a personal problem but a set of common problems, particularly for girls, stemming from the Close Family model.

Kent

Kent is from a midsized northern Washington coastal city. He is "Caucasian" and 22 years old.

> I dreamt that I was at my parent's house and my mother was making a special dinner for my father. My younger sister and I were helping to set the table and set up candles and make sure everything was clean and nice looking....I was a lot younger. While cleaning the dining room, I found a pushpin in the carpet that was sticking straight up (there is no carpet in my parents' dining room). I was concerned that someone might step on the pin and hurt themselves, so I picked it out of the carpet. Right after I had picked that one up, I noticed another pushpin sticking up....Every time I picked up a pin, I seemed to find ten more. The whole time I was going around on my knees picking up pins, my mother and sister were still walking around barefoot in the dining room setting the table and getting things ready for dinner. I tried to stop them and tell them they might get hurt, but they didn't seem to care, and indeed, even though the carpet was completely full of pins sticking straight up at this point, they never seemed to step on one, or if they did, it didn't hurt them. When my dad got home, he suggested pulling up the carpet to shake out the pins.

Name that Text. The dream reminded Kent of two television shows: the 1950's *Leave it to Beaver* and a reality show he watched growing up called *Viva la Bam*. The dream scene, as Kent describes it, is a Beaver family: a symbol of the traditional U.S. family for Kent and for many of my students. In its Beaver form, a boy is at home with his mom (Kent in the dream is "a lot younger," probably under 12, he later remarked). Dad comes home evenings and weekends—a kind of *Father Knows Best* deus ex machina who descends to solve problems as he does in Kent's dream. In contrast, "Bam...is an example of the new family, which is almost completely opposite of the *Leave it to Beaver*. Bam is about 25, and lives at home with his parents and a few of his friends."

Bam lives with an extended family in two senses of the word: Bam is older than the boys who live with parents in Beaver's world; his household includes close friends. Bam's version of the Close Family model counters what Schneider (1968) sees as the basis of American kinship—genetic similarity. In Bam's family, closeness itself is the regent consideration: this model includes everyone to whom Bam feels close. Indeed, many people feel closer to their friends than to family: friends sometimes fit the Close Family model better than relatives do. More specifically, Bam's family combines the Close Family model with what I call the Guyfriends model, as in the U.S. expression "one of the guys." "Guys" may be members of a sports team, a gang, or simply a group who "hang out" and do things together, like Bam and his friends.

In early episodes, Kent remembered, Bam's family lived at the "Homestead," a phrase from U.S. frontier culture, which in Bam's case invokes the U.S mythical past but also what one might call the family's new frontier. Bam's family had to move out because of his pranks, but Bam made a lot of money from his skateboarding videos in reality and bought a big new house—Castle Bam. Is this name a reference to "A man's home is his castle"? Bam is a capitalist Superman; the evidence of his extraordinary powers is money; his skateboard is the vehicle with which he flies through the air. Kent continued:

> Bam and his friends are constantly breaking things in the house and starting wild projects like building a "tree-top casino" in the woods behind his house....Bam and Beaver care for their families very much, but...in different ways....Beaver might help his mother get dinner ready, Bam is very likely to tell his mother that he hates the dinner. To make it up to her, he usually ends up buying her something.

I am reminded here of Baudrillard's (1988) vision of postmodernity as intrinsically fantasy oriented and hedonistic; its mantra "Buy something" to fulfill yourself (or your mother, Bam might add).

Bam's motto is "What will I do next?" The answer, Kent said, was "whatever I want," which usually meant something destructive, off-the-wall, and grandiose. I call this the Impulse-gratification schema. This schema is part of a Bad Boy variant of Supermasculinity.

Model variants, as I define them, share schemas with a major model, but often include an additional schema or schemas that may seem at odds with the model but are not. As U.S. Americans say, "boys will be boys," meaning they may break the rules to satisfy their desires but still observe important principles.[15]

Bam's family is a U.S. capitalist boy's fantasy—one in which he can do and say "whatever," but still have mother love because of his money and munificence. In this "freedom," Bam is a post-Oedipal figure, happily inhabiting a U.S. matrifocal family, which Clark and Lois inhabit less happily. Bam's father is not physically absent, but his son has usurped his role as provider. Kent did not mention him: he is a recessed figure, and the authority he symbolizes, Lacan's (1977a) Law of the Father, is virtually gone.

Here it is useful to return to Marcuse's idea of performance principles, outlined in the introduction. Under early twentieth-century U.S. capitalism (the labor union era), performance principles dictated that men direct their energy to labor and to impulse gratification, which meant drinking, sex, and other "manly" pleasures. I say "men" because there was an alternative set of performance principles for women tied to the Cinderella model, which I consider in Chapter 3. From the late twentieth century to the early twenty-first century "liberation" sported by Bam, people saw themselves as free (like Bam they felt they could, in principle, do whatever they wanted), but Baudrillard (1998) argues that this freedom was virtual: their desires were created and channeled by a global "system of objects."

The first project Kent mentions in describing Bam's antics—the backyard treetop casino—underlines Bam's identification as a twenty-first century capitalist with twenty-first century performance principles. The Comaroffs (2001) argue that the casino is a prime economic symbol of contemporary capitalism—think of James Bond sitting suavely behind the roulette wheel. Rather than "Work hard!" the imperative of the age is, "Place your bets, ladies and gentlemen," in the global stock market. Given that many U.S. State governments and corporations vest employees' retirement in stocks, people have a plethora of stock options (a U.S. synonym for agency), but cannot get out of the game. The image of the casino suggests that Bam (a skateboarding mogul) is as dedicated to the capitalism of his era as his forbearers were to the capitalism of theirs. One might say that gamesmanship, luck, and self-indulgence combine to comprise a less dichotomous and more seductive performance principle than labor and impulse gratification once did.

Images and Motifs. "I think the major motif of the dream is the wife making the husband dinner....I remember the dining room looked very nice and my mom had spent a long time getting dinner ready." Kent's dream seems to be presenting a nostalgic Beaver scene but is not. Beaver and his parents typically ate together. Beaver did not help his mother make his dad candlelit dinners; Kent didn't either: "I cannot recall an instance where my sister and I helped my mother make a dinner for her and my father to enjoy in solitude." Even Kent's mother did not make fancy dinners for his dad because "gender roles are not as concrete as they once were." In a 1950s TV show for example?

Mom and dad's roles in the Close Family are fairly well defined, although increasingly flexible in contemporary gender-bending U.S. culture. Kids' role is less so. In the Good Kid model, growing children are supposed to love other family members (even when they don't feel close); this can be trying with an absent dad, an overinvolved mom, or a sibling who is either competitive or preferred. And, kids are supposed to make a success of their lives: again, this means not to disappoint the "high hopes" parents are supposed to have for their eventual achievements, but this is an extremely long-term goal. In the short run, kids' practical obligations are to "help." In the Beaver family, this apprenticeship was a way they learned gender roles. Daughters helped moms to care for their families. Sons helped dad with more manly chores, like mowing the lawn—manly because such tasks required strength and often an ability to fix machines, which we saw is a motif associated with Supermasculinity.

By helping his mom prepare a romantic dinner, Kent alludes to an earlier era in U.S. American family life, but he takes the daughter's role and, further, contributes to his parents' intimate relationship rather than being an Oedipal rival. The opening dream scene seems an assertion that what Kent wants is a Beaver world, where desire is only between mom and dad, but the pushpins threatened to spoil the show.

The pushpins are the second major dream image. Kent thought they could be "some sort of prank" because in one episode Bam put tacks in a friend's shoes. In the dream, then, the pushpins stand for Bam. A dream image's significance, at least in part, is what it summons in remembrance; what the pushpins summon is Bam. Bam is a U.S. colloquial term not listed in my American Heritage Dictionary. I have seen it in comics where it is an onomatopoetic expression for a loud, explosive sound. I know of only one common use: the joking remark, "Slam, bam, thank you ma'am!" In the dream report,

Kent repeatedly described these pins as "sticking straight up": the pushpins are phallic. The dangerously intruding pins, along with Bam's name (through allusion to ejaculation), raise the subject of sex within the family.

Kent acts the role of a Good Kid in the dream (helping his mom make dinner) but, in a sense, Bam is a Good Kid too. After all Bam helps his parents by giving them a new house. In Kent's dream, however, as in Lois's and Clark's, an opposite represents a major model at issue: the pushpins (a cruel prank) represent the Good Kid (Bam). And these pins intrude themselves in a way diametrically opposed to being a Good Kid. They intrude via the third major dream image, the carpet—significant because there is no carpet in Kent's family dinning room.

An American expression for hidden problems is "To sweep it under the carpet." The pushpins sticking through the carpet suggest an emergence of hidden unwanted feelings, probably incestuous feelings, but here again sexuality represents more than itself: specifically overinvolvement—symbolized by engulfing fog and the sexy skunk in Clark's case, being eaten by the dragon in Lois's, and the pushpins in Kent's.

Anxieties and Wishes. "I was very concerned about my mother and sister stepping on a pushpin and getting hurt," Kent wrote. As in Clark's dream, in Kent's feet are a major image, but feminine feet that counterpoint the pushpins. Neither Kent nor his father is barefoot in the dream. His mother's and sister's naked feet are an example of how dreams change waking reality to express meaning: these feet are in a state of undress and must be to hazard harm. In *And Keep your Powder Dry,* Mead (1942a) argues that in the United States (versus England), women's role is to control sexuality. In the close family, this means to make it invisible. In Kent's dream, his mom fails in this endeavor by enlisting his help with a romantic dinner. Yet, by walking about barefoot, acting "as if" everything is normal, she and Kent's sister play this part (suppressing sex by ignoring it). The context in which they do so, however, contradicts normality (neither Kent's mom nor sister normally go barefoot); hence, they also make this "as if" visible, just as the pins peek through the carpet.

While long hair is probably the most common bodily fetish worldwide (Leach 1958, Mageo 1994, Hiltebeitel and Miller 1998), feminine feet—naturally small like Cinderella's, unnaturally bound, or displayed by high heels—are also a common fetish. For psychoanalysts, fetishes acquire their most important meanings at the Oedipus crisis. Then boys discover that when it comes to gender there are haves and have-nots and infer that, if have-nots exist, they could lose their penises. Typically, fetishes are elongated female body parts or accoutrements that assuage boys' resulting "castration anxiety" by standing in for the lost penis, which they imagine women once had. What do fetishes have to do with pushpins and Bam?

Bam lives in a castle where impulse indulgence has no consequence. This is like the world of the fetish. In that world, boys/men act out forbidden desires but no punishment (castration) follows. If the pushpins stand for Bam, who in turn stands for impulse gratification without consequence, so do Kent's mom and sister, or at least their bare feet, which never step on the absurdly multiplying pins. Impulse gratification is, then, what Freud would call "overdetermined" in the dream: more than one dream image repeats this meaning. With the pins standing for Bam, the accent is on "I want." With the bare feet, the accent falls on a "there will be no consequences." As Kent says: "even though the carpet was completely full of pins sticking straight up at this point, they never seemed to step on one, or if they did, it didn't hurt them." Yet, this imperviousness does not stem Kent's mounting anxiety, a free-floating anxiety Kent also feels in daily life. While Bam is constantly messing up his castle, Kent calls himself a "neat freak." He compared the dream scene to never being able to get all the dust off the floor when nobody cares but you. He likes things in order but makes a conscious effort "not to care" for other people's sake (because he cares about them).

If pushpins are like ineradicable dust, they resemble a pollution fantasy, and yet in pollution fantasies the dirtying element is typically menstrual fluids, not phallic. Cross-culturally, pollution fantasies and rituals correlate positively with close early mother-son relations (Mageo 2005, 2008b). Among the Hua, the Wogeo, and the Sambia, for example, people regard infants and young children as contaminating because they have so recently bathed in female fluids; adult males, therefore, avoid them (Meigs 1984:63–64, Herdt 1987:84).[16] Yet, Kent's dream suggests that he risks anxiety, not so much about females and their fluids, as about his own impulses. Kent wrote, "The dream wish is...to save my family from getting a pin in the foot," but again, only his mother and sister are barefoot. "One might hypothesize that it is also my wish to see someone step on a pin as sort of a cruel prank, but I could never do that to someone, especially my family." If Kent identifies as strongly attached, he also takes vicarious pleasure in Bam's pranks and wants to be cool, as Bam is.

In the dream, Kent directs his care at women's feet, while Bam on TV directs jocular aggression at men's feet. Bam is what I will call a counteridentity. A counteridentity is an oppositional figure that personifies dissociated thoughts and feelings inconsistent with a dreamer's conscious identity and that oscillates in and out of consciousness. In an interview, Kent said he is "serious" and "gets things done and on time," while his sister is "impressionable, silly, and frivolous." Kent's sister, surely, could not be more frivolous and silly than Bam is, but Kent admires him. Kent's judgment of his sister suggests (dissociated) aggressiveness like that enacted generally by Bam and in the dream by the "cruel" pushpins.

The attentiveness expected of Devoted Moms provides, in Foucault's (1979, 1982) terms, a high level of surveillance. Bam's determinedly outrageous behavior and lack of care for what anyone thinks represents resistance to normalization and the repression that goes with it. Although in his paper Kent stressed that Bam "cares very much about his family," in an interview he asserted, Bam "doesn't care"; he just goes on playing baseball in the living room. After all, he paid for it! In this sense, Bam features a Devil-may-care version of the Detachment schema, which is also part of Bad Boy masculinity and that, for economy sake, I simply call the Devil-may-care schema.

Lack of care or concern is also Kent's mother's and sister's attitude in the dream. Kent, in contrast, is "nervous about people getting hurt and do what I can to stop it and failing that, I don't want to watch. I...get upset if people get too close to the edge of a cliff." As in Lois's dream, here a cliff represents the possibility of detachment (which contrasts with Kent's anxious attachments) and risk-taking. Like Lois, Kent repudiates risks and, in his dream, these risks are displaced onto others.

Kent's dream father intervenes to offer a solution, reasserting, one might say, Lacan's Law of the Father—a law against incest. Again, however, I suggest that Kent's anxiety is not about incest per se. The pushpins are metasymbolic; they symbolize incestuous feelings, which in turn symbolize Bam violating the Law of the Father—which I see as social norms in patriarchical worlds. Incest, however, also stands for Kent's overinvolvement with his mom and sister. Overinvolvement provokes an ambivalent reaction: on the one hand, anxious care because the person identifies excessively with another; on the other hand, a reaction *against* involvement. Disgust, for example to a skunk's smell, is one such reaction. Hostility, such as that Kent expressed toward his sister in our interview and in the dream toward both mother and sister through the prankish push-pins, is another.

"It is curious that," Kent observed, "it is my mother and sister that I am trying to protect from these pins. I have a lot of girls in my life (my girlfriend and a ton of other female friends) and I do my best to protect them when I can." Kent's problems with the Close Family model are different from but similar to Clark's: for both, close relations with opposite-sex relatives raise incest issues. For Clark, these issues complicate the development of masculinity; for Kent, they complicate sexuality. Let me explain. Clark's overinvolvement with his mother since his parents' divorce leaves him feeling as if he can't be a man or fill his father's shoes. Kent's overinvolvement with his mother and sister leave him anxious about his impulses—symbolized by his inability to protect their feet in the dream and acted out through his obsessive neatness in waking life.

This anxiety probably stems at least in part from confusion about the Guyfriends versus the Girlfriend model of personal relating. Unlike guyfriends, girlfriends are emotionally intimate with other girls, or physically and emotionally intimate with a boy. A Care schema is critical to this Girlfriend model, which entails a commitment to care for and to take care of others, rather than simple companionship. As the Care schema is also part of the Devoted Mom model, care is another Foundational schema linking models. Larger groups of girlfriends may also have a Clique model that features an Insider/Outsider schema in which a few girls marginalize or exclude other girls (Goodwin 2006). U.S. girls form cliques for the same reason that they become Cinderellas—to gain recognition, status, and other advantages through affiliation—but that is not my concern here.

Like a girlfriend, Kent appears to be emotionally intimate with a group of girls: he listens to his female friends' problems. "Trouble-sharing" is motif associated with the Girlfriend model: it is what U.S. "girlfriends" typically do with one another (Tannen 1990, 2001). In the Beaver family model, moreover, moms and daughters take care of the house and its inhabitants: they clean and make meals. Yet, Kent performs these activities in his dream: he helps make dinner and tries to clean the carpet (he compares picking up pins to cleaning up dust). Kent, like Clark, would like to be a knight who protects or rescues endangered females (his female friends and female relatives in his dream). Protection is another Supermasculinity schema and closely related to the Rescue schema: Supermen are supposed to protect others, but sometimes can't and then they must rescue them. Since the beginning of the feminist movement, however, many U.S.

women don't seem to want rescuing even when they appear to need it, leaving Kent only to listen and assist like "one of the girls." Yet, Kent's memories of Bam's jokes, just as Clark's of living in the forest when he was a boy and Lois's of her mom Halloween costume, alludes to a detached frame (pranks/play) through which Kent might see and accept his impulses in waking life.

Bean (1976) argues that in late-twentieth-century U.S. soap operas, the *Leave It to Beaver* family was constantly collapsing and resurrecting. Kent saw the dream as representing a wish, not for resurrection (evidently, its flaws can no longer be swept under the carpet), but remediation: "The *Leave it to Beaver* family just doesn't fit anymore. Although the family image in *Viva la Bam* is really not accurate, it provides us with an opposite family image. Most families today lie somewhere between Beaver's family and Bam's family." As Grenell (2008) and Fosshage (1997, 1987:299–318) argue, dreams organize and integrate conflicting affect and ideas. In my view, they mediate between personal experiences and existing models and between contradictory models that are likely to emerge in and disrupt everyday activities and relations. Clark's dream mediates between predation and (injurious) self-sacrifice, Lois's between being a "mommy's girl" and jumping without a safety net, and Kent's between Beaver's close family normality and Bam's extended family anarchy. By doing so, dreamers make new connections within those shared webs of significance with which people make sense of their lives.

Constituting the family is a recurrent motif in Kent's dreams. When his own girlfriend is in such a dream, Kent's anxieties recede into the background and his wishes dominate. In one such dream, an old couple gives away plots of land in a suburban neighborhood. He and his girlfriend get one and start to build their house. The grass in the backyard is like a golf course and sits next to a dock with a boat. Perhaps this is Kent's Castle Bam and refers to another problem with the Close Family model: the income it takes to emulate it. "Making it" is always a gamble in a late capitalist order.

Comparisons

Psychoanalysis can show us how personal meaning is; textuality, à la Geertz, demonstrates how meaning is public and shared. Narrative Analysis reveals how meaning is at once intensely personal and widely shared: dreams think about our most personal experiences through public stories and think about the models embedded in these stories through our lives.

In this chapter, we witnessed motifs and images from narratives circulating in U.S. culture enter into dreams—as the hunt and the big footprint step into Clark's dream, jumping into midair and a green and purple dragon into Lois's, and candlelit dining and push-pins into Kent's. These narrative elements represent those larger tales from which they come and fuse these tales with dreamers' life stories: Clark dreams of his dad as Bigfoot, Lois of her mother as Maleficent, and Kent of himself as Beaver. I have argued that, by comparing a group of dreams about a cultural model, one exposes a range of current problems with it. Clark dreams of U.S. father problems, Lois of mother problems, and Kent of son problems. Yet, all these dreams address overlapping issues (mother/child overinvolvement compounded by father absence) because they concern a common model of and for family relations.

Psychoanalysts once distinguished between the manifest dream, the dream as dreamt, and the latent dream, the dream's hidden meanings. In the context of this distinction, Freud (1963) originated the term "dreamwork." Dreamwork referred to the symbolic substitutions that disguised dreams' latent meanings. As I mentioned in Chapter 1, dream researchers have largely abandoned this view, believing instead that the dream simply speaks a language of metaphor not immediately apprehensible to waking consciousness. Dreamwork then becomes the transformations of meaning into metaphors through which dreamers think; this cognitive process, I believe, continues in their analytic/projective work on dreams. Again, I do not mean to imply that the method of interpretation has no effect on dream meanings, but rather, along with Kracke (2003), I believe that the imaginal mind has a degree of independence from conscious processing and may shape the metaphorical dimension of our talk to continue thinking about ideas and feelings with which it is preoccupied. In what follows, I use this new definition of dreamwork.

Narrative Analysis suggests a distinction between the manifest dream and the memories that dream images and motifs evoke for the dreamer, which I call its mnemonic meanings. Such memories may contradict the manifest dream and/or the dreamer's anxious apprehension of it, not because these meanings are repressed, but in order to reframe the problems the manifest dream depicts. Clark's memories of camping alone in the forest as a boy contradict the fears he associated with his Bigfoot dream. Lois's remembered pleasure at her mom's Halloween costume contradicts the anxiety she feels about her Crossroads dream, and Kent's memories of Bam contradict his obsessive attempts to protect his mom and sister in the Pushpins dream. It is often through these oppositions that dreamers tinker with models or attempt to change their relation to them.

A tension between the manifest dream and the memories evoked by its metaphors, I suggest, is what creates forward movement in the dream series, as Lois moves from a perplexing stagnation in the Crossroads dream to her heart-racing jump in her September 11 dream. Evocation provides room for all the ambiguities that the dreamer suffers, for all the confusion about models that are supposed to mean one thing but often turn out to mean another. As obscure as mnemonic meanings are, they are also like an invitation. People sense them underlying dreams' surface; it is their presence that compels people to render an account and to interpret dreams—a compulsion clear in the hermeneutical practices that surround the dream in so many societies.

How can considering dreams in relation to a culture's narrative spectrum help us think about culture and psychology in a general sense? As strategies and practices, cultural models provide principles for acting in the world. As stories, they provide ways of fulfilling desires. Yet, there are critical times when our models fail and visit pain, fear, even despair on culture members. Clark dreams of manhood as unobtainable, Lois of adulthood as an impossible choice, and Kent of family life as inevitably prickly. Dream images and motifs evoke our past in order to mull over troubling models. These ruminations change what things mean to us and, therefore, are likely to bleed back into the public world. As Lohmann (2003a: 206–207) argues, dreams leave "night residues" that shape waking practices. To think of history as a phenomenon large in scale and dreams as small in scale, then, is to miss the mutual indebtedness of culture and subjective experience. What one finds in dreams is not so much history-as-topic as history-as-experience: Clark's, Lois's, and Kent's dreams live through the ongoing transformation of the U.S. family.

Chapter 3

Cultural Complexes and Boyfriend/Girlfriend Dreams

While models are what people use to make sense of experience, I have argued that they also make for contradictions. The last chapter, for example, considered the Close Family model. In this model, close family bonds are supposed to be the foundation of kids' emotional life, but these bonds placed overwhelming burdens on Clark and Lois, and drove Kent to overanxious care. In Clark's and Lois's case, there was a painful discrepancy between what the model promised (two parents playing complementary roles in a child's life), and what they actually experienced: a maternal family, in Lois's case punctuated by paternal visits and rivalry for her affections. For Kent, the presence of two parents did not protect him from incestuous feelings that made no sense within the model—feelings that were supposed to be "under the carpet," but threatened to poke through. When a model generates such confusion and conflict for many people, it becomes the basis of what I call a cultural complex.

I borrow my idea of the "complex" from Jung's (1972) Analytical Psychology in which a complex consists of contradictory inner voices linked by an overarching feeling-toned idea. Inferiority (as in an inferiority complex) is an example of a feeling-toned idea. The person has a voice that says he is worse than others, but probably also another that says it is not his character that is to blame but his circumstances: he has suffered more, struggled against overwhelming odds, and is thereby actually *better* than others. A "cultural complex," in contrast, consists of contradictory voices induced by a cultural model and linked by a feeling-toned idea that is integral to the model. In this chapter, I explore what I call the U.S. "choice complex."

In the United States choice is a feeling-toned idea—feeling-toned in the sense that people have intense feelings about it. Indeed, many U.S. Americans say that theirs is "the land of the free," meaning that freedom is a founding value and a rallying call to action, and they often equate freedom with choice (Beeman 1986:59, Montgomery 1997). In a comparative study of 328 values, D'Andrade (2008:62–63) found that in the United States choice ranks among the top ten (see also Montgomery 1997). U.S. marketing strategies celebrate choice (Beeman 1986) and offer a mesmerizing plethora of options—from countless kinds of cameras on the Web to 50 forms of coffee at the Espresso stand.

Yet, while Americans, like Lois (Chapter 2), tend to claim that they should have "options," we will see in this chapter that they are apt to complain their ability to choose is foreclosed. The obsession with choice that results is comically portrayed in the movie *When Harry Met Sally* (1989). Sally insists on menu options or, rather, options not on the menu. Harry insists on women options and thereby almost fails to recognize that Sally is "the one" for him. Hers is a joke about choice, albeit one she takes very seriously, I believe because it signifies control over her body. Thus in one restaurant scene where Sally has just ordered off the menu, she dramatizes an orgasm to prove to Harry women can fake it. An older woman at another table tells the waiter, "I'll have whatever she's having." Harry's relation to choice signifies his ability to act as an agent in relation to female bodies; at one point Sally jokes that he has had every woman in New York but her.

As in *When Harry Met Sally,* choice emerged as a source of contradiction for my undergraduates in boyfriend/girlfriend dreams, probably because such relationships are one of the first arenas in which young people confront U.S.-style choice. Americans generally feel one's romantic partner must be one's choice; to many, this is an even more essential choice than occupation. I introduce four dreamers in this chapter—two young women and two young men. As in *When Harry Met Sally,* their relation to choice is gendered. For Marilyn *lack of acceptance* by a boyfriend threatens to foreclose options. Betty experiences options and foreclosure in bodily terms: she feels that if she can manage her weight she will be more acceptable to others. For Monroe and Dave, *lack of control* over a girlfriend operates similarly, raising issues of options and foreclosure (Table 4).[1]

In the United States, men dream of other men twice as often as they do of women; women dream of men approximately 50 percent of the time (van de Castle 1994:298).[2] In this chapter, on the *manifest level* of female dreams, men and women are present in equal portions, while only other men appear in my male students' dreams. One of these male dreams is about fixing and the other

Table 4 Boyfriend/Girlfriends and Choice-as-agency

	Marilyn	*Betty*	*Monroe*	*Dave*
Role-played	Boyfriend	Shoe Store	Viking	Cat
Images	Muslim Girl	Lingerie	Carrier	Dog
	Muslim Parents	Hot Rod	Ocean	Ghost
Agency via	Acceptance by Others	Self-Acceptance (Bodily, my shape)	Control (doesn't want)	Control (doesn't have)
Schemas	Marrying Prince	Perfect Fit	Detachment	Detachment
	Perfect Fit	(self)Transformation	Dominance	Dominance
Motifs	Having a child	Shopping	Flying	Flying
	Dressing up	Dressing up	Fixing	Fighting
		Public Speaking	Playing Games	Playing Games
				Watching Movies
Related Models	Cinderella	Cinderella	Supermasculinity	Supermasculinity
	Pinup	Pinup		
Choice	Belongs to her boyfriend	Depends on her shape	Belongs to his girlfriend	Belongs to his girlfriend

about fighting, motifs associated with the U.S. Supermasculinity model. By these two dreamers own analyses, however, their dreams were actually about girlfriend trouble—specifically women acting independently.

Choice is so feeling-charged, I suggest, because for many U.S. Americans choice equals agency, as it does for me as a "pro-choice" feminist. This is the Choice-as-agency model mentioned in the preceding chapter. I think of the countercultural American composer, John Cage (1967, 1983), advocating "giving up choice." Could we do it? I don't think so. Yet, too many choices can inhibit agency. In one episode of the radio show *Prairie Home Companion*, for example, Garrison Keillor's Guy Noir just wants a cup of coffee but can't get one because the kid behind the counter offers him a bewildering array of possibilities (latte, half-caf, etc.) every time he tries to order. Baudrillard (1988) argues that in contemporary consumer culture, choice is a simulacrum of agency: advertisements that dazzle us with "options" distract us from our lack of real opportunities to change our societies.

Inasmuch as the U.S. Choice-as-agency model leads people to seek a superfluous selection of preferences, but diverts them from genuinely improving their circumstances or fulfilling their needs, choice is a performance principle. For the undergraduates considered in this chapter, choice was the idiom of their distress. An insistence that they should have choices often seemed to deflect them from facing the challenges they confronted and from taking effective action to meet these challenges. Their dreams, in contrast, graphically depicted these challenges along with their frustrated demands for choice and in some cases pointed toward possible resolutions.

My examples are all heterosexual. I did not inquire about sexual preferences; at the time in the inland Northwest, this question was still too personal and dangerous to pose in what had been a student/teacher relationship. Some students dreamt of homosexual experiences, but no one reported dreams about a same-sex lover as a "boyfriend" or a "girlfriend," although in a group of subjects as large as mine it is likely that there were such dreams. You may object that my problem here is girlfriend/boyfriend categories and that I might better look at "lover" dreams. "Lover," however, is not an emic category in my data. In U.S. usage, boyfriend/girlfriend implies a quasi-committed relationship, while lover is an erotic term that does not necessarily imply commitment or even affection: "I don't like you, but I love you," as Smoky Robinson sings (1988:130). As a model of intimate relations, Boyfriend/girlfriend is midway between a Dating model, in which participants maintain their right to choose another, and a Husband/wife model, in which participants, in principle, relinquish other possible choices. A person using this model temporarily relinquishes choice by choosing "a special someone," but the parameters and limits of that choice are unspecified and issues for ongoing negotiation.

Dream Play and Dramatic Analysis

My boyfriend/girlfriend material emerged from a set of dreams my students had explored using a projective method I call Dream Play—a method for working with dreams useful for investigating cultural complexes. Dream Play is a form of what Edgar (2004) calls Imagework, which takes images as primary vehicles for self-exploration. In Chapter 1, I discussed hypocognition, Levy's (1973) idea that a common human emotion like sadness may be underrepresented in cultural categories and hence go unperceived. I argued that we can best understand hypocognition, not as referring specifically to emotions, but to all experiences not adequately represented by cultural models. Dream Play uses elements of Jung's (1976) Active Imagination and Perls's (1971) Gestalt Therapy to help dreamers discover such experiences.

In Active Imagination, a client engages in fantasy encounters with dream images to elicit elements of self outside of normal awareness and works with a therapist to analyze these encounters. For Jung, the characters one meets in Active Imagination are often archetypes: they personify universal human experiences. In Dream Play, one presumes that dream images are symbols drawn from a cultural common, blended with personal memory, and used to represent experiences inexpressible in everyday discourses—either because of these discourses' representational inadequacy or because, to express these experiences, would violate social norms.

In Gestalt Therapy, a dreamer role-plays dream images and sometimes acts out dialogues between these images and his or her normal waking persona. Perls (1971), however, was anti-analytical. He saw Gestalt Therapy as a remedy for alienation from dissociated parts of the self. Analysis was a "head trip"—an additional form of dissociation. Participants, therefore, were simply to experience a dream image as an unrealized part of them (a "hole"), not to discuss its significance with a therapist. While Jung insisted that clients identify *only* with the dream ego, for Perls identifying with various dream images was a way of reclaiming the parts of self they represented. Jungians distinguish, sometimes sharply, between these two approaches (Dallet 1982:184). In Dream Play, participants role-play and dialogue with dream images for purposes of personal/cultural analysis, by which I mean understanding how their problems are collective as well as individual.

A *dreamer* who elects this method, first, should find a friend to help her act out a dream. Second, the dreamer picks an image to role-play, which can be any person or object in the dream except her own persona. Third, the dreamer closes her eyes and returns to the dream in imagination, zooming in on the image; she lets this image expand until she converges with it, then opens her eyes. Acting as this image, fourth, she tells the friend about herself and her feelings and responds to any questions the friend may have. Fifth, she switches to an adjacent chair and to her normal persona and asks the image (which she imagines sitting in the chair in which she formerly sat) any questions that have arisen about the image or about its actions in the dream. Sixth, the dreamer switches back to her original chair to answer these questions, and thus begins a dialogue between the image and her waking persona. Or, a dreamer can role-play alone in fantasy. In fantasy role-play, I recommend the dreamer still place chairs side-by-side and change chairs when she changes roles. Seventh, she repeats steps three and four with at least two other dream images. Eight, the dreamer imagines that her dream is about "holes" in herself (unexpressed feelings or unrealized abilities) and guesses what these holes might be. Ninth, she guesses what "hole" in her culture the dream represents—meaning feelings that are hard to express in her social environment or abilities that this environment is unlikely to foster. Last, she uses role-playing and guesses to make a dream interpretation. People act out dreams in some small-scale societies (Tedlock 1991, 1992; Graham 1995), and so Dream Play may lend itself to a number of locales.

There is also good excuse for Dream Play in psychoanalytic theory. For Lacan (1968, 1977a), the superego is the "No!" of the father: it is part of the word-based form of mind that Lacan calls the Sign, as opposed to the image-based form of mind he calls the Imaginary. As a citizen of the Sign, this "No!" controls words best; it keeps us from putting forbidden thoughts into words spoken to others or, internally, to ourselves. It has less control over images. Play sidesteps voices in the mind that forbid us to divulge or even think certain thoughts because they reflect badly on us: they are evil, silly, irrelevant, and so forth. Like the masks of Turner's (1977) carnival, Dream Play permits one to slide into transgressive identities and frees them to speak.

In Dramatic Analysis, a *researcher* selects a number of dreams role-played by dreamers on a common topic, for example girlfriend/boyfriend relationships. He establishes a cultural context by broadly considering this topic in his ethnographic data and in other studies of the culture. Inferring a related model from this material, he considers issues surrounding the model evident in his dream collection and then zooms in on individual dreams. Using projective exercises and, when possible, additional autobiographical material solicited in follow-up interviews, the researcher asks if role-played dialogues help to evoke the contradictory voices of a cultural complex. Next, he consults a dreamer's journal for further insight on contradictions that role-play brings into focus. Last, he considers how dreams and dialogues reflect the dreamer's socioeconomic position and historical moment.

Marilyn

Marilyn is "Caucasian" and 21 years old. She was born in a small Oregon town and moved to a middle-sized city in Washington at the beginning of adolescence.

> I dreamt that I was at my boyfriend's house with my grandparents. My grandma was on the phone with my boyfriend, who was at the hospital. She asked him if the baby was here yet....I knew that he had slept with another woman, she had become pregnant and that they had decided to continue with the pregnancy. I also knew that his mom and dad were at the hospital supporting...my boyfriend, through the birthing process....I imagined the other girl to be a "good Muslim girl" with dark skin that his parent's would approve of. I escaped into his kitchen and began to wash his dishes. My grandfather followed me into the kitchen and I began to cry. He asked me why I was upset since babies are a time to rejoice. I replied that yes, babies were a time for happiness, but that at least he [the boyfriend] had been able *to choose* when he had children. I have to have his kids from her.

Marilyn began by role-playing her boyfriend, Kamil:

> Kamil: I've loved and dated Marilyn for over five and a half years. I have dark skin, hair and eyes and am from a Muslim family. I am happy.
> Marilyn: I don't understand. You are having a baby with another woman. I thought I was *the one* in your life....[Emphasis mine]

The United States has long been an experiment in combining world cultures within the nation. While this experiment began with Western European cultures, contemporary Americans have recast it in racial and religious terms. Now it is not a matter of being half-French and half-German, but ebony or ivory and Muslim or Christian. Probably this is why, when asked about their ethnicity, many students answered with their race. This conflation is evident in Marilyn's role-play where the only adjective she uses for her Muslim boyfriend is "dark." Muslims, of course, are of every possible complexion, but here religion refers to race.

Male dreamers in my collection often, in the words of *The Matrix* (Warner Brothers 1999), endeavored to become "the One": that is, Number One, meaning the best as well as singular and individual.[3] Female dreamers often endeavored to find a significant other—a boyfriend—who recognized them as "the one." This Recognition schema is part of what I call the U.S. Cinderella model of femininity: recognition is what U.S. Cinderellas seek through their romantic other. By trying to become "the one," if through a different route, U.S. Cinderellas also aim at the larger U.S. project of "becoming an individual."

There are two criteria for personal happiness in contemporary U.S. soap operas: choice and commitment (Stone 2004). If choice is a major issue for Marilyn, she imagines commitment is for her boyfriend: in her role-played dialogued with Kamil, he began by doubting hers.

> Kamil: I've had this feeling that you are not in this relationship for the long haul so I decided to find myself someone my parent's will approve of—a good Muslim girl.

In commitment, people, particularly women, often relinquish independence; as Carol King sings, "Where you go, I will follow." To a degree, this lack of independence derives from U.S. woman's role in childcare (Degler 1988:471–473). Marilyn's dream is about having a child. Her rival at first seems to represent a set of values that feature premarital virginity. Marilyn was flabbergasted, therefore, at Kamil's use of language.

> Marilyn: A good Muslim girl! How is she a good Muslim girl when you have obviously had sex before marriage and you're having a baby?
> Kamil: She's dark skinned and a Muslim. She is better than you.

The Good Girl in U.S. parlance, refers to a girl who abstains from sex with multiple partners and who control sex in a boyfriend/girl-friend relationship, for example by not allowing it until both people have declared their sincere attachment to one another. For Marilyn, therefore, the Muslin girl is a contradiction in terms. She also fuses problems of race with problems of multiple religions and standards of conduct—which go way back in the American experience. Mead, writing on what she saw as the moral placidity of coming-of-age in Samoa, attributes U.S. adolescent stress in the 1920s to the panoply of moral choices presented to adolescents—choices that create confusion and inner conflict.

> In religion they may be Catholics, Protestants, Christian Scientists, Spiritualists, Agnostics, Atheists, [and, today, Muslim] or even pay

no attention at all to religion.... [O]ur children are faced with half a dozen standards of morality: a double sex standard for men and women, a single standard for men and women, groups which advocate that the single standard should be freedom while others argue that the single standard should be absolute monogamy. Trial marriage, companionate marriage, contract marriage—all these possible solutions of a social impasse are paraded before the growing children while the actual conditions in their own communities and the moving pictures and magazines inform them of mass violations of every code (Mead 1961:200–202).

Similarly, Marilyn wrote of her dream:

American culture is so diverse.... What is good for one culture and religion may not be good enough for another.... These traditions and standards are used to judge and separate people... but are also used as a way to maintain and ensure the survival of culture and traditions.

In Marilyn's subtext is a fear that she is not good enough and her boyfriend's parents will use their culture to judge her and end the relationship. Like Lois in Chapter 2, Marilyn wants "to please others," but fears she cannot.

Marilyn next role-played the Muslim young woman: "I am small, petite and pregnant with Kamil's baby. I am dark skinned and look more Latina than Arabic, but I am a good Muslim girl for Kamil. I am happy." Arabic is a language, while people are Arab. Marilyn's usage reiterates her lack of connection to Kamil's culture, yet the dream girl sounds like her mirror image with dark skin: Marilyn too is small and petite. In Washington State, dark-skinned people are likely to be the Hispanics, who have long been laborers in fields and groves (James 1968). Like many Muslims, Hispanics often have what mainstream U.S. Americans think of as conservative standards for young women (McKee and Stone 2007:147–162). This good Muslim girl's standards, however, are part of a catfight where marriage in the formal Christian sense of a church wedding and monogamy are surprisingly irrelevant. Marilyn next conversed with this rival, who she named "Her."

Marilyn: How can you do this to me? I don't even know you and you've ruined my life.

Her: That's right, you don't know me, but Kamil does. He's mine and I'm his—for life.

M: How dare you! I hate you for this! I hate your child for this! I
   don't want that child in my life.
H: Well, if you stay with Kamil the child will be in your life since it
   will be in his life.

One could see Her's proxy pregnancy and birth as a depiction of
Marilyn being out of bodily control: the child will be hers although
she never assented to having a baby.

Both Kamil and Her declare themselves "happy." "Happy," like
"free," is a primary U.S. category. According to the U.S. constitu-
tion, the "pursuit of happiness" is an inalienable right. If people
are not happy for very long, others recommend psychotherapy to
them. Here dark-skinned others are happy while white Marilyn
envies their happiness. Is this because she imagines them as enjoying a moral clarity she lacks? They do not see their own position
as ambiguous despite her protests. Yet, inasmuch as Her is uncon-
cerned about marriage and monogamy, she represents the radical
plurality of sexual-moral choices that characterize Marilyn's world
and Marilyn herself. Although Marilyn's appearance and mien are
innocent, she sells sexual toys and accessories as a part-time job: she
is actually a Bad Girl. Marilyn hides this occupation from Kamil's
parents, whom she next role-played.

Marilyn: Why are you supporting him and this girl and this child?
   Why can't you support him and me or our relationship? Why don't
   you like me?
Parents: It's not that we don't like you; we just don't like your
   family.
M: But they've had sex and they are having a baby. How is that bet-
   ter than me?
P: She's a good Muslim girl. She is the best for his future.

One could call Marilyn's dream, "Guess who's coming to dinner," except here it is the white girl rather than the black man who
would like to be invited by her beloved's parents—a gender and race
reversal. Kamil's parents disapprove of Marilyn because her family
is poor and lower class. Like Cinderella, Marilyn wants to marry
hypergamously. While Kamil's family is wealthy, Marilyn has struggled all her life. In her journal, there were several anxiety dreams
about not having medical insurance and one about not being able to
pay for her cat's healthcare.

In role-play, Marilyn complains that Kamil's parents have inconsistent values; in the dream, she is nonplussed by those of her

grandfather. As I mentioned in Chapter 2, my students tended to regard family portraits painted in 1950s–1960s primetime television as representing "traditional" U.S. family values. Marilyn grandparents' generation, one would assume, more than that of her parents, hearkens back to this "tradition." Yet in the dream they have ultraliberal values: they do not see anything wrong with Kamil's infidelity—or is it polygamy? Polygamy is part of the U.S. fantasy of Muslims as the Other.

When Marilyn reverts to her "traditional" U.S. role, retreating to the kitchen to wash Kamil's dishes, her own grandfather choruses what one might expect his parents to say: the birth of Kamil's child is "a time to rejoice." Her grandparents' location, moreover, is Kamil's house—where one would anticipate finding his parents. One might also expect U.S. grandparents (as ancestors) to voice a traditional American view. This reversal suggests that there are no "reasonable" expectations Marilyn can legitimately enforce. Indeed, by inverting Marilyn's U.S. "traditions," her grandparents symbolize how impossible it is for her to sort out a set of coherent standards. Only one thing is clear: she does not meet the standard. This was "the hole" that Marilyn thought her dream represented:

> [N]ot feeling accepted. I worry about what his parents think of me as a person and as their son's girlfriend and possible future wife. I worry about them not liking or approving of me, especially since Kamil claims to see me as part of his future. I also worry that Kamil may begin to view me in the same way that his parents view me; as unacceptable or not good enough.

"The more tradition loses its hold," Giddens (1991:5) opines in his study of modernity, "the more individuals are forced to negotiate lifestyle choices among a diversity of options." Yet, rather than choosing, Marilyn can only hope to be chosen. Lacking shared public values to invoke, what it means to be a woman (or a good girl) reduces to being acceptable to a boyfriend and potential spouse, inscribing subordination in feminine gender identity itself and in the Boyfriend/girlfriend relationship.

Other Dreams

Acceptability appeared elsewhere in Marilyn's journal in embodied terms. In one dream, she is leaving Kamil's house wearing only "hot pink," "boy" shorts. These shorts are a condensation. From infancy in the United States, femininity is colored pink. As these are boys' shorts, they also appropriate a diminutive masculinity. Idealized "girl" shapes in the contemporary United States are often boylike, as is Marilyn's, yet Marilyn's dream shorts are "hot" and connote nudity: she wears nothing above the waist. In her "hot" shorts and partial nakedness, she dresses like a boy in a way that reveals she is female and intimates a sexuality that is both available and, we will see, controlled.

In the Shorts dream, Marilyn "sensed that Kamil's mother was there and that I should impress her....I had to run to my car...in another parking lot far away." A lion chases her. When she arrives, she does not have the key and has "to imagine unlocking the door." I suggested earlier that for U.S. Americans the car is an image for a self-model that is all about transiting and that transiting is one metaphor for transcending birth context—which is what Marilyn would like to do through her relationship with Kamil. Yet, this dream evinces Marilyn's sense that she lacks the key to transiting, along with her feelings of being exposed and an object of aggressive attention. Finally, inside the car she fights and then succumbs to an urge "to return to the house for a robe and high heels." In a robe and heels, Marilyn would be less exposed but still underdressed in a way that alludes to sexuality: robes belong in bedrooms and women wear high heels to display their legs.

In another dream, Marilyn is preparing for a presentation at which she needs to wear heels. Again, in waking life Marilyn is petite, but in the dream every pair "was too small and I had to shove my feet into them." In yet another, she is in a store but too big for all the clothes. These dream problems are reminiscent of Cinderella's sisters who cannot fit their fat feet into the lost slipper. The earliest written version of the Cinderella story comes from ninth-century A.D. China (Bettelheim 1976:236)—the home of foot binding. Marilyn's dreams evoke what I call the Perfect-fit schema, another part of the Cinderella model (it is this perfection that Cinderellas want recognized). In the Perfect-fit schema, a person's display of ideals of body and/or character makes her acceptable (or not) to others.[4] In Marilyn's Shorts and Heels dreams, she enacts the Perfect-fit schema through a Dressing-up motif. Butler (1990) argues that in dressing-up women perform femininity as a self-transformative masquerade. Self-transformation is another Cinderella femininity schema. In *Cinderella ate my daughter: dispatches from the front lines of the new girlie-girl culture*, Orenstein (2011) shows this kind of femininity, far from evaporating with the rise of feminism, is now marketed to younger and younger girls.

I mentioned in Chapter 2 that, in the psychoanalytic view, feet are a common fetish and fetishes are stand-ins for penises that boys once imagined women had. Bettelheim (1976) believes that in Cinderella's story feet symbolize her sexuality. It may seem strange that a phallic symbol should represent female sexuality but, in male-dominated worlds, male symbols become generic. Thus, in a famous essay, Leach (1958) finds that hair, another protruding body part, symbolizes sexuality in many cultures. Cinderella's problem is getting a male to recognize her sexuality, symbolized by her feet. Their diminutive size is what makes them acceptable to the prince. In her Heels dream, Marilyn is not sure her feet are small enough; this, I suggest, is the problem in her Muslim Girl dream too. If Kamil's parents knew of her part-time job, it would really be the end. This job points to a side of Marilyn, visible in her dream journal, which belies her childlike Good Girl persona—the fully sexual and far from conventional woman. Kamil knows this other side. Is this why she fears, "I may be acceptable as the girlfriend, but never as the wife"?

If acceptance (being chosen) is key for Marilyn, this is because she experiences it as prerequisite to choice: relinquishing agency seems the only path to agency. In her Muslim Girl dream, Kamil gets to choose and Marilyn does not—both a mother for his children and a time to have a child. Diversity in the contemporary United States is supposed to give Americans a plurality of "choices"; here it forecloses Marilyn's ability to choose. Earlier in the same night, Marilyn dreamt that she delivered Kamil's baby. He left. She had no support, no job, and didn't want the baby. Evidently, she also associates a scenario opposite to that depicted in her Muslim Girl dream with a foreclosure of choice. For her, being an U.S. "girl" is a no-win situation. If the Choice model is productive of contradictions, in Marilyn's world it belongs to her boyfriend. She is left merely to accept the situation and finds no support from others to do anything but that.

Betty

My second dreamer in this chapter, Betty, is 20, called herself "Caucasian," and hailed from a beautiful resort town in Idaho.

> [T]he dream was about being in a shopping mall with my friend Shirley. We were only there to eat.... The second part was... with

my classmate...Rosalind and some guy. I was looking in an empty
store. Rosalind said she wanted to work there.... [I]t was going to be
a shoe store. The third part was shopping in a mall with girls that I
didn't recognize. I remember being much thinner....I'm very focused
on my weight lately, dieting and working out....We shopped for lingerie...I remember trying different things on. Next, I went to some
house with the girls and some guys. There was a lecture being given
by a woman. The police came and broke up the meeting to arrest her,
but I think she got away. Her car in her garage was bright purple but
covered with mud.... [T]he car looked like a hotrod....The parking
lot resembled the lot I park in everyday for class here at WSU.

Betty's dream begins in a mall, evoking what Baudrillard (1988)
calls the global "system of objects," among which are pretty women.
Toward the end of the nineteenth century, department stores acquired
a place in U.S. middle-class culture (Stone and McKee 2007:35). By
the mid-twentieth-century, "the mall" emerged as a primary venue
of U.S. consumerism and for making feminine gender—just as the
ball field is for making masculine gender. As a U.S. palace of consumption, the mall suggests an underlying oral theme highlighted
by Betty's intention to go there "only to eat." Yet, the dream mall
also reminds Betty that she wants to diet, condensing for her those
contradictions that constellate around choice.

As a gender-making site, the mall evokes the Dressing-up motif.
We saw in Marilyn's dreams that this motif provides a way to enact
the Perfect-fit schema and the Self-transformation schema, which con-
verge in the U.S. Cinderella model and in feminine gender disciplines
like Betty's diets. Cinderella's name comes from her habit of sleeping
among the cinders of the hearth (Bettelheim 1976:236–276)—a habit
opposed to primping and grooming for a date. A potential spouse
(the prince) motivates Cinderella to change from a cinder-covered
girl into a decked-out woman. There is no boyfriend in the manifest
content of Betty's dream. Her present boyfriend, Russell, however,
helped her role-play the empty store, the lingerie, and the hotrod. The
following dialogues begin between the dream image and Russell. The
effect is a trialogue, where conversation comes to include Betty and
underlines Russell's presence as the dream's interlocutor.

Empty Store: Hey, there. What do you think I'm going to be?
Russell: I don't know.
E S: Well I guess anything is possible. I just hope the people who
    bought me are nice. I would certainly enjoy being a busy place
    filled with happy people.

Being "busy" and "happy" are feelings that, especially in combination, evoke a successful life for Americans. So does Empty Store's question, "What do you think I'm going to be." This is a signature question Americans put to children: "What are you going to be when you grow up," with the implied tenet that individuals can choose to be anything they like and thus the Choice model. If girlfriend/ boyfriend relationships are the first life-changing arena in which Americans deal with choice, "What will you be" makes occupation the first arena in which they deal with it in fantasy. In positing unlimited choice, this question also suggests an aleatory situation that can make young Americans feel, we will see as the trialogue continues, uncertain of their future:

> Russell: How do you feel about being next to all these other stores who are already open?
> Empty Store: It makes me sad and somewhat jealous. I'd rather be alone in some ways but having us all together in this mall draws more people. Therefore, the benefits outweigh the costs.
> Betty: I think you are going to be a shoe store.
> E S: That's okay with me. I'm uncertain of my future. We'll just have to wait and see.
> B: How can you take this so lightly?
> E S: Well nothing bad can happen to me. You are the one who is always worrying about everything. Maybe you should see the brighter side for once.
> B: I think you have a point there.

Feeling bright versus worrying seem the poles of Betty's affective landscape. Betty's worries often express themselves as shyness. She is a straight-A student but says it's "a nightmare" to be up in front of a class. Her face flushes and she is always afraid of being wrong. She says she's shy because of her shape. It's not that anyone makes fun of her weight but she doesn't fit the mold. The "hole" she thought her dream represented was

> my true feelings surrounding my weight. I have struggled with my weight for many years but when I am thinner I am always happier and more extroverted. When I am heavier I get uncomfortable....I become accustomed to the introverted lifestyle....I think a part of me doesn't want to let that lifestyle go. Also I tend to be more on the pessimistic side so I don't necessarily believe I can lose the weight...even if I am determined to do it.

While Marilyn's dream "hole" is acceptance by a significant other and his parents, Betty's is self-acceptance. Yet, this apparent difference is really a matter of emphasis: Marilyn's Heels dream indicates that for her acceptance by others is inextricably tied to body issues; Betty's inability to talk in class indicates that for her bodily self-acceptance is tied to acceptance by others. Becoming a girlfriend, a person that a boy recognizes as "the one" for him, often necessitates refashioning one's body along the lines of a "top-model" template.

As the shoe store, Betty would like to attract more people, making her full, an aim she pursues through dieting and exercise. Thinness is key, in Betty's view, to having what Americans call a "full life." Here choices are contradictory in their very nature: to be full, one must be thin—that is, presumably, empty much of the time. Betty experienced a similar contradiction about being a person: she said she wanted "to be who I truly am," while also "wanting to be accepted by others socially. Somehow I need to find out what works best for me and stick to it." Like one "sticks to" a diet?

Why should a shoe store symbolize Betty's worries about her weight? In Bettelheim's (1976:236–276) analysis of Cinderella, shoes are vaginal: one slips an elongated body part into them. Is the empty shoe store, then, a symbol of Betty's sexuality? The shoe store reminded Betty of when she broke her foot in her sophomore year of college. Betty lost 35 pounds in her junior year of high school but, after her foot injury, gained it all back, which made her feel she had "lost control."

Russell worries that he will lose her if she loses weight because then she will have more boyfriend options. "This is simply untrue," Betty wrote, "but I know it is a real concern for him." Yet, in dreams Betty often encounters a man who is not her boyfriend and who she kisses or who almost kisses her. Russell probably does not know of these dreams, but has other reasons to be insecure. Bright young Betty grew up in an upper-middle-class family and proceeded on to college. Russell is a somewhat older mechanic who just got his GED. One might say Russell is in the Cinderella position: he longs to marry up and wants a special other to recognize his real value (shrouded by humble circumstances).

Betty suspects Russell of sabotage. One minute he says he supports her losing weight; the next, he says, "Let's order pizza!" He denies this charge, asserting that he has "invested enough" in the relationship that he doesn't have to be afraid of her infidelity. Russell's phrase underlines the transactional character of "romantic" relationships in U.S. capitalist society. So does Empty Store, "jealous" of the other stores all the while it weighs benefits versus costs of being alone or together. As a metaphor for Betty and her feelings about her body, a store in the mall also iterates this trans-actional character—a secret about love under the sign of capital-ism that "Victoria's Secret" knows well. Betty next role-played the lingerie:

> Russell: Why do you think Betty picked you?
>
> Lingerie: First of all because I'm pink, black and gorgeous. I'm sure you think it's for you, but really it's for her. She's missed being thinner. I make her happy.
>
> R: You seem a little bitter.
>
> L: I am. She hasn't been around in awhile. When she is heavier, she drowns in guilt and worry. I'm glad to have her back though.
>
> Betty: It's so good to see you!!!!
>
> L: You too!!! I've missed you so. How are you feeling??
>
> B: I'm okay, I just wish I felt that I was in good enough shape to actu-ally wear you.
>
> L: I know but I promise it will happen soon. You have got the deter-mination and will power to do this. Just make sure and watch out for those around you who might trip you up on this journey.

Like Russell? Betty claims not to want more choice in romantic rela-tionships, but she seems closer to her lingerie than she does to her boyfriend. For Betty, just as for Marilyn, pink symbolizes a part of her that is both feminine and sexual. As personified by the lingerie, Betty's sexuality seems accessible only through a thin body. The "gorgeous" lingerie, I suggest, represents the U.S. Pinup model of sexuality. "Pinup" is the colloquial U.S. term for the posters and centerfolds that U.S. boys pin up inside lockers or on walls in which young women "show some skin." The Pinup is a model for being a perfect sexual object and for fitting one's own or another's fantasies. In the Pinup model, sex is an agent/object relation and a person is sexual to the extent that she is the ideal object of the gaze.[5] The counterpart of the Pinup model, then, is another model we might call the Voyeuristic Sexuality in which sexuality develops out of a visual experience—the proverbial U.S. teenage boy hiding Playboy under his pillow. Yet, the Pinup model is not only for females, nor Voyeuristic Sexuality only for males.

Students in an undergraduate class I taught on gender in 2004 did a study on weight training at the WSU recreational center. Male stu-dents consistently reported wanting to get "big" and strong. Females reported wanting to get or stay "small" and toned. Both sexes were crafting their bodies—males to be supermasculine and females to fit the tropic slipper or lingerie, but in both cases to fit the visual expectations associated with their gender.

Probably the Pinup took its modern pictographic form among those Marcus (1966) calls "the other Victorians" and their photographs of local and exotic nude or seminude women (McClintock 1995, see also Nordstrom 1995:21, 31, 75). From the original "muscle beach" in 1930s Santa Monica to the open-shirted young "hunks" displayed on enormous posters in Eddie Bauer foyers, however, Pinup sexuality has been a model for males as well. Voyeuristic Sexuality, however, seems less in play among women. Eddie Bauer aside, one seldom sees scantily clad male-pinups splashed over the covers of magazines at U.S. market checkout counters. And U.S. young women, getting everything from new hairdos to liposuctions, spend more time, energy, and money crafting their bodies than young men—an effort to fit-in that fits them into consumer culture but that Bordo (1997) argues also leaves a perpetual sense of inadequacy like that Betty suffers.

Betty's second friend in the dream is Rosalind. Betty is a dedicated student. Rosalind parties and drinks. When she goes to class, she titters about her teachers at the back of the room. In the dream, Rosalind would like to work at the shoe store; in life, she is slim and always beautifully dressed. She personifies the Perfectfit schema, as do the women Betty meets at the lingerie store. In an interview, Betty called them "girlie-girls." Girlie girls, Betty said, always wear make-up and have their hair done; they "look perfect." For Betty, they pointed to the "hole" in her culture represented by the dream: "[W]e are supposed to be individual and independent yet we long to fit in. . . . This often affects our appearance like what clothes we wear or how we do our hair. Weight is a big part of that as well."

Ostensibly, Betty is not a Cinderella. Unlike Marilyn, she did not grow up in poverty nor was she, like Lois, born under the sign of the absent father. Betty worked with her dad in his successful business during her teenage years. One might think she would escape the need to fit the mold that is part of the U.S. Cinderella model. Indeed, her boyfriend would prefer that she did not. There is no individual in Betty's life enforcing a top-down relation of dominance: her anxious need to conform is an instance of biopower, Foucault's (1979, 1982, 1990) term for bottom-up self-policing. Betty's diets and exercises are a Foucaultian discipline, but one that seems closer to what he calls the Roman "care of the self"

(1986), than to what he describes as the twentieth-century's libratory sexual ethos. Betty next decided to play the muddy purple hotrod.

> Car: Why would my owner do this to me?
> Russell: It's not so bad, I'm sure she'll clean you soon.
> C: Are you kidding? She just got arrested...she'll never be back. She's always taken such bad care of me.
> R: True, but your paint is still in perfect shape.
> C: No thanks to her. A friend of hers washes me. Besides under my hood is a different story.
> Betty: Hi, do you want to come back with me? I'd take care of you.
> C: No you wouldn't. You can barely take care of yourself.
> B: That's just rude.
> C: The truth hurts sweetheart.

Does "taking care" stand for calorie counting? Is the mud fattening junk foods? Car seems critical of her owner and Betty, alleging they're equally negligent. Yet, Car is also a part of Betty and one that Russell says is "still in perfect shape." Betty and Russell go to "monster truck" shows where there is "mud racing": lifted trucks splash through pools of mud. Betty loves getting dirty and being free and "can't get enough of it," although she never drives a truck herself. Here mud seems a symbol for sexuality and again evokes Cinderella as the girl who likes to sleep among the cinders (Bettelheim 1976:236–276). Yet, "monster-trucks" in the United States are "Bad Boys' Toys," as bumper stickers on supersized trucks in the Northwest proclaim.

Allison traces a development of toys-as-fetishes and their affiliated stories from Superman in the 1950s to the cyborg heroes in the 1990s, which originated in Japan and became popular among U.S. kids. With Superman, Allison explains:

> [P]hallicism came in and on his body, but with cyborg heroes it is displaced onto removable or detachable things—robots, belts, wands, guns....[T]oday's heroes have powers that reach beyond the body and materialize into tools or machines that could and are operated by more than just men—women and bugs (2001:87–88).

Like other machine extensions of masculinity (guns in Westerns or Thrillers for example), the car has long been a detachable masculinity that men can lose and women can appropriate and thus reminiscent of a Lacanian phallus. As the Beach Boys' song goes, "She'll have fun, fun, fun," what people do with toys in the United States, "til her daddy takes her T-bird away."

Along with Hollan (2003a), I argued in Chapter 2 that cars are a self-symbol for most people in U.S. society. Yet, monster trucks and hotrods are what we might call supercars and represent, not only one variety of what in Chapter 5 I call the Car self-model, but also Bad Boy masculinity. People associate young men with "hot" cars—young men who have often built these cars themselves and use them in what a more rural America once called "sowing wild oats." This identification of young men with supercars does not mean that women, in principle, cannot appropriate the Bad Boy model for which they stand. The police that are soon to show up in Betty's dream, however, suggest that she does not escape a free-floating feeling of guilt about the possibility of appropriating Bad Boy masculinity nor does she escape a fear doing so may have consequences.

Guilty feelings aside, Bad Boy masculinity suggests access to sexuality through a route alternative to Pinup model, a route Betty discovers with Russell and about which her dreaming mind thinks. We saw with Bam (Chapter 2) that the Bad Boy model features an Impulse-gratification schema in which (apparently) breaking the rules is not "really" bad and a Devil-may-care schema in which one acts without care for consequences. Gilligan (1982) demonstrates that many U.S. women have a care morality and the Care schema is part of the Devoted Mom and Girlfriend models. There is probably, then, a contradiction between Betty's sense of herself as moral, someone who "takes care" of herself and others, and her actual behavior, which at least with Russell is carefree.

If the muddy hotrod represents Betty's newfound sexuality, additionally it is "bright" and a metaphor for intellect. It belongs to the woman lecturer, who exercises agency that Betty cannot—talking in class. This lecturer speaks at a classroom-like gathering outside of which, Betty told me, was the university lot where she usually parked for class. Betty described the house where she gave the lecture as "beyond informal"; it was a "comfortable" versus "scary" place where Betty said she would have felt free to speak. What the lecturer does in the dream (and for a living) is precisely what Betty won't let herself do. The lecturer's muddy hotrod makes Betty's splashing-through-mud sexuality into a symbol for agency to achieve. In many cultures sexual agency, like that which Betty finds with Russell, is a trope for other kinds of agency, like speaking in public, and tends to change in tandem with them (Mageo 2002a).

For Betty, these two forms of agency are associated with guilt and fear, which her dream and role-play dramatize. In the dream report, police break up the meeting to arrest the woman lecturer who owns the hotrod. Betty told me, "I think she got away." In role-play, however, Car says the police took her away. Betty explained that the woman must have done something wrong before the dream began, but she did not know what it was. Betty's dreamwork (the symbolic renderings of the dream itself along with her projective/analytic work on it) trace an interlarding of biopower versus top-down social power. Her exercises and diets aim at fitting her into the dream lingerie and are a form of biopower enforced in bodily ways by Betty herself and by her peers. However, the appearance of police suggests that when Betty's agency (as personified by the lecturer) takes form as action in the public world, she fears a top-down form of social power.

I, of course, am a woman lecturer, and one who urged Betty to speak in class. Betty, by choosing this dream for her final paper and coming back to talk about it in an interview, was probably trying to engage me in the dream problem. Am I the woman who got away? The dream lecturer's car is bright purple. Grunge was fashionable during the study period and students sometimes remarked on the bright colors I liked to wear. Purple has always been one of my favorite colors. I wear it a lot. I do all I can to make my classroom informal and comfortable so that shy students like Betty can speak. Our relationship, brief as it was, may have underlined for Betty that she might exercise more successful agency herself.

Monroe

Monroe was 28, identified as "Caucasian," and came from a small town in coastal Washington. He served in Operation Iraqi Freedom but disapproved of that war.

> I see the main figure in the third person perspective, and it is a Viking. I am living in some sort of village and from this village I fly (...I have a jetpack) to an aircraft carrier which has broken down. At the carrier I do all sorts of work to fix it, working with many people..., After I have finished fixing all of the problems...there is a party on the dock....[T]he aircraft carrier leaves, and I shout out to it—"Hey, you're supposed to bring me with you!" I run to the end of the dock and jump off and start to swim toward the vessel, even though it is

foolish and I will not make it. I eventually get tired and start to go under.

Monroe sees the Viking in the third person—a character he takes to represent him. This perspective implies detachment, a schema reiterated by the Viking's ability to fly. Again, to fly is to detach from earth and presumably from what goes on there. To sink is to be subsumed, as the Viking later is by the sea. Over the course of the dream, then, Monroe's detachment suffers symbolic decay. Monroe wrote that the dream resembled:

> [A] computer game that I had been playing the day before…called "Empire Earth"—you can set out little persons or vehicles such as Roman Legionnaires or World War I tanks and have them fight each other…, Everything seemed all choppy and angled as if it were a computer generated image.

Usually games are for fun and do not have real life consequences: they also suggest detachment. The legionnaires and tanks are all pawns in Monroe's play, which presupposes a dominant, indeed Godlike, position. This position probably makes it easier for Monroe to confront the identity distonic material that is the dream's focus. Monroe first chose to play the Viking with a friend.

> Friend: So what are you like, Viking? Describe yourself.
> Viking: Well, I am a tough Viking living in my seaside village.
> F: I see that you have a jetpack.
> V: Yes, I know, it makes me unique.

The Viking is a condensation—a throwback to an earlier kind of warrior plus a futuristic kind: one who has extraordinary technological power—a jetpack. Inasmuch as the Viking represents Monroe, one might guess he sees himself as modern but also as a little old fashioned and that his identity as an individual ("unique") is to some extent premised on this combination. The Viking, of course, is also a Superman: he combines the extraordinary power to fly (by virtue of a prosthetic) and detachment, both of which are Supermasculinity schemas. Monroe's friend continued:

> Friend: Why did you try to swim after the carrier when it left?
> Viking: I had to try, I feel that the carrier still needed me, it was not complete….

F: Why didn't you fly to it after it left.
V: I was probably out of fuel.

While Monroe feels the carrier needs him, he drowns because he needs, not "the wind beneath my wings," but the carrier beneath his jetpack: he is incomplete. Monroe next played the carrier.

Friend: So tell me about yourself, aircraft carrier.
Carrier: Well, I am your typical large aircraft carrier, but I am broken down and part of me is on fire, I need somebody to repair me.
Monroe: What happened to you?
C: I think I was attacked, but the enemy is gone, so I had better get back out to sea so I can find them.

Although the aircraft carrier has no present enemy, it continues the battle motif that Monroe began in fantasy in his Empire Earth game. This battle fantasy moves up through history: from Roman Legionnaires to World War I tanks to the dream's World War II aircraft carrier. In World War II, the sky became a major battle site and aircraft carriers were vital supporting weapons. This progression suggests that Monroe's game, dream, and role-play continue one fantasy process.

Monroe thought that the carrier stood for his girlfriend. In the two years they had been together, they "had done some traveling and I met all sorts of people through her." Monroe's surmise makes sense. Traditionally, ships are named after women. Monroe wrote that the dream represented "the recent realization of my former girlfriend of two and a half years [is] leaving for a job over on the east coast. . . . I had since recognized a drifting apart," like the carrier and the Viking. Notice the distancing use of "the" rather than "my" in reference to Monroe's realization and "a" versus "our" in reference to "drifting apart." "Former" is also a distancing word, given that the girlfriend was still his and in Pullman. Here Monroe seems to be trying to get a detached outside-the-frame perspective like that with which his dream begins. Monroe continued:

Monroe: Why did you leave the person that fixed you?
Carrier: I respect him and all, but we don't fit in the same context, a Viking and an aircraft carrier, come on!
M: But he did have a jetpack and flew all the way over from his town to fix you!
C: Yes I know, but it was time for me to move on. I have things to do.

As Clark was a mechanic in his dream, so is the Viking in Monroe's dream: he fixes ships. We saw the fixing motif offers a way to enact the Problem-solving schema, which is also part of Supermasculinity. Fixing aims at control, but fails to produce it for the Viking and presumably for Monroe as well. Part of Monroe's discomfort may be that, like Russell, he finds himself in the Cinderella position: wishing that a significant other would recognize him as valuable (that is, as the Viking who "flew all the way over from his town to fix you"). More relevant to the Carrier, evidently, is that the Viking does not fit her "context." The problem, Carrier intimates, is that while she is relatively modern, he is not. The Perfect-fit schema may not be part of Monroe's gender model but he is not immune to perfect-fit expectations. Earlier I argued that once models are in popular circulation, in principle, anyone can appropriate them. Intentionally or not, however, people use all applicable models with which they are familiar to understand their feelings, thoughts, and actions. If the person disidentifies with such a model, however, this usage tends to be subtextual and implied rather than conscious—as is Monroe's use of the Cinderella model and its Perfect-fit schema.

The Carrier/girlfriend says that she has to "move on." Chapter 4 explores this Moving On model of personal progress, which assumes a willingness to shed past relationships and circumstances to solve life's problems. Monroe said she

> had been expressing a great deal of dissatisfaction with her current job...and seemed to be suffering a bout of depression. She had ceased to say "I love you"...probably *chose* not to....I knew that it was going to end although I had no desire for this to happen and pretty much ignored the problem. She would ultimately leave the relationship early on in the month of December as she feels her move would be too stressful, to my dismay. [Emphasis mine]

In other words, to avoid stress Monroe's girlfriend intends breaking up with him before she actually departs Pullman and has even set a date for the breakup! She definitely has a Detachment schema. So does Monroe. Again please note his distancing language: a tentative "she would" rather than a definite "she will," "leave the relationship" versus "leave me." As in Marilyn's dream, here choice is the issue but belongs to a romantic other. Indeed, for Monroe attempting choice is foolish—like trying to cross a vast ocean with a jet-pack. Next Monroe played the ocean.

Friend: Describe yourself to me, ocean.

Ocean: I am a large body of water that is vast and will take a lot of time to cross.

Monroe: What do you think of somebody trying to cross you?

O: Ha, that would be very foolish, I am here for a reason, to create borders that someone should not cross.

Ocean confirms that Monroe would be foolish to attempt a crossing, but the Viking only needs to fly to Carrier, not across the Pacific! As an unbridgeable distance, moreover, Monroe's ocean is at odds with Western ocean symbolism. Thus, at the opening of *Civilization and Its Discontents* ([1930]1964), Freud describes an "oceanic sense" in which the bounds of self dissolve in infantile or mystic bliss. Monroe's ocean is the ultimate barrier; it is like a wall that tells him: You can't fix this problem! Monroe thought:

> I am...the Viking with the jetpack, who jumps in the water to follow after the carrier, even knowing that his goal is futile. In real life I recognize that she has been searching for an opportunity to start a career with her degree—which until now has been difficult. I can't hold her back without coming across as the type of person that seeks to control others, and I am definitely not like that at all and I could not be with someone who would tolerate such a person even though I would rather that she stay in the area....In my culture, it is expected that when an opportunity comes up for someone, any person...attached to them should be gladly willing to let that person go to chase their dreams.

Monroe felt that this expectation created a "hole" in the "person that is being left behind" who might "find it hard to express the desire to keep the one who is leaving them close by." While Monroe wrote that the ocean represented his personal "hole," he didn't say what that was. Is it, true to classic ocean symbolism, Monroe's emotions? Monroe's friend astutely asks why the Viking didn't just fly to the carrier: why did he swim? Does diving into the sea suggest an inability to distance himself from his emotions? Yet, neither can he express them.

> While in real life I follow the old saying—"if you love something, let it go," I also have an unshared desire to follow her to Virginia. I have to believe that this is something commonly faced by career minded couples in the United States. The ratio of men to women in the workforce is continuously becoming more even, and finding a good job often can require searching in a place that is far from what you call

home. Many including myself still desire to remain with someone
that they have invested a great deal of time in, but this is hard to
express when you also want to respect the freedom of a loved one.

Monroe's romance, like Russell's, is under the sign of capitalism:
what is distressing is a loss of investments. Evidently, he was more
open in his paper than with his girlfriend. There is, I suggest, a connection between the absence of women on the manifest level of this
dream (that is evidently all about a woman) and Monroe's reluctance
to share his feelings. His girlfriend is symbolically submerged in the
dream: she is one of the latent meanings. In his daytime interactions, his feelings for her are submerged: he does not express them.
Betty and Marilyn believe their path to choice and agency is through
acceptability, which in both cases hinges on playing the role of a
woman. Marilyn hopes that she is acceptable as a spouse role; Betty
would like to dress in acceptable feminine drag. Monroe (and we
will soon see Dave too) believes that to exercise agency/choice is to
control another. Monroe, moreover, construes expressing his feelings as an attempt to control another and to foreclose her options.
The result is the drifting apart depicted in the dream. Monroe's
Supermasculinity model seems directed at exercising agency (winning battles, fixing ships, etc.), but does not help him reach his goal
(the carrier)—a fact that both his dream and projective work illu-
mine. In his silence Monroe, like Marilyn and Betty, seems impelled
by a form of biopower, but in his case one that structures, not sexuality, but emotion.

Dave

Dave identified himself as "Korean/German." He was 20, and from
the larger Seattle area. He remarked that the dream "was like the
ending to a movie that I kind of knew."

> I was deep in a cave with rocky walls. It was difficult to move
> around, because the cave slanted downward....[I]t was pretty
> dark....Looking down the cave I saw a dog and a cat fighting. The cat
> seemed to be winning and this troubled me because I think that the
> dog was mine....I went down to try and save it but the cat was really
> strong....There was a lot of blood....[A]bove me there was the same
> dog barking at me and growling, this dog seemed very evil....He
> wasn't injured like the other dog...its intentions were to hurt me.
> Then all of a sudden the dog turned nice again, so I left my dog to the

cat. I started going up to the dog, but it turned evil again.... I felt safe, like I knew what was going to happen as I crawled... out of the cave. At the cave's mouth I found my little brother waiting for me. He tried to pull me out, but I told him to wait because I knew something was coming behind me... a small doll.... I had my boots on so I kicked the doll... the doll exploded on contact. I got up and out of the cave and knew that this was near the end of the movie.... [E]verything... had become like an old three-dimensional video game. I saw the man flying in who looked... like a weird gray ghost.... He said... didn't you like this ending instead of just some generic one?... I told him that it was very good for an early 80s movie. Then he said that the math for the movie actually began in 1963. I wanted to fly around the screen... but the movie ended.... I came out of the movie and was in... [Temple's] house watching it.... I was trying to see the ending to the movie again, by pressing the skip button on the credits.... I really wanted to fly in the screen, but couldn't get back into the movie. Then Temple said something about watching... porn.

The dream dog is Dave's pet. U.S. kids often first learn about and practice friendship and parenthood in the pet-person relation. A pet is supposed to be a committed and affectionate companion but is also like a child that must be cared for and gently coerced into appropriate behavior. We will soon see this dream is about parent-hood for Dave, or its obviation. The Pet model can be particularly important for U.S. boys because, at least in the Beaver version of close family, after early childhood (from a psychoanalytic viewpoint after the Oedipal crisis), boys may not express much direct affection toward their parents (even though they care about them). Then their primary model for expressing of care and attachment may default to the Pet model. This is the model that Dave as dreamer rehearses and tries to use to address the life situation the dream concerns.

The dream frame, a movie, suggests the Detachment schema. Yet, one normally watches movies and Dave is in (and then out of) this movie making his status as detached ambiguous. Indeed, experienc-ing something people usually watch counterposes detachment and indirectly suggests attachment, like the Pet model. Nonetheless, Dave decided to analyze this dream because: "it was weird to feel safe in a dream that... was almost like a nightmare." His statement underlines the relation between detachment and risk-taking. Detachment, a sense of remove, can make scary circumstances feel safe and hence permits action. "Kind of" knowing the movie suggests control: proverbially in the United States, "knowledge is power," and Dave seems unlikely to face disconcerting surprises (that could threaten his control). Yet, the opening bloody battle scene is intrinsically surprising and does vicariously threaten his dominance: it is an unnatural fight between a dog with whom he identifies and a preternaturally powerful cat.

The choice Dave originally confronts is whether he should stay detached or come to the dog's rescue. Rescue, like detachment, evokes the Supermasculinity model. When Dave climbs up the cave's rocky walls, he finds, not the dog, but his brother. Indeed, there was a less coherent version of the dream in Dave's journal in which the dog at the cave's mouth turns out to be his brother. So, the dream plays out the fraternal variant of a Knight tale and the cat is the monster Dave would slay. Supermen intervene on the side of justice to rescue the weak. Here the dog is the weakling and Dave starts to intervene to save it, but he cannot decide to do so because he sees "the same dog" at the cave's mouth that is evil, then nice, and then evil again. The result is that, rather than helping the situation make sense, Dave's Supermasculinity model recommends contradictory courses of action between which he vacillates.

Probably because Dave already knew something about the dream dog (that it was his), he decided to first role-play the cat.

Cat: I'm Orange and White stripped and very large. Large and strong enough to take on and kill a dog, while keeping someone else from pulling it away. This is my cave and you can't come in, I want you to leave me to kill this dog. I hate this dog and I'm going to end its life as soon as I can deep in my cave.

Dave: Why are you killing my Dog?

C: I don't want it to live because it is in my cave and I don't want it or want you to have it so go away. Why don't you just take that other dog behind you? It looks just the same.

D: I don't want that Dog, it's evil and is not mine, and I want my Dog. I'll just take it from you.

C: There is no way, I am way stronger than you are because this is my cave and in my cave I have all the power.

D: Why don't you care about how I feel?

C: Because this is not your choice.

On the manifest level, the human dream images are all men—Dave, his brother, the ghost, and Temple. Yet after role-play, Dave concluded Cat was his girlfriend. The powerful cat, like Monroe's independent carrier, suggests a reversal of traditional U.S. gender roles. Does Dave, like Monroe, find himself in the Cinderella position, wishing another would recognize and care about his feelings? At the time, Dave's girlfriend was pregnant with his child:

> I think that I might want to keep it subconsciously. Although I do know that having this baby would be detrimental to my school and family life.... [T]hat is why I am trying so hard to pull the dog out of the cave.... [E]ven if I told her that I wanted it, I think that she would kill it anyways. Killing the baby goes against my moral beliefs, but I know that ultimately the decision is up to her. This is why...she is the cat....In her cave she has all the power, and if her decision is to kill the dog, that is what is going to happen. The doll, when it comes out of the cave...might be her trying to reel me back in and help her with it [the abortion], but I don't want to since I want to keep the baby. So when the doll comes up I kick it away.

So, according to Dave, the cave stands for his girlfriend's womb, getting an abortion is killing his dog, and the cat and doll too represent his girlfriend. Dave says that "even if" he shared his feelings she would still have an abortion: evidently, like Monroe he was not as open with her as he was in his paper. Next Dave role-played the dog.

> Dog: ...I'm fluffy and nice. I want to get out of this cave, but this awful cat is overpowering me and I can't get out, I need your help. Please just give me a chance to live....
> Dave: Dog I really want to get you out, but I can't....
> Dog: Keep trying. I'm almost dead, don't let me go.
> Dave: ...[A]s hard as I try this cat won't let you go.
> Dog: I'm too weak to fight, this cat is overpowering me and won't stop attacking me, isn't there anything you can do?
> Dave: I'm sorry; I'm powerless to help you.

The dream Dog's moral ambiguity clouds its right to life: evil is not a word Dave uses for Cat, despite its murderous intent. Dave wrote of this interchange:

> [T]he hole in my culture that this dream represents is that men don't have *a choice* in whether or not to keep a child even if it is theirs. Women can decide whether or not the child will be born without having their partner's consent....[W]omen have all the say...so it is very difficult for me....Watching television it seems that...in America males do not want their children or want to deal with things like child support. I see all kinds of shows where guys say things like "I'm not the baby's daddy." So these things in my culture make it very

hard for me to say that I want to keep the baby, because it should have a chance to live.

Before the pill and Roe vs. Wade, men's rights in paternity were secure: women could not reliably prevent nor terminate pregnancy, but for decades now women have had basic control of their bodies, which may leave men feeling that they don't have a say. As in Monroe's dream, here the issue of expressiveness is key, but with a twist. While Monroe refuses to express himself so as not to control another, Dave does not bother to express himself because he cannot exert control.

Dave's frustration at his lack of control over his girlfriend seems enacted in kicking the dream doll; this scene replays yet reverses the earlier cat/dog fight. A girlfriend/doll relation is congruent with U.S. symbolism. In the 1940s and 1950s, girlfriends where sometimes called "Dolls" in colloquial speech. Barbie is the archetypal U.S. doll. While there are Ken dolls, most miniature people toys that boys play with today are called "action figures." Yet, dolls are also reminiscent of babies, a role they often play in girls' games. By kicking/exploding the doll, does Dave also intimate ambivalence about the baby? Last, Dave role-played the ghost.

> Ghost: I can fly, I know a lot of information, and I am very impressed that I know so much. I'm gray and oddly shaped, like a ghost from a game you played at your Uncle's house. This game scared you then, but doesn't anymore.
> Dave: Who are you?
> G: I'm your Uncle here to show you this movie, aren't you impressed by the graphics?
> D: Sure, but I think that they are kind of old.
> G: Well they are very good for their time don't you think.
> D: What is your purpose in my dream?
> G: I'm here to show you that the movie does not always end like you think it will.

Dave portrays the ghost as overly impressed with himself. He claims extreme knowledgeableness that suggests, along with his ability to fly, Extraordinary Powers, which is a Supermasculinity schema. Inasmuch as the dream is a movie he is showing (and bragging about), the ghost's position is dominant and he is in control. Yet, by implying the ghost's knowledge is braggadocio and treating him, albeit politely, as passé, Dave reveals mixed feelings about Supermasculinity: he would like to emulate it, to fly as the ghost does, but he also frames the model as inflated and dated. This ghost reminded Dave of his recently deceased uncle who was a recurrent figure in Dave's dreams at that time.

> [W]e were taking him to all the places he wanted to go before he died. When I woke up from that dream I almost wanted to cry. I would have used that dream, but I dreamt it over at my girlfriends' house, and had nothing to write on.

As a character in a game who flies, the ghost doubly evokes the Detachment schema, but he also evokes a memory of attachment, which is what Dave feels toward the dream dog and toward his unborn baby. By melding a public symbol of detachment with an experience of attachment to a father-figure, Dave's ghost condenses the contradictions that characterize the Supermasculinity model for him. Dave's failure to fly may represent an inability to detach from his current life situation or, possibly, a critical response to the Supermasculinity model evoked by it. Yet, the dream ends with Temple's proposal that they watch porn, suggesting Voyeuristic Sexuality and, like the doll, objectification: unlike dogs or cats, dolls are objects, even if the dream doll walks. Through the dream, Dave tries to use the Pet model of attachment to understand his feelings, but it is simply not up to the moral complexity he faces with his girlfriend, leaving him to lapse into depersonalized agent/object relations.

Playing with Choice

For Marilyn and Betty choice comes with being accepted, which is contingent upon their bodily control. When one's gender model is Cinderella, one seeks to fit that tropic slipper: the expectations of some idealized other who, like a prince, has the power to radically change one's life, along with one's status and wealth. Yet, if Marilyn says she wants to be accepted as a wife and as the mother of Kamil's children, she also sells sex toys. Betty says that she wants to lose weight but likes to have fun in the mud. For Monroe and Dave, choice is a matter of having control over another, "having a say," which Monroe supposedly doesn't want and Dave supposedly does. Yet, Monroe feels like he is drowning and Dave can't decide who is evil. When I question these dreamers' sentiments, I do not mean they are wrong in their self-assessments, only that they also have contradicting feelings united by a feeling-toned idea—choice.

If these young men and women approach choice through different idioms, moreover, they share common issues. Surely, Marilyn's problem is like Dave's—she doesn't have a say. In the dream, her grandmother talks to her boyfriend on the phone; she does not. Betty's problem too is one of expression: she has no voice in class. Having a voice, in turn, represents her ability to pursue a career like that of the lecturer. If Monroe and Dave don't talk of acceptance, both feel rejected. Monroe was not asked to come along. Dave identifies with the dog that his girlfriend is getting out of her cave. Both, moreover, are controlling themselves through silence about their feelings.

In personal life, all Americans are prochoice—their choice. Everyone wants it, but none of these four dreamers feels they have it. The question for them is: who gets to choose? In other words, there appears to be a "limited good" underside to the Choice model in which the person who makes her own choice deprives a significant other of choice. While these young women's choices founder on their inability to fit the expectations of others and these young men's, on keeping silent when they can't legitimately seek control, their dreams suggest alternatives. Marilyn and Betty, like Cinderella before the prince, are dirty little girls: they both have a positive-participatory relation to sex that is anything but ladylike, symbolized by selling sexual toys and mud racing respectively. Marilyn's entrepreneurial venture is paying for her education and Betty is enjoying a wild ride despite her size and shape. Their dreams and Dream Play lead Monroe and Dave toward a realization that the Supermasculinity model is letting them down and that a possible solution lies in expressiveness.

All four of these dreamers fear rejection: Marilyn, Monroe, and Dave by a romantic other; Betty by others in a general sense and possibly by a future ideal romantic other. These fears trigger a rehearsal of gender schemas and models. Marilyn (the girlfriend but never the wife) starts washing dishes (taking care of her boyfriend's place). Betty (who can only window-shop for lingerie) worries about not taking care of herself (eating junk foods). Monroe as the flying Viking mechanic rehearses detachment and fixing. Dave as the movie-watcher also rehearses detachment and contemplates entering into a struggle for dominance. Yet, in their dreams these gender schemas and models produce confusion and contradictory or uncertain outcomes, rather than sense and efficacy. In effort and effect,

I suggest, these dreamers interrogate their schemas and models and Dream Play enhances these interrogations.

Under normal circumstances, Marilyn might have been reluctant to share her feelings about Muslim others. Betty might not have spoken of her feelings about her weight and talking in class. Monroe and Dave wouldn't even tell their girlfriends what they felt. Foucault (1990) argues that psychotherapy is a kind of confession. Confessing in the religious sense brings guilt and shame. Do people escape these emotions in therapeutic confessions? Dream Play achieves therapeutic effects through acting out. In the Dream Play recorded here, dreamers are assertive rather than ashamed even though they are discovering "holes" in themselves. What they discover, moreover, is as much about their society as it is about them. Such discoveries grant a kind of absolution for apparently idiosyncratic failings and summon individuals to a greater awareness of how their culture bears, often uncomfortably, on their personal lives.

Chapter 4

Holographic Dreaming and "Moving On" in the U.S.A.

Contemporary psychologists investigate the dream's role in memory.[1]
Yet, our existential experience of the dream is one of forgetting—
of being immersed in a reality that seems to stretch back in time to
an origin beyond remembrance. At the next moment, we wake and
the dream vanishes from the horizon of consciousness, sometimes
completely but even when we retain it, our reports to a friend or
confidante are often faltering. By mid-morning, if we do not record
or relate them, dreams are usually well beyond recollection. This
amnesia, I argue in this chapter, offers clues to those memory processes that do indeed define dreaming.

Dreams are full of missing pieces. These missing pieces, like
something the dreamer has forgotten, prompts a search into the
deep resources of memory. In Clark's dream (Chapter 2), for example, Bigfoot is missing from the dream; the dream quest is to find
him. Bigfoot represents Clark's dad. Clark's dreaming mind elicits
memories of their times together to fill in this absence. I do not
mean that upon waking Clark knew what his dream was about.
In U.S. culture, many people do not give dreams a passing thought
and never discover meaning in them. Yet, dreams speak their own
language—a language of figures that connects memories to models
whether or not people try to render their scenes and meanings into
words.

The missing pieces of dreams, I propose, represent daily instances
when an undercoded experience grazed consciousness. The missing
element symbolizes what we could not make sense of because it was
beyond whatever model we brought to bear at that instant. Within
the dream, a figure with a missing piece catalyzes memories of past
times when we experienced a similar problem with the model and
memories with the potential to supplement the model that we found
wanting in the present.

According to Lacan (1968), the infant's experience is fragmentary: just a series of disconnected events. In the mirror phase, which occurs around the age of two, the child's imaginal mind begins to organize this rubble in whole images. When we learn language, according to Lacan, the logical/practical mind displaces the imaginal, which recedes into the background (1977a). Yet, the parts of our experience that fall beyond the scope of our models remain in rubbles. In dreams, the imaginal mind goes on trying to organize this fragmentary remembered experience by revising and extending our models.

The Gestalt psychologists of the first half of the twentieth century thought that incomplete visual figures, a set of dots suggesting an elephant for example, compelled people to fill in the absent parts (Murray 1995, Petermann 1932). Likewise, I hold, the fragmentary visions of dreams compel people. Yet, dreamers strive not so much, or at any rate not merely, for a perceptual completeness as for a completeness of meanings. Completion, of course, is a hypothetical point: meaning systems never achieve closure, but are processual (Derrida 1978). The movement toward repair/elaboration, however, impels dreams forward.

States (2001) describes dreams as metaphors in motion. What are they moving toward? I will show that dreams' fragmentary figures are in motion in the sense that each successive figure reconfigures a predecessor via a new metaphor that enlists additional memories, which constitute a mnemonic commentary on a dreamer's problem with a cultural model. What the dream/dreamer seeks through such commentaries is a memory that can patch the missing part of its predecessor. In these efforts to fill absences, dreamers produce new connections among personal memories and to cultural models—connections that make these models more workable and, therefore, have the potential to change them for others too.

In the dream, bizarre figures (figures with missing pieces) operate as a self-protective disguise against anxiety-provoking memories, just as Freud ([1900]1964) saw it, but at the same time as an invitation to reconstruct them. The action of the dream itself derives from a compulsion to complete the blurred figures of the dream world. Freud ([1900]1964, [1916]1963) tells us that some dream meanings are *overdetermined*: they are symbolized redundantly. I agree, but suggest that dream figures are *underdetermined* in a way that continually compels their replacement by a new figure, which iterates but also supplements an incomplete meaning—a compulsion that continues in dream reports and interpretations. Yet, such innovations are not necessarily conscious. In dreaming and in working on dreams, people think in figures that their verbal minds, at least at first, do not comprehend.

The reiterative nature of dream replacements resembles what Dreyfus (1984) calls "holographic memory." In holographic memory, the person remembers events as numerous superimposed pictures of relevant past scenes that come together to suggest a new way forward. Dreyfus's example is a chess game in which a master sees in memory all similar chessboards she has formerly played. The dreamer, likewise, is confronting a "move" in life, one associated with a cultural model, and "sees" a series of figures, each representing a new set of memories superinscribed, as it were, upon the last. States (2001:101–102) says that each part of the dream is "holographically endowed with the power of the whole." By this, he means that dreams are associated with "emotion-laden events" for the dreamer, each "capable of carrying the full emotional import of that particular history." The uniting element of these histories, the basis on which dreams select them to think about a possible real world "play," I argue, is not an emotion per se but a model that shapes both how we think and how we feel about our experience.

The Selfscape Method

In this chapter, I draw upon exercises students did using Hollan's (2003a, 2005) ideas about what he calls "selfscape dreams." A "selfscape" dream is especially vivid and easy to recall; it depicts the individual's current state of body, personality, and relations with others, and integrates new experiences into emergent self-schemas. Here Hollan draws upon a host of ideas in psychology and psychoanalysis—most significantly, Kohut's (1971, 1977) concept of "self-state dreams": that some dreams are directly related to the dreamer's current life situation, to alterations in their conscious and unconscious sense of self, to their sense of well-being, as well as to dramatic shifts in self-esteem and psychological balance. Also important is Noy's (1969, 1979) view of the dream as a nondiscursive, emotional, imaginal language, which plays a central role in psychological growth and development, and Damasio's (1994, 1999) that dreams are neural representations of the body, self, and world, which need continuous updating and modification. Hollan also cites Fairbairn (1952), who sees dreams as dramatizations or "shorts" (in the cinematographic sense) of inner reality that depict unconscious

relationships among part-selves and part-selves relations to internalized representations of others, ideas indebted to Jung's (1967,
1968, 1970) work. To these insights, Hollan adds Levy's (1984):
dreams often represent hypocognized material. Rather than understanding hypocognition as referring to underrepresented emotions
like Levy, or to experiences that cultural models fail to represent as
I have (2001a, 2003), for Hollan (2003a:69) hypocognition refers
to "widespread social anxieties" that people in a culture ordinarily
suppress or repress. I call the projective exercise that I developed
from these perspectives, "The Selfscape Method."

First, the dreamer guesses how the dream reflects his current life
situation and is a dramatization of his inner life. Second, he asks
how it reflects alterations to his self-esteem and sense of well-being.
Third, he questions how it represents his relations to others, either
closeness or estrangement, and the emotions that go with these
states. He also considers if the dream depicts his relationships to his
part-selves and their relations to one another. Next, he asks how the
dream represents his ideas about himself—his self-schemas. Last, he
considers how the dream depicts emotions, widespread anxieties, or
other experiences that people neither talk nor think much about in
his culture.

Holographic Analysis

As in Narrative Analysis, in Holographic Analysis too, a researcher
first assembles a set of dreams on a common topic and, through
ethnographic data and other studies of the culture, infers a cultural
model from this topic. For consistent data, I recommend selecting
dreams that dreamers analyzed with a single method, one that helps
them provide life history and associational material. Here again,
dreamers' journals provide a valuable additional source. Second, the
researcher zooms in on a specific individual and a dream. Third, she
reflects on what is missing from an opening dream figure. Fourth,
she explores how this missing part relates to memories the figure
evokes for the dreamer, both day residues and memories from the
dreamer's past. Fifth, she considers how these memories highlight
an inadequacy in the cultural model at issue or in the dreamer's use
of the model. Sixth, she asks how the next dream figure represents
its predecessor: how it resembles this figure yet enlists new memories
with a further potential to throw light on inadequacies in the model
or the dreamer's use of it. Seventh, she repeats steps three through

six with each major dream figure, tracing how the dream raises questions in the form of absences and answers them with memories that address these absences. This chapter's structure follows the steps for Holographic Analysis using data and interpretations that dreamers developed via the Selfscape Method. The instructions I gave them did not suggest that their dreams had "missing parts," nor did they discover such parts in their analyses.

Moving On

In this chapter, I consider a U.S. model of and for personal progress that I call "Moving On." In the Moving on model, progress is tantamount to moving up socially, economically, and professionally, which often entails a departure from past relations and an allegiance to future possibilities. Indeed, using this U.S. model often entails "a race to the top." It is by moving on, along with hard work and merit, that Americans putatively transcend birth context and status, the social roles and affiliations that go with them, and even social categories that they often construe as biological such as race or gender. A willingness to transit is particularly relevant to young adults like my students who typically find themselves between their natal families on the one hand and careers or marriages on the other.

Moving on is what D'Andrade (1984:95) calls a U.S. Success model in which a person with ability works hard and competes to reach "an outstanding level of accomplishment." It relies on the Close Family metamodel and two of its component models, the Devoted Mom and the Supportive Dad. We saw in Chapter 2, Devoted Moms promote accomplishment by rewarding a child's efforts with recognition. Supportive Dads provide what Winnicott (1967) calls "transitional space": a safe space within which the child can practice risk-taking, necessary to succeed in a high modernist order and a prerequisite to effective use of the Moving on model in which the person ventures into the unknown.

Moving on is a middle-class model. Most of my students' were from middle-class families. Their role in the Close Family should have buttressed their Moving on model. We saw in Chapter 2 that Good Kids realize their parents' high hopes, meaning that they go beyond birth context, surpassing their parents' achievements. In fact, malfunctioning close families often stood in the way of my students moving on. Thus, Clark put off graduation and moving in with his girlfriend, both of which would represent personal progress for him, because of his involvement with his mom. The Moving on model demands a readiness to shed or at least loosen former relationships and to undertake risks. Lois cannot move on in her recurrent dream because she is afraid of loosening her relationship with either parent and is risk-avoidant. Monroe's problem (Chapter 3) is that his girl-friend has a Moving on model: she doesn't mind shedding her past, while he is a bit old fashioned and does mind.

Models evolve in a group where members, because of shared patterns of socialization, are likely to possess knowledge and desire that promote using these models and where, because of the group's socio-economic position, members possess real opportunities to use them. Yet, Moving on often means leaving one's place of birth, family, and friends—that is, going beyond the group with which one shares socialization patterns and opportunities. In this sense, the Moving on model has an inherent contradiction that makes it a likely subject of dreams. Dreams tend to fasten on such contradictions as well as on times when socialization and opportunity have not conspired to help the dream use a model.

The dreamers in this chapter were seniors about to begin a major life transition from undergraduate school to professional training or a job. I call them George, Dolly, Madison, and Betsy (Table 5).

Table 5   Missing Pieces and Moving On

	George	*Dolly*	*Madison*	*Betsy*
First Figure	Best Buddies	Franklin Driving	Frazzled Bride	Speeding Car
Absence	Development	Destination	Preparation	Care for Consequences
Memories	Perfect Family	Ministry Camp	Leaving WSU	Goodie Goodie Sister
Second Figure	Ascending Mom	Rushing Cars	Absent Father	Driving Martha
Absence	Family Feeling	Connection	Support	Care for Outsiders
Memories	No-account Relatives	Busyness, Loneliness	Judgmental Dad	Her Clique
Third Figure	Fridge	Stairwell Race	Fiancé	Angry Man
Absence	Father	Risk-taking	Transitional Space	Listening
Memories	Selling House	Twin Sister	Sexual Joking	Party Train

To the extent that moving on is not really in their interest or in line with their feelings, for them moving on is a performance principle—one that, as dreamers, they question and challenge. George's dream concerns moving up in social status. Dolly's is about moving beyond feelings from her past. Madison's dream is about (not) moving forward into a career. Betsy dreams about moving fast—moving for its own sake.

George

George was 21 at the time of the dream and described himself as "Korean/Croatian/White." Redundantly specifying Croatian and White is a way George underlines diversity—an important family value for him. George grew up in the larger Seattle area.

> I was in the living room of the television show, Arrested Development. I am laughing with Jeff and Thomas while sitting on some living room chairs. My mother comes into the room, seeming very serious. I rise and follow her upstairs.... [S]he shows me to a refrigerator where she has mapped out my Korean family's lineage on a family tree. She points to them and looks at me gravely.

Figure 1: Best Buddies

The dream opens in a set from "Arrested Development," which was also George's title for the dream. "I have been having references to Arrested Development in several of my dreams," George remarked. The Moving on model is about progress: this title suggests an inability or reluctance to use the model. Development, then, is the missing element in this first scene. The dream begins via a return, possibly to the point of arrest and to people George misses, Jeff and Thomas: "These two are my best buddies, and we always make a point to watch the show together." Boarding at university is many U.S. kids' first experience of moving on from youthful friendships. Hanging out with Jeff and Thomas is a figure for lost boyhood conviviality and suggests the Guyfriends model in which companions share being together and a common focus on something other than their relationship. Yet, Jeff's and Thomas's status as "best buddies" suggests something more.

One normally watches TV rather than living in a TV program: this first figure is bizarre. In Lois's and Monroe's dreams, they are

watching from outside the dream frame. I argued this outside perspective signifies detachment, which Lois needs and Monroe loses.
Like Dave in Chapter 2, George experiences something people usually watch: he is inside of something that people are normally outside. In Dave's case, I suggested that this ambiguous frame (outside
yet inside) signified the Detachment schema held up to question. In
George's case, the TV show is a kind of double negative and again
a way of questioning detachment, but this time as a part of the
Moving on model.

Jeff and Thomas reminded George of a family he left behind. In
his preschool years, George lived in his paternal grandmother's big
Seattle house because his mom and dad had careers. During the
holidays, both sides of his family celebrated there. Three cousins
were his age, two of whom were half Samoan (his paternal aunt
married a Samoan). His maternal relatives were Korean. George
felt the family of his early childhood was "perfect." This extended
family, what one might call a One-world Family, is George's alternative to the Close Family model, which in his case was plagued
with typical problems (mother/child overinvolvement and father
absence). People often have an alternative for a hegemonic model
that has not worked well for them. Such alternatives range from
enduring models that are simply not as common as prevailing models, to models that enjoy a passing popularity (in fantasy) like Bam's
family model, to more private models. George felt his family was
special and unique, adjectives that also captured his sentiments
about his Korean side. "I actually studied much of the culture in
school, and I attended... a full-submersion camp where I learned to
speak some," George told me.

Figure 2: Mom Ascending

The next figure to enter the dream is George's mom. George's
memories of his mom resemble his memories of Jeff and Thomas.
When George left his grandmother's house and came home to live
with his parents, his mother hung around home. They sometimes
watched TV together, as George did with Jeff and Thomas. Yet,
while laughing with his buddies reminded George of good times, his
"serious" mom marks their departure in the dream. "Good spirits"
at the opening, George wrote, "change with the introduction of my
mother," who, "if anyone ever was a bearer of bad news" would
have "the biggest impact upon me." Good spirits, then, refers to
the joy in companionship he experienced with Jeff and Thomas and

earlier with his extended family. This joy is also the missing part of his dream mom.

"I begin in the lower floor of the house and am brought upstairs by my mother," George observed, "I am moved from one level to another...Moving up, to me, would suggest an improvement in my standing." George's mom was socially upward bound—an orientation symbolized in the dream by upstairs/downstairs topography. She is the only member of her natal family who left the Olympia area and now "pushes my [close] family to separate ourselves from those family members. I have an actual, physical split from them because we live so far away, almost to say that we are not like them." Koreans do not draw sharp lines between nuclear family and lineage; this distinction is a feature of the U.S. Close Family model. His mom's detachment from family members who are not improving their "standing," then, represents a loss of warm affective bonds, which George also experienced going away to school and before that when he left his grandmother's house in Seattle. These loses symbolize what is missing from the Moving on model for him—attachment.

George had this dream shortly before Christmas. His close family had not visited his mom's Korean family at Thanksgiving and was not planning to visit at Christmas either: "It just seemed wrong," George remarked, "I felt like we were shunning them." While George thinks that "our society has begun to undermine...reverence of family units with respect to our development," he has come to share some of his mother's negative attitudes toward his Korean relations: "I feel somewhat ashamed....It's hard to be around them...feeling contemptuous. I start to judge...when I am confronted with my actual roots, I feel hostile....We love our families, but we are taught to be ashamed of...stupidity, poorness, alcoholism."

George's hardworking and generous Korean maternal grandmother met her Croatian American husband during the Korean War. George thinks his granddad was in the army because he has seen photos of him in a green uniform. George loves and respects his grandmother, but he too finds visiting difficult these days: she's caring for a grandchild who is in the terrible twos and not developing well, which makes her home a "madhouse." This chaos represents George's current impression of his extended family. His grandmother's adult kids have problems with substance abuse, messy divorces, several don't work, and one has a gambling problem—trash covers her house. Even on his dad's side, everyone is divorced except the aunt with the Samoan husband. George idealizes his family's diversity, but these days he disapproves of most of his relatives: this contradiction arrests his moving on.

Figure 3: The Fridge

The next major dream figure is a fridge that "acts" as a lesson board and represents what was missing in George's memories of his mom: a validation of his larger family. U.S. Americans often post pictures of family and friends on their fridge, but the dream fridge displays George's entire Korean lineage. This fridge evoked memories of what was missing in George's close family—his dad.

George's parents never fought, nor did they talk about their emotions, but they almost separated when he was 14. He then learned that his dad "did not listen" to his mom. His parents played out this problem around their fridge. Although George's dad made a good living, their home was rundown and George's mother felt "untended." She wanted a remodeled kitchen but, for his dad, that was always "on the back burner." The fridge in the dream was the one from their old kitchen; the dream took place in their old house, which his dad sold when he found out that remodeling the kitchen would cost more than getting a new house. George regrets this: he loved that spacious property with its creek and cow pasture.

George was not close to his dad. Unlike George and his "best buddies" in the opening dream scene, George's dad did not like to be stationary. In daytime, he worked; at night, he was out running errands or doing chores. Busyness is a schema proper to the Moving on model: to the degree that U.S. Americans have internalized Moving on as a performance principle, they are constantly busy or think they should be. Busyness can get in the way of close relationships. Indeed, in the opening dream scene, loitering symbolizes such relationships. In contrast, George says his dad "always goes off to do his own thing, leaving my mother and me."

George's dad sometimes planned times with him; even then, George did not feel close to him. "This upcoming break, we have planned a hunting trip," but now George would like to "get out of spending time with him." In another dream, George is "stricken with grief" because he has to tell a blonde female friend that he can't go to a school event because he has to go on a hunting trip with his dad. In yet another, George is "afraid to tell my father that I will be absent.... I feel so pressured to perform when I am around him, I find it very disconcerting when I am alone with him for too long. I often get stressed and tense, and eventually end up getting angry." George had an absent father, from whom he would now like to absent himself.

By alluding to George's memories of his dad's coolness, the fridge reconfigures his mom's coolness to her lower-class relatives. George's dad stands for an unwillingness to nourish close family with personal time or money and a readiness to sacrifice what is valuable in the past—like a spacious property with a creek and pasture. This readiness is what makes George ambivalent about Moving on. The dream refrigerator summons memories that amount to a mnemonic commentary on this model and on George's reluctance to embrace what he experiences as a big block of ice.

This dream leads back through a series of missing pieces—from missed friends, to a missing "perfect family," to a missing dad. The dream tries to repair the Moving on model by altering the significance of George's mom. Although she leads George up and away from Jeff and Thomas (from hanging out and from Arrested Development), by schooling him about his Korean family tree, she acts like an anthropology professor and may be a stand-in for me and for George's recent memories of my class. I am a Samoanist. In class (as in this book), I often contrast Samoan culture to U.S. middle-class culture. George once came up to my office after class to tell me that he had Samoan relations and recognized what I was saying. I could tell that he was proud of his diverse background and pleased at my surprise: a student who appeared to have Asian ancestry had Samoan relatives. In the dream, George's mom points gravely to a Korean kinship chart that George probably studied in his "full-submersion camp," but may also have learned about from her, whether she subscribes to Korean family values or not. The dream melds George's missing friends and family with a more positive way of moving on (or moving up)—an education that aims at greater understanding of cultural differences.

Dolly

Dolly was 22 at the time of the dream and was "Caucasian/American." She grew up in a small town outside of Yakima.

> I was driving somewhere with my cousin, Franklin. He's *huge* (tall and heavy). We're not that close and he's younger than me. He was driving a van and we were going to a familiar place, although I have no idea

where it was. We started out by taking a route different from what we normally take—a country route—so after a while we thought we might be lost. Then I started seeing all kinds of land markers of things we would pass on our way to this familiar place (like an old shack), but we were going the wrong direction, so I told him he needed to turn around. He turned around in a really small town, and immediately we were in a mad rush of cars. All of a sudden we were in a stairwell racing with all the people who had been in the cars to get down the stairs. I think for a while we were on bicycles, but eventually we were just running. Franklin is so huge he would just jump down a flight at a time.... [W]e were racing to be first out of the house and Franklin and I were a team. Eventually as he went to jump, I pushed him over to the middle of the stairwell, and he grabbed something to hold...hanging in midair. He was only a couple of flights from the bottom, but he was too scared to let go...so he just kept swinging.

Figure 1: A Road Going Where?

Dolly's dream is what I call a Car dream, a dream in which major action happens in and through a car, explored at length in Chapter 5. For Dolly, however, the figure of the road or route soon becomes more salient than the car itself. The road has long been a major figure in U.S. popular lore, music, and movies because, like the car, it offers freedom—an escape from the intractable problems of real places and people. Roads are also supposed to "lead somewhere." In the dream, however, "somewhere," is a missing part and a source of contradiction: although their destination is "familiar," Dolly had "no idea where it was." The "different route" that she and Franklin take represents Dolly's lack of direction: she fears they are lost. Next, the landmarks repeat her disorientation: although recognizable, they indicate that Dolly is on her way to the wrong place.

In Chapter 2, I suggested that cars and roads symbolize a U.S. Traveling self-model in which the self is a vehicle of constant movement forward: this model meshes with Moving on. Thus, Americans may remark, "He's really going somewhere," suggesting that forward movement destines a person for success. Yet, there is often an opposition between the road and home—as in the following song by Heidi Muller, *Good Road* (1989).

It's a calling, a strange compulsion
That makes us leave our homes and take music on the road....
Good roads, good roads, wishing you a good road
May you find your comfort in friends along the way.

Probably the songwriter wishes friends for the traveler because U.S. roads are notoriously lonesome: like tumbleweeds in Wild West movies, roads remind Americans that there is an opposition between moving on and having "roots."

Dolly and Franklin travel in a van. Vans usually have rows of seats and often carry groups, although not in this dream. At that time, Dolly was missing a group: "I had just finished going on a retreat with a Christian group on campus where I was able to relax and rest." She remembered that the previous summer too she went to a Christian ministry training camp. "I made friendships and formed relationships with the people there like I hadn't ever experienced before. By the end of the summer we were like family.... We lived together, worked together, ate every meal together, and played together." Going back to WSU, Dolly felt "very lonely and at a loss for a long time."

Dolly's loneliness after ministry training camp reminded her of high school before she became a Christian. At that time, her mom left her dad. Her best friend and her beloved grandfather died of cancer. Her aunt went into a coma. The small town where they lived was conservative; her friends and schoolmates were Christian. She alone was an atheist because she didn't think a good God would make her so unhappy. Yet, with encouragement from friends, she then turned to Christianity. At the time of the dream, her Christian family had become Dolly's alternative to the Close Family model.

Franklin personifies Dolly's lack of direction. In the dream report, she says that she was driving but she was not: Franklin initially pilots the van. In Chapter 5, we will see that female dreamers are twice as likely as males to describe driving as a joint activity even when they are behind the wheel. Dolly's wording accentuates her (missing) agency, a lack that Franklin helps to explain. He is a younger cousin who did not finish high school because he couldn't bring himself to go to class. "Franklin has social anxiety disorder, depression," Dolly wrote, "and is very insecure with who he is." He is quiet and shy and has little interest in others. He reminded Dolly of high school. Then Dolly too was shy and afraid to talk to people she didn't know. She traces this insecurity to her close family situation, a situation that illustrates what is perhaps the most intractable problem with the Close Family model: it makes a child dependent primarily upon two fallible people—sometimes very fallible.

Dolly's mother was alcoholic. Her father was a workaholic and generally an absent member of the family. Both her parents grew up in alcoholic homes. Franklin signifies Dolly's resulting insecurities.

Dolly's driving with Franklin in the dream implies that insecurities originating in her family experience impair her ability to move on. The dream amounts to a mnemonic commentary on the source of her problem.

Figure 2: Mad Rush of Cars

A mad rush of cars belongs in a big town or city but in the dream the van is in "a really small town." Dolly remarked:

> [I]t's a really strange and fast-paced dream...and...reflected a lot of my internal state at the time—physically, emotionally, and mentally.... We're always in a hurry to get somewhere or do something, which is a common theme in my life because I have so much going on....I think the dream reflects the stress my body was going through...feeling rushed to get to the destination, stressed about school and life, but not really having time to process...it all.

Rushing is a good stand-in for insecurity/anxiety because people who feel chronically insecure and anxious readily panic. When panicked, people rush around. In another dream that semester, Dolly was "in a rush...panicked and terrified," because she was moving to China for a year with a bunch of people and had forgotten half her luggage in the car; there were draconian luggage restrictions. She had to leave her "essentials behind, like my hair dryer and curling iron." As a minister-to-be, it seems odd that Dolly's "essentials" were hair-care items. As in Clark and Betty's dreams, I suggest, here hair represents sexuality, which in turn represents agency. The traveling and rushing in this Hair-care dream are attempts to exercise agency—to take the lead, as Dolly does with Franklin and as she hopes to do in her ministry.

If Franklin initially stands for Dolly's missing ability to connect with others, the Driving Somewhere dream resignifies this meaning through the rush-hour traffic: in traffic, many people are together yet apart at the same time. In the dream, Dolly wrote, "there were hundreds, maybe thousands, of people all around me...but...they were just bodies. This is a reflection of an ongoing theme in my semester—being and feeling alone. I am surrounded...by people *every day*, but I have never felt more alone in my life." Yet, in another dream that occurred the same night, Dolly relishes being alone. She "lived in the attic of a house. I loved living there alone, but later in the dream, one of my friends moved in with me and I hated it because my room was so tiny." A few days later, she dreamed that her dorm room was unlocked. A friend, acting as if it was not a "big deal," tells her that many people went inside. Another girl probably steals from her. This dream reflects lingering insecurities, which make Dolly want to be alone even while she feels isolated.

Figure 3: Stairwell Bicycle Race

The Franklin Driving dream next *reconfigures* the mad rush of cars as people racing down the stairwell, Dolly now one of them, first on bicycles and then running. Dolly believed that the running figures symbolized her "estrangement...at one time I felt as if there were several people at the same place in life with me, and I wasn't ever traveling alone. Sometimes I feel as though I am racing to catch up with them....It doesn't surprise me that I wasn't sure where I was going...or why I was racing, because in my real life I wasn't sure when an end would come to the busyness." This day residue suggests that Dolly's childhood and adolescent insecurities may not only be holding her back but making her race even when she knows neither where nor why. While the Busyness schema is integral to the Moving on model, when the practitioner lacks direction, it can get in the way, not only of close relationships, but also of actually moving on.

Dolly said that in the dream race she felt competitive: she wanted to *move past* others. Along with her mistrust of relationships, Dolly believed, "comes a need to compete with people, thinking that in order to be acceptable and loveable I need to be 'the best.'" These statements are general, but Dolly grounded them in a specific memory. She has a twin sister with whom she's competed all her life. Jung (1972:90–113) held that dreams counterpose, and thus compensate for, the dreamer's normal waking attitude. Dolly's attitude is that she often feels alone, wants to live in a caring Christian family, and needs to slow down so that her emotions can keep pace with her experience, but her dreams suggest that she has individualistic feelings too: she would rather win the race than babysit Franklin.

In the stairwell, at last Dolly knows where she's going—outside. Yet, this remains a vague and unexplained destination, simply a finish line, signifying arrival in the figure of escape. In her attempt to be the first, Dolly pushes Franklin downstairs, which does not result in progress but in suspension: he hangs in midair too scared to let go. Does this reflect the dynamic of her own personality: pushing herself beyond her emotional margin of safety, making her feel chronically insecure (like Franklin)? Dolly wrote:

> Franklin gets stuck after I push him off the stairs. This is how I often feel with my emotional state—stuck. I am afraid to move forward because I'm afraid of getting hurt. . . . I pushed Franklin off the stairwell, who represents so much of what I don't like about myself. It was almost like I was pushing those things away from me, because they are slowing me down. I don't think my motive in pushing him was to get him out of my life, though; it was more that I wanted him to catch up to where I desired to be.

Pushing away suggests distance and hence detachment. Like Lois, Dolly appears to need not attachment, but the detachment that would make risk-taking feel safer and more playful, which the second dream scene's frame supplies. A bicycle race, after all, is a kind of game, not a life and death contest, even though Franklin apparently fears serious injury.

At the time of the dream, Dolly was longing for her Christian family. In the dream, she is with a relative, huge Franklin, the driver of the van, designed to carry groups. Affiliation is what Dolly thinks she wants, but in her dream, Franklin's mode of progress is undirected and cumbersome. Dolly says that feeling alone increases her need to compete, and the dream depicts competitive urges. Yet, Franklin, who signifies Dolly's insecurity, isolation, and urgent need for care, stands in the way of winning, rather than making her competitive. Franklin also evokes Dolly's fear of falling; this is the threat that he depicts—falling down the stairs—a fear that leaves the dream hanging in midair.

We saw in Lois's dream (Chapter 2), a fear of falling can signify a fear of flying: both motifs allude to the Risk-taking schema, integral to Moving on. We also saw that an inability to take risks is often associated in the United States with an absent father: dads are supposed to provide transitional space where kids can practice risk-taking. Dolly's workaholic father was emotionally and physically absent during her childhood. The stairwell, as an open in-between place, is yet another dream symbol for transitional space. Franklin, then, also represents Dolly's missing ability to jump into midair, to take risks, which holds her back and keeps her from finding her own direction.

Dolly's dream is a personal history presented in figural memories that begins with feeling lost, no direction home, at the root of which is her fragmented family. When she arrives at the small town, symbolizing the Christian community where she stayed the previous summer, Dolly begins to take the lead. She tells dysfunctional Franklin that he needs to turn around (a metaphor for turning her life around?). In the process of finding a direction, she ends up busy, indeed constantly racing. I suspect many U.S. Americans are familiar with this course of "development." Dolly wants to progress (to success!), but the dream suggests a regressive part, personified by Franklin, impedes her use of the Moving on model to move past others and satisfy her own competitive needs—a situation symbolized by her dream's ever-shrinking vehicles of progress, from a van, to a bicycle, to feet.

Madison

Madison was 21 at the time of the dream. She grew up in the Tacoma area and is "Caucasian."

> It was the big day and I was a wreck. I didn't have time for hair and make-up and my dress was ugly. When I walked down the aisle, my dad wasn't there and my fiancé walked me down....I didn't understand why I was getting married at all. The weirdest part was my fiancé, a high school acquaintance who also goes to WSU. We were never great friends but we are friendly to each other when we do see one another.

Figure 1: The Bride-as-a-Wreck

In the dream, the Big Day just happens without any anticipation on Madison's part, which reminded Madison of her current life situation. "Throughout this semester the reality of leaving college has slowly dawned on me. I will be moving to Seattle with my best friend and I'll be working for Saks."[2] In *Educated in Romance* (1990), Holland and Eisenhart argue that there are two alternative modes of progress for U.S. women: moving into a career and moving into marriage. By using moving into a meaningless marriage as a metaphor for moving into a career, Madison's dream asks if Moving on is development or devolution. Madison thought:

> The dream shows that I am weary about such a dramatic alteration in my life. It does this by showing me that I am so worried about my appearance. This could have something to do with the fact that I am working for...a...prestigious department store...I will have to look my best.

Madison's substitution (weary for wary) may be a misspelling or a slip that conveys her feeling that she is not up to major life "alterations," a word for what one does to clothes, for free if one buys them at an expensive department store like Saks. While many U.S. men explicitly aspire to masculinity, few people, male or female (with the possible exception of male transvestites), explicitly aspire to femininity. They may use baseball metaphors for success like "batting a thousand," but seldom sewing metaphors. Femininity is usually a tacit aspiration, yet one that many U.S. girls and women fervently pursue via perfect clothes and hair. A wedding day is the ultimate dress-up occasion: the day when, for many young women, looking perfect merits a wholly disproportionate investment of resources—a Cinderella occasion even for families that can scant afford it. Young men in my sample didn't have wedding dreams. No single event, moreover, requires more preparation (for a girl) than a big wedding. "In the dream," Madison wrote, "my mind wouldn't get off the fact that my hair wasn't done and I never even put make-up on for the day," which left her "feeling ugly and unprepared as well as nervous." Preparation, then, is the missing part of this first figure. Madison believed the dream showed that she was unready for "the move from college to the working world." Moving into that world, like marriage, involved a "huge commitment," and was "a huge step in one's life."

Another of Madison's dreams suggests a relation between looking perfect and Madison's inability to genuinely Move on.

[E]veryone around me was turning into creepy looking dolls. There was a man controlling all of this and his reasoning was that he thought the world was a terrible place and that everyone needed to become perfect. The man used radios and televisions to turn people into dolls.... [T]hey were half plastic, half human. I had not been turned into a doll; I was running around with my sister and my roommate's mother and grandmother. The grandmother was turned only half way into a doll, while the transformation was taking place, she was thinking about her husband and her life she had led.

Why do radios and televisions effect these transformations? Probably because these are the advertising devices by which people are recruited into Baudrillard's (1988) "system of objects," among which are pretty women. For girls, intense recruitment begins in adolescence. Thus, Madison commented: "Teenagers these days are so wrapped up in shopping and looking good that they are drawn to the malls." Does Madison speak from experience—that is, from memory? Malls, she wrote, were a "black hole that seems to grasp hold of people." The nature of this black hole is: "greed" and wanting "to be so attractive and own lots of things...believing that is the best way to live a successful life." This is the Cinderella way to success: a girl makes herself "so attractive" that a prince gives her "lots of things." This dream resembles a feminist analysis: a man is controlling the dollification process; his principal is everyone needs to be perfect, but the only people transformed are female—into "dolls," a word likely to be used for girls' toys.

As in the case of Betty's gorgeous black and pink underwear (Chapter 3), the mall evokes the Perfect-fit schema, or as Madison put it, "the constant pull to think about the way one looks." Madison thought:

> The dolls represent perfection...the toy "Barbie" is not even realistically proportioned yet everyone idolizes the image she portrays. The doll significance also dates back to my childhood and the fact that I had many growing up, now that my sister is at that age she is intrigued by them as well.

Madison's dream continued with her 13-year-old sister who "wanted so badly to be in a clothing store." Next Madison and her sister were in a clothing store and her sister "was trying to fit herself into a pink backpack." "Trying to fit" evokes the Perfect-fit schema; it also suggests Madison's sister was adapting to a pattern she did not fit—again like Cinderella's sisters who cut off their toes and heels. Madison mentioned that pink was her favorite color when she was a teen: this 13-year-old resembles Madison's teen self.

In longer dreams, I (2007) have argued elsewhere, just as major dream figures repeat while also varying a preceding figure, so also each scene symbolically reiterates and varies a preceding scene. If the clothing store/backpack scene replicates the doll scene, for example, Madison's Doll Dream comments directly on shopping/trying to look perfect as objectification (becoming "half plastic"). Yet, in this dream, the people turned into dolls "weren't attractive looking at all. They looked more like creepy troll-like characters." Weddings are times girls are supposed to look as perfect as only dolls can. In her Wedding dream, Madison's messy hair, lack of make-up, and ugly dress may represent resistance to dollification and to her new job in a top-drawer clothing store.

Figure 2: Walking without Dad

"My dad isn't there," Madison wrote, "and I am nervous to be walking down the aisle with someone I barely know." Madison's dad is the missing piece here. "Around my dad," she continued, "I am nervous and feel as though I am trying to impress him." Madison thinks her dad's absence "represents all of the anger and frustration that we have in our relationship," because of their "problems in communication." My students tended to describe problems with their dads (even their moms' problems with their dads) as "communication problems," just as George says his father didn't listen to his mother. Communication problems stood for dads' inability to deal with feelings—their own and those of family members. The alternative to "communication problems" was "opening up."

Madison's dad was distant and judgmental. He did not support her decisions. She wanted to be a grammar school teacher, but her grades were poor. He said that she should get into an apparel program. That would have required putting off her graduation, so she switched to general studies instead. Now she sells children's clothes,[3] but misses life at WSU: not having to pay for things, having many friends, learning. She feels she didn't take advantage of her freedom then; it didn't seem like freedom, but in retrospect she says it really was. By recommending that Madison take the safer course, rather than "following her dreams," as U.S. Americans say, Madison's father failed to foster risk-taking. In the United States, a readiness to take risks is necessary to pursue a career. Madison did not pursue one; she just did what her father told her to do as best she could. She couldn't do an apparel major but she got a job in apparel. In U.S. terms, Madison was like a robot—a doll—rather than a Free Individual who chooses for herself. Madison's problems, then, are with practicing the Free Individual model and a closely related model, the Choice-as-agency model. The free individual is in touch with her "true self" and hence "knows what she wants." On this basis, she makes meaningful choices among options.

As Madison walked down the dream aisle, she "didn't understand *why* I was getting married at all." Walking, then, resignifies her missing preparation as a lack of intentionality—of a reason why. At the time of the dream, Madison was about to walk down a new life course in retail but had no idea why she was doing it. Where her personal motivation might have been there was a lack, an absence. She remarked: "I am graduating from college on Saturday and still trying to figure out what I believe in."

Figure 3: Walking with a Fiancé

In the dream, Madison's inappropriate groom (Ben) stands in place of her absent dad; he reconfigures the absence signified by her dad and is an attempt by her dreaming mind to enlist memories that can fill this absence. Ben is Asian. He has never even been a close friend. Why, then, might the dream use him to resignify Madison's dad? Madison described him as someone who "has been through high school as well as college with me, he has made the transitions with me.... I believe that the dream is trying to tell me that even though those were big transitions I still have people in my life to carry on."

The only other-than-causal contact Madison had with Ben was as a freshman. She and her roommate would instant message with him. It was a three-way joking around. She remembers that he said things like, "[Y]ou and her shouldn't make out." This standing joke about homosexuality (and the three-way verbal-sexual play it enacted) anchors Madison's memory of Ben in practices that many contemporary young Americans consider alternative and edgy. Here edgy sexuality is a metaphor for risk-taking, which Ben fostered under the auspices of forbidding within the frame of play. As in Lois's and Dolly's case, the missing element is risk-taking, which Ben evokes in memory and hence configures.

When fathers do not provide transitional space, Benjamin (1988) argues women may indulge in sexual fantasy to provide it for themselves. Benjamin's example is a pornographic novel, *The Story of O,* written by Pauline Réage. O's lover demands she stay at "the Castle," a palace of perilous sexual experimentation involving whipping and other painful abuse. Yet, this castle is Réage's fantasy and in this sense a safe place where she can do dangerous things. Madison recruits Ben as dream fiancé because sexual fantasies, like those he playfully initiated, are a memory of a safe space in which Madison once practiced risk-taking, a place in her past where it was fun and not so frightening.

In Chapter 2, we saw that romantic relationships are probably the first setting in which young Americans face important choices in fact, although an anticipated occupation may be the first stimulus for significant choosing in fantasy (because adults ask kids "What do you want to be?"). Madison's dream wedding symbolizes the latter kind of choice (occupation) via the former (romance), and this very substitution underlines the problem. In prefeminist days, women were choosers in the realm of romance and marriage, even though they were supposed to exercise choice only after a man pursued them and proposed. Men made career choices. By symbolizing career choices via a wedding, Madison's dream seems to revert to an older model. Just as Dave's Pet model was inadequate for contemplating parenthood, Madison's Wedding model seems an inadequate vehicle for forwarding a career. Nonetheless, in and through her dream, Madison thinks about her problem with Moving on through a series of figures.

First, her appearance on the surprise wedding day configures her lack of anticipation of a major life change—the end of college—along with her lack of preparation for a career. Second, through the absent figure of her dad, the dream summons memories of his failure to support her. This mnemonic commentary sheds light on her inability to take personal responsibility for her future. Last, through Ben, the dream finds memories of risk and experimentation, which is what Madison needs to effectively practice Moving on.

Betsy

Betsy is 20, "Caucasian," and grew up in a remote small town in inland Washington. There were about 45 kids in her high school graduating class.

> Martha and I were driving down a dark highway going very fast. We were coming up on a car, getting ready to pass. I hit the back end of the other car. The man slowed way down, trying to get my plate numbers. I clearly saw his face and he was extremely pissed and was pointing for me to pull over. Being that we were on a dark, scary road, there was no way I was going to stop. I sped back up and passed him. He started chasing us, riding on our tail. We started going over a hundred miles per hour, and didn't slow down until his lights were not visible. All of the sudden,...my lights were off....All I could see was the moon shining through the trees as we flew by them. I knew we were going to crash. Then, we did. We were side-ways off the road, being held up by the trees. All I did was turn off my car, so that man would not find us. That was my only worry.

Figure 1: Speeding Car

Betsy's dream, like Dolly's, is a Car dream: the dream's major action happens in and through a car. Betsy wrote, "I think that the car represents my body. It is going extremely fast down the road....Lately my life has been in fast mode, trying to study for finals, move and get a job." In Chapter 3, we saw that Betty's purple hotrod was a phallic symbol: a detachable sign of masculine identity and privilege that women can appropriate. Does equating her body and her car suggest Betsy identifies with masculinity? In life, Betsy normally goes by a shortened version of her birth name (which is not Betsy); this nickname is a boy's name. I don't mean that Betsy was actually confused about her gender; for her identifying as masculine was a way of rebelling against gender conventions. Indeed, Betsy calls herself an "American Rebel." Rebels represent an important instance of Bad Boy masculinity—for example James Dean racing his car in *Rebel without a Cause* (Warner Brothers 1955).

The reliability of sex/gender differenes and their accompanying psychological difficulties has long been controversial. Feminist scholars like Lutz (1990) and Tavris (1992) offer data that contest reliable variance in emotion, identity, or action, while evolutionary psychologists interpret small (and possibly statistically insignificant) dissimilarities as evidence of biological disparity (Hyde 2005). In this book, I argue that the question is not one of reliable behaviors or biologies, but of models, albeit models differentially fostered by experiences in infancy and childhood. When a majority of children in a culture or subculture share an experience in infancy or early childhood, that experience is likely to become the basis for a cultural model through which peer cultures (re)socialize kids, whether or not an individual child's personal experiences strongly support the model. Yet, deviating family experiences, we will see in Betsy's case, can support resistance to normative models. By the time people are adults, if not before, moreover, most are familiar with a variety of cultural schemas and models. They can experiment with and combine these resources (barring laws or conventions that forbid it), including those usually ascribed to the other gender—which Betsy does.

Betsy loves to drive fast, just as she does at the opening of her Speeding Car dream. "In some kids there is [a] need to be extreme," she wrote, "and never think about the consequences." Care for consequences is the first missing element of Betsy's dream. Like a Bad Boy, Betsy has always defied them:

> My favorite season is winter because I especially love to drive in the snow. My Subaru and I can handle anything; the more challenging the better....When I was in high school, I dated a guy with a fast, all-wheel drive car. We went out every day in the winter to do this....From the time I was a little girl to the time I graduated, I have

loved the excitement and thrill of driving fast in the snow; knowing
each time you learn something about your car and how it handles,
knowing that you could crash, or that you could just get in trouble.

We found this Devil-may-care schema in Kent's dream in Bam's Bad
Boy pranks and in Betty's dream in the lecturer's lack of care about
the muddy hotrod. Betsy knew, "I was breaking the law," but she
felt it was not "like bank robbers, it was simply...a need of excitement and thrill." Here is the Impulse-gratification schema, which
also characterizes Bad Boy masculinity. The dream reminded Betsy
of high school when she sometimes played hooky to go wakeboard-
ing, another wild ride. She drove fast then too and her hometown
police knew who she was.

Betsy contrasts herself to her sister who has always been a "goodie-
goodie," a U.S. expression for girls who conform to the expectations
of those in authority. Betsy's sister was successful in school and is
now successful in her profession, like Betsy's mom who works full
time and makes more money than her dad. Her mom "wears the
pants in the family." Betsy's sister elicited another memory—a high
school teacher who told Betsy she was "nothing like her sister." Betsy
has always wanted to prove that she's smart to people like that. If
Betsy has something to prove, it is different from what many male
rebels want to prove: that she is as good as a goodie-goodie woman.

In Betsy's memory of wheeling wildly in snow, a boyfriend provides a transitional, risk-practicing space, but this time not because
Betsy's father didn't do so. She learned her love of cars and driving
from him: "When I was young my dad used to take us kids out on
the snowy roads and flip around just for fun....Every time I am
out it gets me excited and thrilled to be spinning around." Flipping
around with the kids in the car, Betsy's dad exemplifies the kind of
rough physical play with kids that Benjamin (1988) attributes to
dads. Betsy not only associates her dad with thrills but also with
love. In another dream, for example, a demigod lover takes Betsy
and her dad to Hawai'i. "When we appeared there were new cars
waiting to take us around. A Ferrari for my dad and an Exterra for
me." Betsy can't wait for Dad's weekend—a WSU fall event when
dads visit. Electra is her story.

Figure 2: Driving Martha

In the dream, Betsy drives with Martha, who was sleeping in Betsy's
bed with her that night. "In the dream, she may be a comfort to me

in the sense of just having someone there, not being alone. I think [she] represents how I like to have company at all times." Here Martha appears not as Betsy's girlfriend (someone with whom she is emotionally intimate), but rather as constant company; she also stands for Betsy's clique. "I have a really tight...group of friends," Betsy told me, "I am comfortable with that, and I really don't want it to change."

We saw in Chapter 2 that girlfriend groups in the United States may have a Clique model of personal relations that features an Insider/Outsider schema (Goodwin 2006). Unlike most U.S. femininity models, the Clique model combines a Dominance schema and a Detachment schema. In cliques, girls may use conversation as well as nonverbal communication to marginalize, exclude, degrade, and generally distance those outside their group (Goodwin 2006:210–240).[4] Betsy thought that, because of her clique, she did not "give other people a chance." Having a clique allows Betsy to disidentify with others, to keep them at a distance rather than empathizing, like the distance she tries to put between herself and the dream driver. Inasmuch as Martha is a stand-in for Betsy's clique, she represents Betsy's missing care for consequences as a lack of care for outsiders, like the dream man she rear-ends. Betsy mom was absent and, therefore, she suffers from an inability to care rather than from the inability to take risks common to so many dreamers in this volume.

A problem with Betsy's moving-fast version of Moving on is that it leaves no time for other people, particularly those outside of one's immediate circle. Even those in one's clique (like Martha) can be distracting: "My friends want me to go party, like the guy wants me to pull over, but I know I can't. I have to stay strong...stay on-track," by which Betsy meant she had to study, graduate, and get a job. As representative of those who pull Betsy offtrack, then, Martha anticipates the figure of the angry man.

Figure 3: Angry Man

The angry man recasts Betsy's lack of care about outsiders in an active and hostile form.

> In a way, the guy represents people in my life that I am afraid to get close to or let get close to me....I know this isn't good, just like me not stopping after I hit the guy, because I am coming off as kind of rude and some day I might need a favor from someone I acted that way towards or need someone to stop after they hit me....The guy represents me in a way that sometimes I feel that no one is listening

to me, like I wasn't listening to him in the dream when he wanted me
to pull over.

In other words, Betsy has the same problems that men who identify
with the Supermasculinity model do: she too has "communication
problems" and can't deal with others' feelings. Like George's dad
(Chapter 2), she is detached from others and doesn't listen to them.
Betsy's communication problems stem from her fear that she will
"take an emotional hit" from others: "I will try and tell them how
I feel, like the guy, but they just keep going or doing it. This always
makes me upset, like the guy in my dream was."
    Betsy takes a defensive posture because she feels ignored and,
one might say, run over. The result is moving away from others.
So, lack of care (for consequences) is a correlative of thrill-seeking,
but also comes from being in a clique, which presumes insiders and
outsiders, outsiders about whom you don't care and to whom you
don't listen, as Betsy didn't listen to the angry man. In the dream,
Betsy's unwillingness to listen, in effect, is an unwillingness to take
responsibility for her actions. She doesn't stop to assess the damage
or exchange insurance information; she only wants to escape, as she
wanted to escape her hometown cops in high school. At the time of
the dream, she felt that others were "obstacles" that kept "trying to
distract me from my responsibilities."

> I keep driving to get stuff done....In a college culture, many people
> my age are on a path trying to get through school with good grades,
> in order to get a good job. Many people at this time run into...pres-
> sures of drinking and, or, doing drugs. Some people get around this
> and some don't. The guy could symbolize the "party train" wanting
> me to pull off the track....In my current life situation I am trying to
> stay on path to get through school, move, and get a summer job, like
> traveling on the road to get to my destination, but there are many
> obstacles.

Trains, particularly party trains, imply a collective mode of transit. This shift in metaphors (from cars to trains that go offtrack)
reiterates that for Betsy traveling down "the road" means ignoring
or escaping others. Ever since high school, driving fast has been a
symbol of escape for her: "Being from such a small town, it was the
only thing to do to get away from our problems." Escape repeats
not listening in an extreme form: one moves from acting as if one is
absent to literal absence.

Betsy's relation to the Moving on model, then, is moving as escape. This relation is all-American and illustrated by what is the most important cinematic motif in U.S. macho movies (versus "chick flicks")— the car chase. In a car chase, police often pursue a malefactor or, alternatively, a rebel who is, for whatever reason, on the wrong side of the law. In the dream, Betsy's need to escape drives her to crash. Crashing is an important motif in another of Betsy's dreams:

> I was driving up the grade from the river, coming back to town.... [O]ne of my best friends, and my boyfriend, Ross, were all passengers in my Subaru. There was a snowstorm and visibility was limited. All of the sudden, I was going off the road. Ross, from the passenger seat, grabbed the steering wheel and put us back on the road. We were then going in reverse. As I was trying to keep us on the road while driving in reverse, we went around a corner and there were multiple cop cars.

In high school, the police were on Ross's case too: they ticketed him when he had done nothing wrong. Like Betsy, Ross is very smart. He got an almost perfect score on his SATs. Since Betsy came to university, however, she doesn't feel smart. She can't easily keep up in classes and has gained weight. "Guys don't look at me in the same way," she says. Why should males' failure to gaze (and by implication the Pinup model of sexuality) be significant when Betsy is a rebel? For her too Cinderella is a default model. Ross inherited money. She sometimes phones him to say: "Come and get me. I give up, come and take care of me." Crashing is what Betsy is afraid of doing in school and reconfigures her need to escape as an inability to "stay on track," that is to care for herself.

Betsy is trying to move on, but her dream suggests she is in danger of going nowhere but off the road. She may have mistaken movement itself with making discernable progress. Betsy's problem with the Moving on model is not with the model per se but with one of its dangers. To the extent that people internalize Moving on as a performance principle, they may take pride in moving for its own sake. Models are ways of making sense of one's life, not ends in themselves.

The night before our interview, Betsy dreamed that she missed a meeting with an African American teacher who reminded her of a Rap artist. She associates this Rap artist with me: he wears bright colors and so do I. This is a transference reaction. Betsy admitted she was anxious about and anxious at our interview, probably fearing I would judge her like the high school teacher who compared her unfavorably to her sister. Betsy's dream surprised me because she was a charming and dedicated student. I thoroughly enjoyed her tomboyish bravado but, as an outsider, I lacked a view of where Betsy was going. Her dream may have compensated for her intrepid waking attitude by signaling she was heading for a crash and was less in control than she wanted to think.

Remembering Missing Pieces

Moving on in the United States is a way to make personal progress: to move beyond whatever circumstances, conditions, or feelings, might otherwise hold one back. Yet, this model recommends that George rise above his ethnic past, that Dolly race beyond her deeper feelings, that Madison embark on a life course, ready or not, and that Betsy ignore others' claims to care. In other words, the Moving on model inspires action by promising success, but also generates predictable problems that people's dreams address.

Freud saw the dream as the remainders of the day. Dreams are also cultural remainders, elliptically referring to troubling shared experiences—as all these dreams are troubled, albeit in different ways, by a cultural model, Moving on. Ricoeur (1981:254) remarks that repressed experiences people remember in the psychoanalytic encounter are those that "at the time" they could not fully integrate "in a meaningful context." Such failures can be collective: dreams fasten on fissures in cultural meaning systems, holographically duplicating fragments that intimate larger wholes, prompting dreamers to seek missing parts through a series of figures. Each new figure copies what is lacking in a predecessor and evokes additional memories that clarify the problem and hint at a solution. By integrating models with personal experiences, dreams comment on what we need to repair the assumed world we share with others.

In George's dream, laughing with Jeff and Thomas configures missed close relations, particularly those "perfect family" relations he remembers from childhood and the positive sense of self that went with them. His mom, hanging out with him watching TV, reconfigures these close relations but, additionally, represents a willingness to leave birth context behind: she is close to George but distant from her natal family. The fridge adds more memories of distant relations with close family—memories of his father's emotional distance, but also of Korean family models that can help George amend his U.S. Moving on model. Franklin configures Dolly's lack of direction and stands for insecurity and the family history from which it comes. The mad rush of cars ties this insecurity to Dolly's current busyness but also to the loneliness that Dolly has long experienced. Finally, the bicycle race connects her insecurity and loneliness to memories of sibling rivalry, and through these memories to a desire to win incongruent with her conscious desire for union with others. In Madison's dream, her appearance at the wedding represents a missing piece, preparation, and stands for Madison's present job and her inability to genuinely move on. Her father's absence at the wedding reconfigures this lack as an absence of support, offering a pictorial analysis of Madison's problem with this model: she did not get the early fostering necessary to use it. Madison's fiancé, who jokes about unconventional sexuality, is an attempt to find in memory the risk-taking transitional space her father failed to provide. In Betsy's dream, care is missing from her driving. Memories of Martha remind Betsy of her clique and of her tendency to ignore outsiders and their demands. The angry man further reconfigures Betsy's style of moving on as escapism, which threatens to drive Betsy offtrack (Table 5).

The waking mind seeks logical solutions. The dreaming mind seeks missing pieces of memory and puzzles them together like Levi-Strauss's bricolageur (1970, cf. French and Fromm 1986). These puzzles are about shared models that dreamers use memory to repair. Dreams assemble an implied whole by creating figures from the debris of personal history, melding this debris with culturally shared symbols like blackboards, bicycle races, weddings, and cars. The visual contradictions that often mark these figures stand for problems with a model. In Betsy's dream, for example, speeding with her lights off is a contradictory figure for moving on that suggests that, when one can't see where one's going, forward movement only gets you off the road. This holographic movement toward representation and elaboration, Wagner (2001:26) believes, "displaces or dislocates" all "congealed" metaphors. Dreams' missing pieces display an ongoing dislocation of cultural models within the self. Partial figures stand for incomplete models and compel dreamers to reorder meaning-laden memories. In pursuing a hypothetical, if missing, whole dreamers grope for a point just beyond the horizon where a model will finally work.

Dreyfus (1984) says the aim of holographic memory is not retrospective: the chess master looks back but only to discover potential directions latent in a present situation. In a quest to find what was apparently lost, like George's lost bonds of affection or Dolly's lost direction, dreamers anticipate new models that can better accommodate their on-the-ground experiences and ever-changing worlds. In this sense, dreams have a prospective function, as Jung (1972) and Basso (1987) claim. Yet, dreams are not only prospective for individuals, but for their societies, because they participate in a culture-wide conversation about the incomplete portrait of reality offered us by our cultural models.

Chapter 5
U.S. Traveling Self-Models

Many psychologists and anthropologists think dreams depict people's sense of self.[1] Hollan (2003a, 2005) argues that dreams offer us the nightly news of the self, updating its relations to internal and external worlds. I want to go further: dreams offer us news updates about cultural self-models in flux. What I am proposing here is, first, we hold shared self-models in figurative form just as we do other cultural models. Second, as in the case of other cultural models, dreams depict and develop self-models, particularly models beset by contradictions, which act as irritants and thereby stimulants to individual dreaming. And, third, how a self-model is changing in a culture can be discovered through a technique I call Figurative Analysis.

In review, I define a "figure" as an image, such as a car, plus an instrumental motif that is functionally constitutive: for cars, traveling is an instrumental and constitutive motif; for houses, sheltering is instrumental and constitutive. To say that a motif is instrumental is not to say that the action to which it refers always happens in a dream; it often appears, but even when it does not, that action defines the dream. In a Car dream, for example, a vehicle may be broken down, yet travel defines the scene by its absence. Some figures will not recur across a set of dreams, although they may be significant symbols in daily life, as the fridge is in Kent's dream, and one can interpret them in light of this significance. Different figures would emerge as more or less consequential in different cultures or subcultures, while other figures would probably be inconsequential or missing and new figures would surface. Some figures, such as homes/sheltering, probably occur in people's dreams everywhere, although, perhaps, not with the same frequency.

Not all figures are self-symbols: a figure represents the self only if it is a common object of identification as well as critical to people's practical and emotional lives. Whether or not a person takes a figure/model as an object of identification has much to do with social positioning. For my students, for example, parents in dreams were not self-symbols, but the Good Kid was still a likely self-symbol for them. Cars, in contrast, are self-symbols, for an extremely broad band of people in U.S. society and Car dreams are this chapter's subject.

In Figurative Analysis, one takes a self-symbol's frequency in a dream collection sampled across a group to index the salience of a shared self-model. Figurative Analysis compares dreamers' use of these symbols based on a variable that people in the culture studied regard as significant—for example relative age or socioeconomic status. Such variables split a set of dreams sharing a figure into subgroups that conceive or use the figure in different and revealing ways. In the Figurative Analysis to follow, I take gender as a basis of comparison.

My students regarded gender as a primary marker of difference. Thus, none of my U.S. male students ever wore a dress or any item (a barrette, for example) that Americans regard as feminine, nor did they wear snug, contoured clothing as many of my female students did. In Samoa, in contrast, status often outweighs gender as a marker of difference; some clothing items (particularly fancy foreign items) indicate status. Since missionary times, Samoans have worn such items or dressed their kids in them without regard to gender to vaunt family status aspirations (Drummond 1842, Schoeffel 1979:110). This was true despite the presence of male transvestites. Even simple convenience can outweigh gender: when I resided in Samoa, a man might wear his wife's muumuu if all his clothes were dirty.

Certainly, my U.S. students regarded other variables such as age, race, and income as affecting personhood, but most were similar in age and were Caucasian. All attended a reasonably priced public institution; there may still have been significant differences in family income among them, but I feared they would not feel comfortable divulging this data on signed consent forms and so did not request it. Students, moreover, don't always have accurate information about family income.

Figurative Analysis may remind readers of Hall's and Van de Castle's (1965) Content Analysis (van de Castle 1994:291–310, Domhoff 2001), which measures comparative emotional and behavioral characteristics of groups through dream collections. In Content Analysis, the analyst scores the manifest content of a dream set on nineteen preestablished scales: sixteen empirical scales and three theoretical scales, the latter borrowed from psychoanalysis. Hall and Van de Castle (1966) assumed these scales corresponded to universal variables and compared variations in cultural groups and subgroups identified by factors such as age, gender, and culture.

Cultural anthropologists since Geertz have favored letting analytic categories emerge from ethnographic data, although Geertz (1984) himself believed that certain categories such as "person" had comparative validity. A Figurative Analysis focuses on the manifest content of dreams but allows emic figures and their particular features (rather than etic scales) to emerge from a set of dream accounts collected in ethnographic context.[2] By "features," I refer to typical issues associated with a figure in dreams. Thus, "accidents" was a common feature of Car dreams. I also refer to conceptual elements of dream reports. Many male dreamers, for example, saw driving as a singular and independent activity, while female dreamers were equally likely to see it as singular or as an activity two or more people shared. This chapter shows that a figure's recurrent features reveal its local meanings and common feelings about a corresponding model. A cultural analysis of dreams needs to begin with local interpretive frameworks, which prominent figures and their features can provide.

Figurative Analysis

An ethnographer using this method first gathers dreams from members of a cultural group and then reviews the resulting collection for figures that are

(a) Pivotal to the plot of around 10 percent of dreams in the collection,
(b) Appear in diverse cultural material—popular entertainment, commerce, law, politics, and so forth,
(c) Treated as objects of identification and surcharged with emotions, desires, and needs.

Second, the ethnographer explores what the figure represents for group members. Through his data, along with other studies of the culture, he asks: What ideas and feelings about the self does the figure symbolize? How do these feelings derive from cultural history or reflect current socioeconomic and sociopolitical conditions?

Third, the ethnographer assembles a subset of all the dreams where key events happen in or through this figure and delineates recurrent features within the subset. How do these features illustrate alternative versions of this self-model favored by different subgroups within this set or problems with this model that may be common or variable?

Fourth, the ethnographer zooms in on individual dreams that evince recurrent features and works with dreamers to interpret this material. He asks how these dreams differently address model problems discovered in feature analysis and explores dream transformations of the figure that defines the set. Comparisons are clearer when using dreams that dreamers have analyzed themselves using a single method. Of the methods presented in this volume, I find Dream Play most useful for eliciting material outside of dreamers' normal awareness. I, therefore, selected dreams for closer analysis that dreamers had worked with using this method, supplementing student papers with additional associative and life history material from interviews and with other dreams from students' journals.

Car Self-Models

Cars were pivotal figures in 19 percent of the dreams in my collection.[3] This frequency is no surprise. Cars are necessary to U.S. lifeways, and advertisements attest they are objects of emotions, needs, and desires (Jennings 1990). The car is a key dream symbol in the manifest content of my students' dreams because the United States is a "traveling culture"—a culture in which, for many, transiting is as time-consuming, routine, and significant as dwelling. In such cultures, people often regard modes of transit as symbolic of the self.

There is a diverse array of traveling cultures, from nomadic cultures to diasporic ones and, no doubt, a wide range of subjectivities that characterize them.[4] In the United States, moreover, there are other figures for travel that suggest related self-models (for example airplanes/flying), although these figures appeared much less frequently in student dreams. Because this chapter focuses on cars/traveling, for economy sake, I call the Traveling self-model considered here the Car self-model.

Since their invention, cars have been Americans' favorite mode of travel: "See the U.S.A. in your Chevrolet," as Dina Shore put it. We all have them—all genders, all classes, and when we grow too old to drive, how painful the sense of impairment and loss. In the United States, getting that first driver's license is a more real "coming of age" than menarche is for young women—that hidden passage marked neither by ritual, by discourse nor, for many, by any visible change in sexual status or behavior. But a car! From the beginning of Fordist distribution, cars have represented new freedoms and financial responsibilities, a new station.

Cars traveling are a figure for the Free Individual model: the self as free, autonomous, and bound beyond birth context (in transit). Yet, we saw in Clark's, Betty's, and Betsy's dreams that cars can symbolize masculinity too. Through a Figurative Analysis of Car dreams, this chapter asks: if cars are a masculinity symbol, but also an important self-symbol in our car-crazy culture, where does this leave women? In answer, let us look at how Car dream features differ for women and men in my collection.

Car Features

For investigating car features, I use all car dreams in students' final papers and journals. My students had 171 Car dreams: 106 from women, 65 from men; these dreams came from 45 women and 36 men. Here, I refer only to this Car dreams subset (Table 6).

Table 6   Recurrent Car Dream Features

Feature	Males Dreams (n = 65)	Female Dreams (n = 106)
We drove	15% (10)	35% (37)
I drove	45% (30)	30% (32)
Accidents	18% (12)	22% (23)
Accident as driver	50% (6)	30% (7)
In car, not driving	17% (2)	43% (10)
Witnessing accident	33% (4)	26% (6)
Control problems	8% (5)	10% (10)
Compromised roads	14% (9)	9% (9)
Compromised cars	11% (7)	9% (9)
Stolen	3% (2)	3% (3)
Misbehavior	6% (4)	12% (13)
Police	12% (8)	13% (14)
Physical Aggression	30% (20)	13% (14)
Bodily Harm		
Executed by male	15% (10)	2% (2)
Executed by female	2% (1)	1% (2)
Threatened by male	8% (5)	8% (8)
Threatened by female	2% (1)	3% (3)
Property Damage		
Executed by male	12% (8)	0% (0)
Executed by female	0% (0)	2% (2)

Some dreams contain more than one type of aggression.

Male dreamers use the singular ("I") for describing driving in 45 percent of their Car dream accounts, while female dreamers use it in 30 percent of their accounts. Female dreamers use the plural ("we") in describing driving in 35 percent of their accounts, while males used it in 15 percent of theirs. In other words, "I drove" dreams were significantly more likely for men, while "I drove" and "we drove" dreams were close to equally likely for women. As a motif, "We drove," suggests a more porous, less-bounded version of the Car self-model. Female dream accounts did feature the driver's separate identity if the driver was a male who intended the woman harm, if an underage male drove, if a problematic mother figure drove, or if the dreamer was attempting to escape the scene of a crime. All four of these conditions probably evoke defensive (versus porous) boundaries but for different reasons. In the first three defensiveness is evoked by fear: of injury to oneself or to another in the first two cases, and fear of engulfment in the third, which we also encountered in mother-daughter relations in prior chapters. The fourth instance suggests that for my female undergraduates guilt also evokes defensiveness.

In male dreams, female drivers presented problems. In one, for example, the dreamer's girlfriend asks to drive; he says "No," gets out of the car, and walks away. In another, a young man rescues a young women driver whose car catches fire after an accident. She gets mad, tells him to "mind his own business" and that "she could get herself out of the car." This dream illustrates a current issue with the Supermasculinity model in Car dreams: for Caucasian males, this model seems to have lost its association with the hero who "saves the day" and rides off into the sunset. Two Chicano males had the only successful male heroism dreams in my Car dream set, probably because in Chicano culture the car remains a strongly positive male identity symbol (Bright 1998). In one, the dreamer pulls a friend who has driven into a lake to safety. In another dream, he drives, first a car, then a motorbike, then a Hummer to rescue his girlfriend from a terrorist kidnapper. The other Chicano dreamer, dressed in "a futuristic military suit" protects civilians from a large vehicle. In his second hero dream, he rescues a younger version of his brother and they drive off together. Two Caucasian women had car-heroism dreams, which in both cases amounted to "helping" at the scene of an accident.

Accidents were the most frequent Car dream feature (approximately 22 percent for females and 18 percent for males), suggesting that people perceive the Car self-model as inherently dangerous; its mobility suggests rapid progress, but this progress is chancy and often comes to a bad end. This frequency also suggests that the Risk-taking schema is integral to the Car self-model. In women dreams, accidents were more frequent when someone else was driving (69 percent), whether the dreamer was in the car or witnessed the accident from somewhere else. In two female dreams, for example, the dreamer watches an underage male have an accident. In male accident dreams, there was a 50 percent chance that the dreamer was driving. This statistic reflects social reality. In 2009 an anonymous insurance agent from a major U.S. insurance company told me that an 18 year old male will pay 18 percent more for car insurance than an 18 year old female because statistics predict he is more likely to have an accident. The agent added that when comparing singles, women always pay less, although the difference goes down to 5 percent by age 24.

A control schema is also part of the Car self-model. Getting a driver's license and a car are primary to what U.S. Americans call "being in control of my own life," which is necessary to an identity as a Free Individual capable of choosing a road forward. Yet, car control problems were common, occurring in approximately 10 percent of women's and 8 percent of men's dreams. Both men and women had difficulty maintaining control during floods, snow, hard rain, and other inclement conditions and also when driving a boyfriend's or girlfriend's car, probably because the latter symbolized confusion about autonomy. Men had control problems when their car was a supercar—a kind of car that did not appear in female dreams. While one dreamer's boyfriend gives her a "muscle car," she attributes no superpowers to it. A supercar, as I define it, goes extremely fast or is a car-spaceship. One young male drives a car that travels 500 miles per hour but later wakes up within the dream to discover he was in a coma. Here an accident is a missing dream element. Another drives his Jetta past stars and meteors, while another's car is a "star fighter, the spaceship that Darth Vader flew"; it has a "wings button" and glides "down over the sea of cars."

In male and female dreams, roads compromised by traffic or weather obstructed the dreamer's progress (9 percent of female dreams and 14 percent of male dreams). What these roads suggest is that, while the Car self-model conjures up rapid advance, people often experience such advancement as thwarted. Compromised cars, immobile because of inadequacy, constraint, or damage represented a related but less frequent problem, occurring in approximately 11 percent of male dreams and 9 percent of female dreams. For males, other males' aggression or female intervention could compromise a dreamer's car. An enemy, for example, throws a garbage can into one male dreamer's windshield. In another male's dream, a man tries to take the dreamer's parking place by ramming him out of it. In yet another male's dream, a female teacher wraps the dreamer's car in saran wrap as an April fool's joke. Is this symbolism sexual and the plastic wrap a big constraining condom?

In women's dreams, a male's inability to fix a car or the structural inadequacy of the vehicle itself might compromise it. In one woman's dream

> [T]he car I am driving isn't my car at all. Everything is made of wood and it starts to fall apart. I try to drive it carefully back to work, and barely make it. I then start to frantically search for my car, but it is nowhere to be found. I think to myself that maybe Ahab [her boyfriend] has it, and I start to go inside. I then get the feeling to look over my shoulder and I see Ahab there, with my car and a yellow balloon.

Here the dreamer's car loss is troubling but she discovers the trouble is illusory—even a happy surprise. In a male dream, the dreamer likewise loses his car; he too becomes frantic, then angry, and rolls down a hill as a ball.

Males and females dreamt of male threats of aggression in equal numbers (8 percent of male dreams and 8 percent of female dreams), but males feared confronting actual male aggression more than women did. Thus, males execute bodily harm in 15 percent of their car dreams and in 2 percent of female dreams. In a female dream, for example, a white man climbs on and clings to the roof of her car, then stands in the driveway and growls at her beside a growling Rottweiler who becomes a black man. Men damage property in 12 percent of male car dreams, but in no female Car dreams.

Females seldom do bodily harm in dreams (2 percent of male dreams and 2 percent of female dreams). Neither do they tend to threaten bodily harm (2 percent of male dreams and 3 percent of female dreams). While they do not damage property in any of my male dream accounts, they do in 2 percent of female accounts. If women are less likely to commit acts of aggression in Car dreams, they are somewhat more likely to misbehave in other ways (12 percent of female dreams and 6 percent of male dreams). One dreamer's best friend robs a bank and holds her hostage. Later, they take the money and go shopping. For females, car misbehavior also involved sex or deserting grandparents. For males, it involved pranks. One male, for example, moons a waitress at the drive-through fast-food restaurant. For both sexes, the car was a place for illicit smoking.

Police appeared in 12 percent of male and 13 percent of female dreams. In female dreams, police just watched or pulled the dreamer over for misbehavior (speeding, having sex in a car, smoking, poor driving, etc.). In 6 percent of male police dreams (but no female dreams), the officer acts unjustly by planting evidence or siding with the villain. My students stole cars in only 3 percent of women's and of men's dreams, a statistic that might be higher for a more urban or less middle-class demographic. One of my male dreamers "hijacks" a truck but then it turns out he is in a video game. In one woman's dream, the dreamer and her friend steal a car but then it turns out only the friend has stolen it. In another, a woman steals a car along with a friend who is driving but who keeps getting depressed and slowing down. The dreamer takes the wheel but the car won't go. Both of these female dreams suggest guilt, which the dreamer displaces in the first case and that evokes a fear of apprehension in the second.

Car Dreams

The frequency of most Car dream features is similar for male and female dreamers, yet the orchestration of these features differs, suggesting that a computational approach (while a good start) is insufficient for understanding how men and women experience the Car self-model.[5] There are two important exceptions: physical aggression dreams and "we drove" dreams.

Aggression. Using a much broader demographic than mine, Goodwin (2006) finds openly aggressive verbal and nonverbal behavior among white, Latina, and African American girls of middle- and lower-socioeconomic status. One of her main research sites is the playground. Yet, hopscotch or jump rope don't pit girls against one another physically as, say, football does boys. Domhoff and Schneider (2008) recommend a sample of at least 125 dreams to reveal significant common dream features. In a random sample of 125 dreams from my larger dream collection, physical fights appeared in 17 percent of male dreams and only in 2 percent of female dreams. Granted, my data is from mostly white, middle-class youth in a particular region of the United States, but these results are similar to those of other dream studies.[6] Physical aggression in Car dreams also reflects a U.S. cultural reality: men are much more likely then women to commit violent crime.[7] Social aggression, rather than physical aggression, is common among women (Cairns and Cairns 1989:323, Goodwin 2006). To commit social aggression is to exclude, ostracize, or defame another, which in childhood and adolescence girls in cliques often do.

The car is a figure for a male-identified self-model, versus a gender model: traditionally in the United States men were drivers when they were in the car. Yet, nowadays, the car does not configure a model of how males should be but a model of how people should be: free, autonomous, and mobile. Because this self-model resembles social conceptions of maleness in many respects, cars may suggest scenes of a male-associated type of aggression, physical aggression. Social aggression appears only in two women's Car dreams (out of the entire 171 dreams). In both cases, the driver and passengers ignore the dreamer and leave her behind.[8] Even when physical aggression appears in a women's car dream, when women initiate such acts, they tend to represent social aggression. Thus Betsy's dream (Chapter 4), by her own interpretation, is about ignoring those outside her group even though rear-ending the angry man symbolizes this social aggression.

Inclusive Driving. "We drove" dreams indicate that women's Car self-models tend to have inclusive boundaries rather than the "sacred" boundaries that Hollan (2003a, 2005) associates with cars as a self-symbol.[9] I am reminded here of my fieldwork in Samoa. After a drive there, the passenger politely remarks, "Thanks for driving" and the driver responds, "Thanks for your support," as if driving were a joint enterprise. In riposte to theorists such as Gilligan (1982), who distinguishes moral orientations between U.S. males and females, Kondo (1990:33–34) points out that Western women are still "solidly within a linguistic and historical legacy of individualism." What I see in my female students' Car dreams is not what Markus and Kitayama (1991) would call a "sociocentric self," based on an identification with group concerns, but rather a "personal" self based on an identification with intimacy. To clarify, I turn to the development of self-models in Western European history.

In the West, a tendency to regard the self as inner dates back to the Industrial Revolution. In small farming villages, people cooperate to survive, as in Somerset Maugham's beautiful account of bringing in the harvest in *Of Human Bondage* (1915). The Industrial Revolution in Europe and America, however, broke down many stable agricultural communities. Levy (1973, 1974) argues that values that had once been communal needed internalization. Foucault sees evangelical religious practices as achieving this effect (1988, 1990). Evangelicals preached that original sin sullied people's souls. People were good, therefore, only through constant introspective vigilance (Davidoff and Hall 1987:88). The attention thus directed illumined and helped to develop internal space, creating a psychic valise in which people came to port their values.

In the early days of the Industrial Revolution, an industrialist's wife might be his assistant and even second-in-command; his home was often adjacent to his factory and its central room, the factory office (Davidoff and Hall 1987). As industrial fortunes developed in the nineteenth century, home and factory drifted apart and became public and private respectively. In the public realm, men strove for gain against one another. Hence, they learned to define themselves and their interests in counterdistinction to others. Freud ([1930]1964) called this singular form of self the "ego." Bourgeois women voluntarily exited or were evicted from the public realm. In the domestic realm, they began to create the bourgeois family and a culture of interpersonal relations (Davidoff and Hall 1987:317–396).

These two sociohistorical experiences suggest two models, which I see as components of a Traveling self metamodel. One is the Free Individual model discussed in prior chapters: singular and separate from context, and thus ready, in principle, to transit. The other is a model I call, borrowing Benjamin's (1988) term, the Intersubjective Person, who discovers herself primarily in and through interpersonal intimacy and is ready, in principle, to bond with another individual and to travel together. Intersubjectivity is crucial to Western models of intimacy, which portray the most profound form of bonding as between two individuals who recognize one another as uniquely valuable and as "soul mates," that is, as emotional kin. Not all models of intimacy are intersubjective. In Turner's (1977) idea of communitas, for example, groups of people experience intimacy-as-communion. Indeed, I have felt this type of communion in Samoa where it is cultivated and suspect that sometimes U.S. Americans at ball games experience it with others rooting for the home team.

In the United States mothering practices foster the Intersubjective Person model. Thus, Winnicott (1967) documents facial interchanges between Western mothers and babies that precede verbal communication. This experience of recognition develops through the face-to-face position in which mothers hold babies. Western mothers and babies gazing into one another's eyes, I suggest, becomes a shared metaphor for intersubjectivity. Is this why U.S. lovers sometimes call one another "baby," or "my baby"?

Chodorow's work (1974, 1978) suggests that gender-identity formation in the context of mother-child intimacy is likely to favor internalizing the Free Individual model and the Intersubjective Person model differentially for boys and girls. Because males are often distant figures, boys tend to construct gender by defining themselves against mother. An oppositional self-definition enhances a sense of self as different from others and lays the groundwork for the Free Individual self-model, historically associated with men and public life as a venue in which separate individuals compete with one another. Boys, then, also tend to reject what mother represents to them, interpersonal intimacy, in preference for competitive peer relations (Chodorow 1974, 1978). Girls tend to construct their gender through identification with mother and, therefore, have less reason to reject the Intersubjective Person model and what Brown and Gilligan (1993:3) call a "sense of connection with others" as a basis for self. Thus, Tannen (2001) in her video recording of early childhood interactions in the United States shows little girls embracing one another, gazing into one another's eyes, while boys sit uncomfortably with chairs parallel, gazing off into space as they talk. For this reason, the Intersubjective Person model, while not a model of femininity, is female identified, just as the Car self-model is male identified.

Family and gender models, of course, are in flux in the United States, as this book documents. I am not, furthermore, arguing for what Goodwin (2006) calls a dualistic model of gender—which portrays the sexes as natural opposites—although Gender-as-dualistic is an important U.S. metamodel. I mentioned in the preceding chapter that the degree to which sex is predictive of psychological differences has long been controversial. My argument is, when early relations are different for girls and boys within a certain cultural or subcultural group, the result is common same-sex experiences. These experiences become the basis of practices and rituals in childhood and in adolescent same-sex peer-groups because they are what most kids share. In turn, these gendered practices and rituals promote certain cultural models, whatever a child's biological proclivities or individual family history might be. Kids, furthermore, just as adults, can use any model with which they are familiar, although in fact individual temperaments, internalized norms, negative sanctions, and lack of opportunity may prevent conscious identification with a model to differing degrees. Models and people's opportunity to use them, however, change through time.

Even when there are strong barriers to using a model assigned to another group in waking life, many people try out such models within the safe space of dreams, particularly those associated with power and privilege. In dreams, they also think about the possible real world consequences of such appropriations. In prior chapters, young women have conducted these experiments in Car dreams. Betty (Chapter 2) and Betsy (Chapter 4), for example, contemplate the consequences of using the Devil-may-care and Impulse-Gratification schemas, both elements of Bad Boy masculinity. People also continue to practice and extend those models that they have learned in their gender cultures and try to combine these models with others. Thus, "We drove" dreams attest to my female students' efforts to combine the classic Car self-model, which features clear boundaries, with the Intersubjective Person model, which does not.

Car dreams in my collection suggest that presently there is a "singular autonomy" version of the Car self-model and an "inclusive autonomy" version in which individuals flow easily in and out of oneness with another. When boundaries expand to include another, this larger entity can act "autonomously" on a basis of volitions, desires, and needs that participants share. I now zoom in on three individuals whose dreams display the Car dream features mentioned above—Hester, Reb, and Scarlet (Table 7).

Table 7 Car Dreams Features and Variants

	Hester	*Reb*	*Scarlet*
Agency	we drove	they drove	I drove/he drove
Accident	in car not driving	dreamer not in car	witnessing accident
Compromised Car Control	earthquake	attacked by	underage male
Road	earthquake	off-road	drive-by
Aggression	by nature	by a car and males	accidental, by a male
Traveling Self	intersubjective (learning singular autonomy)	free individual (longing for intimacy)	intersubjective (questioning singular autonomy)
Hero Role	saves, but no victim	fails to save	expert intervenes

Hester

Hester was from Las Vegas, Caucasian, 28 years old, and in her senior year. In her dream, she travels with a boyfriend and a girlfriend, but rather than specifying the driver, she says, "we were headed out on the start of a road trip." While her account suggests inclusive autonomy, Hester achieves singular autonomy in the dream.

Our car was at a complete stop on a road with heavy, bumper to bumper traffic. Suddenly the ground began to shake beneath us, and the flat road...dramatically dropped downward. The nose of our car now looked down a steep hill....[O]ur car seemed...almost vertical to the road. Somehow, though, our car was managing to hold onto the road.

Our windows were rolled up, but I could hear screaming all around us. Terrified, I turned to look out the back window. Other cars on the road were beginning to lose their grip and were hurling down toward us...as if...falling off a cliff. On the side of the roadway, in a patch of grass...lay a baby, possibly a one-year-old. I panicked and began screaming, "Oh my God! There's a baby! There's a baby!" Before Arthur or Pearl could turn to look, a minivan came crashing down, hitting the baby....I began to bawl, uncontrollably, and covered my face with my hands. The van, taking the baby, came to a crashing halt nearly 200 yards below us, where the road had evened itself out.

Now our Camaro is parked in a store lot. Arthur stayed in the car, and Pearl waited outside with me. We both stared up at the cliff, which used to be our road. I told her, "I have to go up there, and tell someone about the baby. Someone has to bring some help." I started to climb the road, as if I were a rock climber. The road was no longer made of concrete, but...of cold, dead flesh. My hands and feet clung to it, and it would rip and tear as I climbed. I reached another man on this wall of flesh and I told him about the baby, and that we needed a rescue team. He told me there were too many people hurt, and a rescue team couldn't be sent down for one baby.

I returned to Pearl, and the two of us decided to make our way down to the van, to see if there was anything we could do. We reached the van safely, and I opened the back two doors to find a woman....She was lying on her back, dressed in a Quaker's outfit. To me she looked like a pilgrim. She had bright red hair and freckles. There was blood coming into her eyes from her forehead, but her eyes were wide open, staring at me. It was very gory, and frightening.

I asked her, "Where is the baby?" She responded very softly, "She's right here." Crawling toward me, from the front of the van, came a toddler, possibly a three-year-old. She crawled right into my arms. I snatched her out of the van, holding her tight to my chest. I placed her down on the ground, and knelt to look into her eyes. She was the most beautiful child I had ever seen. Her skin was porcelain and her hair was bright white. For many seconds we just stared at each other silently. The woman in the van got out and said in panic, "Where's my baby?" I yelled, "She's right over here!" I picked up the toddler and handed her to the woman. I then awoke.

Female ecstatics in Sri Lanka describe themselves in trance as "shaking below" (the waist), which Obeyesekere (1981) sees as orgasmic. The dream earthquake has orgasmic implications (as Hemingway [1940] put it, "the ground moved"). The dream offers a sequence: an orgasm, then a baby, and later a mother figure with a toddler. One might regard this sequence as a feminine version of coming-of-age; this view is coincident with Hester's own. She thought that one "hole" the dream represented was a fear of letting "go of my youth" and of making "the transition into adulthood, true independence. I must make this transition on my own and for myself." Hester also believed the dream represented:

> [C]onfusion about when exactly to let go of our youthful ways. In our culture there is no ceremony marking adulthood, no specific age, or dramatic celebration. Eighteen does not necessarily make every teenage boy a man, or a young girl a woman. We are left to wander, and wonder, what exactly it is that makes us an adult. I know that I have reached a point in my life where I want very badly to feel like a grown up; my culture expects this of me at 23. But I do not feel any different than I did four years ago. Many of us may not be ready at 18 to be "grown up" and independent, but our world tells us we should be, which for me has led to anxiety, fear, and some guilt.

Witnessing the accident by the side of the road, Hester's boundaries quickly expand to include the endangered infant. When the minivan hits it, Hester begins to "bawl." "Bawl" is a U.S. term for infantile crying, identifying Hester and the baby—an identification that develops when moments later the three-year old crawls into her arms and gazes into her eyes, a trope for intersubjectivity.

Hester's modifier, "uncontrollably," explicitly conjoins bawling (her identification with the baby) with control problems. A control issue is implied at the dream's opening in Hester's car "managing to hold onto the road," while other cars are "beginning to lose their grip...as if...falling off a cliff." "Losing one's grip" is a U.S. colloquial expression for the loss of control and implies that the Car self-model leaves Hester feeling unprotected—as the baby on the patch of grass is unsheltered and exposed.

If the dream is a "road trip," it begins with motionless cars. Hester's dream cars are in a traffic jam, evoking scenes from modern life: freeways, crowded streets, and so on. The dream also begins with Hester witnessing an accident, a common problem that speaks to the dangers inherent in the Car self-model—in Hester's dream, a danger to an infant-mother dyad, symbolic of intersubjectivity. Soon her boyfriend's Camaro is "parked in a store lot." The traffic-jammed cars depict a problem that the parked car reiterates. While the Car self-model is all about mobility, for Hester, as for many of my car dreamers, progress was often impeded. Indeed, to move ahead in the dream, Hester leaves one car behind, although she finds another.

The dream car belongs to Arthur; one presumes he drove, but Hester does not conceive the situation in terms of his agency: he is silent and passive throughout—a bystander who Hester, later analyzing the dream, saw as a "hole." In Car dreams, dreamers often refer to cars as if they are agents. In Hester's earthquake scene, her car has a "nose" and "looked down a steep hill," like cars in cartoons that have headlights for eyes. This car is a cyborg (Haraway 1991, Bright 1998). Hester's car also hangs onto the road, just as she does in the later climbing scene, suggesting an identification between Hester and the car. For Hester, the road too is animated. While it appears dead as she rips and tears her way upward, it has been a violent actor up to this point, first shaking, then angling down, then evening itself out, and it is made of "flesh."

Fear and bravery are the dream's emotional poles; it begins with terror but Hester is brave/independent throughout. Indeed, Hester's dream, like Lois's (Chapter 2), is a visual pun on the Cliffhanger. A Cliffhanger is the U.S. colloquial term for a movie genre more recently called a Thriller. Indeed, Hester remarked, "Even now when I read it, the dream plays like a movie in my mind." Thrillers are an important contemporary genre probably because modernity is a high-risk environment in which, as Giddens (1991:7, 37) argues, "reappropriation and empowerment intertwine with expropriation and loss" generating "programs of actualization and mastery," where dread, in the form of "being overwhelmed by anxiety," threatens "our coherent sense of self." In Thrillers, the audience vicariously confronts risks and dread, symbolized by mortal threats to a hero and related others, threats that the hero converts into a program of mastery.

Cliff climbing evokes another classic U.S. genre: the success story in which one climbs "to the top." In the United States, success stories are career stories. Hester was confronting a transition from college to the "working world." As in Lois's dream, here the cliff (with its threat of a fall into open space) stands for adulthood as a risk-taking enterprise and for the transitional space kids must internalize to feel capable of undertaking risks. In Hester's words, her dream is a way of "wonder[ing] what exactly it is that makes us an adult."

This dream Thriller begins with Hester and Pearl staring at the cliff together, but Hester tells Pearl, "I have to go up there," not "we have to go": she begins by shedding her intersubjective mode, at first only to seek help. Hester is reluctant to assume the status of a rescuer, saying, "Someone has to bring some help." Here the hero is singular, individual, but unidentified—an absent identity that Hester is unready to assume.

Next, Hester undertakes the challenge represented by the cliff: crawling up cold dead flesh. This climb is a parturition sequence. Hester's hands and feet cling to the wall as if she and the wall are one flesh from which she must rip and tear herself away. Not only does this parturition, I believe, signal an identity revolution, but also Hester's remedy for the boundary confusion likely in the intersubjective version of the Car self-model. Hester's efforts to detach from the wall also suggest the Detachment schema, which is part of the Free Individual model. The man Hester meets climbing the wall of flesh abjures responsibility for rescuing the baby, telling her that he cannot send a rescue team. This man, of course, is helping others but his values are collective, whereas Hester's are intersubjective: she must rescue an individual baby. The gender other, I suggest, to a degree always represents "the Other": the opposite of intersubjectivity is not individualism (that is its counterpart) but a collective orientation—in this case triage. This man also underlines that Hester alone is on the line.

After her climb, Hester returns to Pearl so that together they can climb down to the minivan. Having achieved detachment and separateness, inclusive autonomy now works for Heater, although Pearl is more "along for the ride" than a partner. One might see Hester's descent as a return to an earlier sense of self and as an effort to protect what is valuable in her past. What Hester finds in the van is not a baby but a little girl. Hester first chose to play this girl who she calls "Baby."

Baby: I am 3 years old. I have white skin and white hair. I am a beautiful child, angelic looking.

Me (Hester): Are you all right?
B: Of course I am. I knew you'd come for me.
M: Who are you?
B: I am you. Don't you recognize me?
M: I thought I'd lost you.
B: No. I'm not hurt, not one scratch on me.
M: Who is that woman?
B: She takes care of me.
M: I love you, and I was so scared!
B: You saved us, there is nothing more you can do.

Here, by identifying with Baby, Hester again suggests regression but this regression is a recherché—an effort to remember/recapture an earlier self, which the dream portrays as threatened by the Car self-model. Cars "hurling down toward us" appear to crush Baby before a womblike vehicle (the minivan) snatches her. Hester fears that she has "lost" this "baby" self—presumably, that self she first surrendered in love and trust to the mother/child relationship ("I knew you'd come for me"). Inasmuch as mother-child gazing is a trope for intersubjectivity, it is remarkable that the women mothering Baby has bloody eyes—eyes that "were wide open, staring at me." This injury, presumably, comes from the accident and represents the problem with the Car self-model initially symbolized by the earthquake and then by hurling cars.

In the dream, Hester too acts like a mother after the U.S. model, holding Baby to her chest, kneeling down, and gazing into her eyes. If this dream is about claiming an adult identity, is it a mother identity? As if seeking an answer to this implicit question, Hester next chose to play the mothering woman, naming her "Woman." Hester says that she "looks like a pilgrim"; one might call her a historical U.S. traveling figure.

Woman: I am in my 30's. I have bright red hair and lots of freckles on my face. I am dressed like a Quaker, wearing only black and white. There is blood running down my face from my forehead.
Me (Hester): Is this your baby?
W: I am responsible for her.
M: Why are you dressed like that?
W: Because I walk with God.
M: I wasn't expecting to find you here.
W: Why?
M: She seemed so alone.
W: Do I make you angry?

M: No, but I am sad.
W: It is ok to love her. I'm sure that she loves you too.
M: I just wanted to keep her.
W: She's not your responsibility.

When Hester opens the van, she discovers the Quaker and the child. The Quaker is in a prone position; she does not appear to be an agent—certainly not the van's driver. Yet, by making Woman a Quaker, Hester not only appoints a properly American symbol of spiritualism to be her pilgrim but also a type of woman who exercised what was, for her time, an astonishing degree of agency. In the mid-seventeenth century, Quaker preachers migrated from England to the United States.; nearly half were women (Dunn 1979:119). Women generally had authority in the church because Quakers believed the conversion experience restored men and women to an equality they had enjoyed before Adam's and Eve's fall (Dunn 1979:119). I am not suggesting that in her waking mind Hester is aware of this history. Rather, she draws upon a cultural common of figures that is historically inscribed. We use such figures in dreams as if we understood these inscriptions, just as we use words as if we understood their nuances—nuances we might be at a loss to articulate.

Clearly, Hester's Quaker is not one of those puritanical pilgrims with their *Scarlet Letter* models of femininity. The term "Quaker" is descriptive of bodily quaking: it derives from its founder's admonition to "tremble at the word of the Lord" (Morris 1979) and "quake" puns on the dream earthquake that, I argued above, implies orgasm. The Quaker's red freckles and hair, furthermore, imply passion. Hester finds the Quaker's bleeding "very gory, and frightening." For women, sexual coming-of-age is concomitant with bleeding—menses and defloration—both of which suggest porous rather than "sacred" boundaries. The dream displaces this coming-of-age blood from lower to upper. From a psychoanalytic perspective, an upward displacement of sexual symbolism is classic. Decapitation, for example, may signify castration and a big nose may signify a big penis. Blood, in fact, fastens Woman's two apparently opposed meanings, spiritualism versus sexuality. "She was bleeding from her forehead," Hester wrote, "like Jesus on the cross." While "Woman" appears to need saving, she is actually a female version of the savior. In Hester's words, Woman

acted as a comfort for me, letting me know it is ok to love...who I used to be...telling me that God is also watching over me, taking care of what I cannot.... I like the idea of a higher power, a protector, and sometimes I forget how important this really is to me.... Since our culture so greatly encourages independence, then it is no wonder why individuals my age may feel lost and scared when we cannot live up to our culture's ideals.

Hester's dream illumines a conflict between the autonomy vital to the Car self-model and scary feelings of abandonment. These feelings are predictable in a world where everyone is supposed to "stand on their own two feet," as U.S. Americans say, particularly for those who identify more with intersubjectivity than with the ego. Hester moves to resolve this disharmony by displacing her need for protection onto a flexible symbolic concept, God. Some psychoanalysts call displacement a defense. In classic psychoanalytic theory, defenses help a person remain unconscious of anxiety. Hester's projective work, in contrast, helps her to become clearer about her anxiety and helps to resolve it.

Similarly, French and Fromm (1986) argue that displacement is the modus operandi of dream cognition and represents a form of problem solving. Difficult problems are represented through *less* intractable examples that bear a metaphorical relationship to the dreamer's case, but that the dreamer can more easily think and feel through (see also Westen 1994, Grenell 2008). Is living through an earthquake and climbing a wall of cold dead flesh to which you stick like a fly to the proverbial paper easier than transiting to the world of work? Possibly not. Hester's dream *magnifies* the real problem, although accurately represents how she feels. This magnification comes about by alloying Hester's personal memories with a shared U.S. narrative (the Cliffhanger or Thriller). Shared narratives symbolize collective memories. My point is that Hester is working on and contributing to the solution of *collective problems* with the Car self-model, which are also her own.

Let me review and elucidate this view of Hester's dreamwork. Hester's dream initially represents an intersubjective version of the Car self-model through a car that three friends "drive" on a road trip. While at first the car is motionless, soon the road shakes violently, which leaves a baby and a mother figure exposed to a crash. This sequence suggests a problem with the intersubjective version of the Car self-model, which moves Hester to try out schemas from other models such as detachment and rescuing. When Hester reaches the van, she discovers the female in question (here the angelic girl) is unscathed. Baby, nonetheless, confirms Hester's identity as a rescuer, telling her "You saved us." This plural again evokes intersubjectivity, which Hester fears she may endanger by moving on: "I have reached an important part of my life where change is inevitable, but I am afraid to lose...relationships as I now know them." But Baby assures Hester, "I'm not hurt, not one scratch on me."

Establishing that what she values in the past is safe, Hester begins exploring her identity as a savior through Woman. While Baby and what she signifies is unaffected by the hurling cars, Woman, the dream's personification of mothering, is harmed. It makes narrative sense that, through this identification, Hester decides (at least for the present) against a mother identity. Woman, moreover, tells Hester that Baby is "not your responsibility." Next Hester begins to develop another aspect of her dream pilgrim—the pilgrimage: she decides to play a character she called "Road."

> Road: I am a highway. I am made of black concrete with yellow lines.
>   There is something below that is making me shake violently.
> Me (Hester): Please stop! You're scaring me.
> R: This will only last a minute.
> M: But you're hurting everyone.
> R: You are fine! You should feel happy, lucky even.
> M: I feel only panic and horror.
> R: Soon this will all be over, and you will again be happy.

Cars are the most obvious figure for U.S. Traveling self-models, as in the science fiction joke where cars are the earth's most prominent inhabitants and outer-space beings, observing global life, think all would be well if the cars weren't ridden with those awful parasites! Yet, we saw in prior chapters that roads are a venerable figure for Traveling self-models as well. The road has long been a major figure in U.S. fantasy because, along with the car, it offers an escape from the intractable problems of real social contexts. Does it also suggest a Traveling self-model more compatible with intersubjectivity? In answer, let us turn to a favorite U.S. children's traveling movie, *The Wizard of Oz* (Metro-Goldwyn-Mayer 1939).

Dorothy begins her transit inside a tornado passively riding her house through the air like a wildly out-of-control plane, crashing on and killing a witch. Earlier, we saw that in fairytales witches symbolize mother figures that threaten to erase the boundaries of the self, particularly for daughters. As Dorothy kills the witch, however inadvertently, the plot symbolically asserts her autonomy, yet she begins her intentional journey by "following" a yellow road (as Glenda the good witch and the munchkins urge her to do), rather than "being her own boss," to invoke another U.S. colloquialism. Dorothy quickly becomes the core member of a traveling party—the scarecrow, the tin man, and the lion, who represent the members of her extended family back in Kansas. Thus, Dorothy's intersubjective form of autonomy is porous and inclusive.

Like Dorothy, Hester's first reaction to transport is panic but after Dream Play Hester wrote, "The road lets me know that I should be excited for change....Transition is difficult for me, but I do know that I'll soon be comfortable and find happiness in my new adventures." The road is, after all, a "transitional space" and, therefore, a symbol of what U.S. Americans need to "make it" to successful adulthood. Through the dreamwork, Hester realizes that "fear is not failure and...my subconscious [is] cheering on my own independence. Being scared of the future doesn't mean it still won't happen."

Hester's dream anticipates the transition to postcollege life, practicing for it like play practices for adulthood—miming its threats and dangers. Traveling self-models, which involve moving beyond the limiting worlds of home and known relationships into an uncertain future, often seems at odds with protecting one's capacity for attachment and intimacy. This dilemma is an underside of the Car self-model, and is one that Hester—embarking on her own road yet feeling, as Dorothy says clicking together her ruby slippers, "There's no place like home"—faces daily and nightly as well.

Reb

Reb was "white" and 25 years old. He was born in New Jersey; his family moved from there to the Seattle area.

> I found myself at a party...guests included ex-girlfriends of my roommate and myself....Our ex-girlfriends were talking to other men with the apparent intention of making us jealous....I decided to walk home. It was cold and snowy outside and it soon became quite difficult for me to walk....I climbed up a hill and began to cut through a parking lot to save time. Some twenty or thirty feet away sat a car with its parking lights on. Inside sat two men...discussing murder. Upon recognizing me, the men turned the ignition switch and drove straight for me....I ran in erratic patterns to prevent the car from staying behind me....The two men then got out of the car and headed for me....I promptly incapacitated one of the men while holding the other at bay. I next fought the other man. I struck him with a heavy blow and flipped him several feet in front of me. I knew

that he was not dead, so I took to running again. As I ran, I saw the man get back up and pull out a gun from his jacket. I run faster than before and resumed an erratic pattern, this time to avoid a bullet instead of a car. All of a sudden a beautiful women appeared in front of me...running from the man with the gun....I felt it was my duty to protect her. I next saw the man fire the gun....I dodged the bullet but instantly knew I had failed to protect the women. The bullet had struck the women square in the chest. I turned to see her lying motionless on the ground. I was horrified.

Reb's dream, like Hester's, resembles a Thriller; the role he fails to play is that of the classic superhero who rescues a beautiful, defenseless woman. Again as in Hester's case, one might see Reb as dreaming about coming-of-age symbolized by sexuality. While Hester feels scared by what sexuality/adulthood represents (signified by Woman's bleeding, a breach of boundaries), Reb's problem is separating sex from aggression, which the Car self-model complicates: in his dream, the phallic car *is* a weapon. I am not suggesting that Reb is violent toward women. He struck me as gentle, gentlemanly. We will soon see that while role-playing himself in a dialogue with a character he calls Woman, Reb assumes an exalted, one might say knightly tone, but he also expresses a hostile-critical attitude toward women generally, an attitude the dream configures as the car-weapon.

The dream opens at a party, a U.S. venue for finding a girlfriend. In Chapter 4, I argued that figures in dreams are progressive: they form a series in which a succeeding figure repeats and elaborates the meanings signified by a preceding figure. In this dream, the series begins with Reb fleeing the party women (former girlfriends) who make him "jealous": they stir hostile/sexual feelings, which he construes as their intent. He avoids confronting them only to confront these feelings in new forms, first as the snow, which makes walking difficult: ice replaces and stands in for indirect or passive aggression, which Reb attributes to the women but that they also elicit from him. Almost immediately, however, the dream replaces the obstructing snow with the car driven by the murderers. Reb is not driving: he is not in control. A duo drives, neither an individual nor two people joined in intersubjective communion, but two men locked in a common purpose like players on a team. The car/murderers are after Reb but intimate a hidden aim by what they actually accomplish— shooting a woman.

In this scene, backwards/forwards transformations identify the car, the murderers, and the bullets. Visually, the dream replaces the car with a zoom in on the murderers, returning thereafter to the car, which serves as a vehicle of their murderous intent. In the fistfight to follow, the murderers again replace the car. One murderer then draws his gun. Reb dodges the bullets, running in the same erratic pattern that he uses to avoid the car. As with the party women, here avoidance is the name of the game.

Reb first role-played the party women who he impersonated as one character he named "Women."

> Women: Why did you leave? Are you jealous? Are you afraid of confrontation?
>
> Reb: I'm not jealous or afraid of confrontation. I just thought you two were ruining the atmosphere of the party, and it also seemed like you were trying to cause trouble.
>
> W: We weren't trying to do anything, you are just immature!

In his dream report, Reb describes the party women as manipulative ("making us jealous"). In Dream Play, Women (who is a composite of these characters) directly provokes confrontation. Probably, she melds a longstanding U.S. stereotype of women as seeking control indirectly (Tannen 1990, 2001) with a more contemporary experience of them as confrontational. In waking life, Reb knew the party women. Leaving them individually nameless in role-play suggests he is playing out feelings toward "women" rather than to any individual—a suggestion born out by the car, which Reb next role-played.

> Car: Don't worry, there is no need to run away, I won't hurt you if you give up escaping me. I am an eventuality!
>
> Reb: What do you mean when you say that you are an "eventuality?"
>
> C: I represent the realization that the only way to avoid wicked women is to accept that they are all wicked. Thus, you should stop pretending to be surprised and offended when women behave like they did earlier this evening!
>
> R: You are wrong! It is the actions of men with false beliefs such as yours that cause women to end up loosing their faith in men. No man or woman is born wicked.

Car begins by making the same accusation that Women made: Reb is avoidant—he runs away. Car also voices Reb's negative view of Women as "wicked." The problem, Reb avers, is really caused by men with false beliefs—misogynists like Car, who feel hostile to women (as Reb did at the party).

Many see the conscious ego alone as having motives—reasons and aims for action. Theorists since Jung (1967, 1968, 1970), however, have viewed the self as composed of subselves with identities of their own, identities that people may not recognize (see also Hollan 2000). Reb, for example, fails to recognize the car and murderers as forms of that hostility he felt toward the party women. While marginal or repressed in conscious life, in dreams and other states where imagination supercedes reason, these partially or entirely dissociated identities emerge to personify feelings and ideas that counter conscious identities. In Chapter 2, I called these counteridentities. Thus, Hester's conscious identity is frightened about the road forward and how it will affect her intersubjective connections to others but, in Dream Play, her counteridentity, Road, is excited for change and sees it as an opportunity.

Reb's dream represents his critical attitude as murderous hostility, hostility in stark contrast to the idealistic sentiments he next expresses in his dialogue with the murdered dream woman, whom he named in the singular as "Woman."

> Woman: Why didn't you save me? I appeared by your side as I thought you would be worthy of my love, but you were only concerned with yourself, and now I'm dead!
>
> Reb: I was compelled to protect you from the moment I saw you and if I could do it again, I would have taken the bullet to save you. When the bullet fired, I panicked and dodged it, but it was not because I cared more about myself than you. I know that I should have saved you and now I will always think of what could have been. True love.
>
> W: I forgive you, but I am still sad. I thought you could save me.
>
> R: There is nothing I can say that will make right what has happened.... [F]ate is cruel and we are victims of this cruelty. What makes this cruelty so unbearable is the thought that it was my own doing that should have caused you to perish, even if it was an accident.

In an accident dream mentioned earlier, a woman whose car is in flames rebukes the male dreamer who tries to save her—as Woman also rebukes Reb in role-play. Even though Reb is not driving, apparently he occasions Woman's death by dodging the bullet, a U.S. expression for avoiding confrontation. In his analysis, Reb volunteered: "Although I deny that I am afraid of confrontation, it is at least true that I go to extensive means to avoid conflict." In contrast, Car heads straight for it. Reb thought the car expressed "an inner conflict between an idealized view of women and a more sinister

view, which was held by the car and presumably by the two men."
Reb's wording ("an inner conflict") implies this conflict is inside
somebody—but Reb does not say it is within him. Reb believed that
the dream "sadly reflects my outlook on the prospect of finding
true love," namely that "the actions of careless men may darken the
hearts of women so that they might not love as they once did." In
other words, women may indeed be "wicked," as Car says, but they
are not to blame.

In Reb's dream, Woman represents what I have called the
Intersubjective Person model, which revolves around intimacy with
a special other. Just as everybody in the United States is supposed
to be committed to "getting somewhere," everyone is also supposed
to want (sooner or later) intense interpersonal connection, and
Reb does. The dream depicts what Reb experiences as the conflict
between the Interpersonal Person model and the Car self-model, the
latter conflated with his personal aggressiveness. This aggressiveness
is at least partially beyond the limits of his awareness. I say partially,
because Reb is aware of his anger in response to the party women.
Yet, he is unaware, at least before role-play, these feelings generalize
to Women. Sexual-aggressive feelings compel him to avoid women
(as he does in the first dream scene) and put his possible relation to
a loved other (his capacity for interpersonal intimacy) in jeopardy—
jeopardy symbolized by Woman's death. Reb appropriately worries about what all this means for his future with the woman of his
dreams. At the time of the dream, Reb did not have a girlfriend. He
wanted one, but feared that his standards were too high. By implication, he was highly critical of women, as he was at the dream party
and as Car was in role-play.

I argued earlier that the Car self-model is symbolically male, but
Reb's gender does not mean he has an easy identification with it. In
rejecting Car's viewpoint, Reb distances himself from the Car self-
model. What does this say about Reb's experience of this model?
Reb sees it as masculine: in his dream, men drive the car; it is a
vehicle of their hostile purpose. This purpose combines sexual and
aggressive feelings—a combo Reb fights, at first successfully but
then ineffectually through "dodging" the car and bullets, which
again sounds like wanting to avoid confrontations. Tannen (1990)
found U.S. boys avoided "eyeballing" each other; she believed they
were avoiding confrontation. Intersubjective gazing, however, is a
loving recognition, not confrontation. To the extent that men in a
gender culture equate one-to-one connection with confrontation,
they may also tend to experience intersubjectivity as a competitive

relationship in which people try to dominate one another. Thus, Reb sees the party women as trying to control his feelings.

Other dreams in Reb's journal also featured masculine hostility and wicked (sexual) women. In one, Reb fights "a tough looking woman" in a country store who enters the back "wearing extremely revealing lingerie."

> I then asked her why she wore so little clothing in a public store? I felt bad, as I had been thinking of that question but had not intended on asking her. She promptly assumed an attack position, and began to assault me, using an advanced martial arts technique. I would normally never strike a woman, but she obviously was a threat to me. I somehow instinctively countered her attacks, and soon knocked her down. I was very confused!!

In this dream, the woman's aggressiveness is initially sexual, but her attempt to physically compete and dominate soon replaces sexuality. In the Murdered Woman dream, a masculine version of the Car self-model represents Reb's dissociated hostile/sexual feelings. While, in Dream Play, Reb does not identify with these feelings, in this Country Store dream and in other dreams in his journal he enacts hostility toward (sexual) women. It seems likely that the desire and aggression that women evoke in him provoke intimacy avoidance and prevent him from moving on in his personal life. Reb's alienation from the Car self-model also reveals linkages between the sociocultural world and the self. It is hard to change ourselves in part because we cannot do so without changing cultural models, giving them back to others in new forms.

Scarlet

Scarlet was "Caucasian" and was 21 at the time of the dream. She was born in Anchorage, Alaska.

> I'm driving along this road behind a car and then the car somehow crashes and hits 3 trees. I park and run to see if the people are okay and its 3 kids, two Mexican boys and a white girl, there's glass everywhere and blood from head to toe on one of them. I call 911....The ambulance comes and they act like its nothing and I am just in a panic.

Like Reb's dream, Scarlet's seems to be a "failed heroism" dream, not because she fails to save others but because it is an open question throughout the dream and dreamwork if anyone needs saving; in any case, the rescuer role is claimed by "experts."[10] Scarlet believed the bleeding Mexican boy stood for her boyfriend, Butler. If Scarlet marries Butler, she will be part of a Mexican family: his half sister is Mexican; so are his nephew and niece. Like the injured boy, Scarlet associates Butler with an intervening expert.

> Butler has a heart arrhythmia....Ever since I found out...I have been very stressed and have anxiety about not being in control....As much as I want to fix his heart and want him to be better I can't, and I really should trust the professionals to do that....Butler is seeing the top doctor in the nation for his heart problem...I still question whether he diagnoses Butler properly.

Ambulances are normal part of life for Butler's family. Scarlet remembers an incident when his heart became arrhythmic and they called for an ambulance. His sister was in the bathroom putting on make-up because the ambulance man she knew would be coming was cute and she wanted to look good. Scarlet was sitting there shocked and scared.

In the dream, blood is everywhere and for women blood often symbolizes a breach of boundaries, but Scarlet is driving alone. In an immediate sense, her boundaries are clear and responsibility rests easily in her hands. In life she has struggled to erect and maintain her boundaries. During high school, Scarlet rose at 5:00 AM to work out six days a week. Her mother once gave her a Slimfast shake for breakfast; she was "very upset" about it. Once her mother told her sister to "watch sweets"; the sister cried. These seem strong reactions to singular incidents and small counsels, which implies for these sisters that larger issues—"sacred boundaries"—were at stake. Scarlet believes she has become "less compulsive" about exercise; if she stays up late and misses a work-out "it's okay." Her sister now works with an eating disorder prevention program.

In Chapter 2, I argued the Close Family model tends to create overinvolvement between mothers and children. This involvement can exacerbate boundary problems for girls because their gender likeness to mom supports mutual identification, symbolized in childhood fantasy by eating/being eaten. Many U.S. adolescent females' eating disorders involve practices and rituals through which girls try, as in the Car self-model, to take independent control over their own bodies (Gremillion 2003)—to do the driving themselves. If anorexia aims at agency in an oral register, however, in the United States it is also evokes the Perfect-fit schema along with the dieting and exercising through which female adolescents often aspire to a top-model body, not merely to autonomy.

In Scarlet's dream, there is an additional boundary problem— empathy. Scarlet's family took three spring-break trips to Mexico when she was in high school: one to Cancun and two to rural Mexican villages. Later, Scarlet was a student leader in a church group that she inspired to help poor people in Mexico. They traveled to a village and built a house for a woman with three kids in a week. Scarlet was shocked to discover people living in reeking shacks built out of old doors, fences, or cardboard boxes. Watching people scavenge to survive in the village dump, she remembered Americans lounging and spending freely in Cancun. The village also had a "migrant house" where people learned how to sneak across the U.S. border safely, and a long fence with crosses, each cross signifying someone who died trying to get across. One cross was for a boy who was Scarlet's age when he died. She still has information about him at home. Scarlet's empathy, then, is at odds with the Free Individual version of Car self-model, which puts responsibility squarely in the drivers' hands, be he a Mexican boy or an ambulance man—the character who Scarlet first chose to play.

> Scarlet: Can't you see these children are hurt and need immediate attention?
> Ambulance Man: They aren't hurt badly enough to go to the hospital.
> S: They are bleeding from head to toe!
> A M: That doesn't require them to go to the hospital.
> S: They need tests done, they were just in a severe accident.
> A M: This is not a severe accident; you want to see severe come in our ambulance everyday. Then you will see severe accidents.
> S: You don't think that blood running that much is a big problem!?

Here again, running blood signifies breached boundaries and a problem with the Car self-model.

> Ambulance Man: Trust me, I am a trained professional. These children are fine.
> Scarlet: I feel like this is a huge problem for these children and I cannot trust you.
> A M: You need to trust me. You are overreacting and you aren't a professional so stop telling me what is wrong with these children.

Ambulance Man is a voice in Scarlet's cultural world and in her "head." He articulates what I call the Hysterical Female model: in this model, a woman or someone acting like a woman reacts emotionally rather than rationally and hence overreacts. Scarlet, who is tall, strong, and smart, did not seem particularly emotional to me— caring yes, emotional no. Yet, Ambulance Man's voice dominated her interpretation of the dream. She thought the hole the dream represents was as follows:

> I need to take care of everything. I don't trust the correct people to take care of things; I have to do it to make sure it gets done.... [S]ometimes everything is okay and my reaction is much stronger than the problem....I didn't take a second look and realize even though there was blood all the children were okay....I didn't realize that the ambulance and emergency crew know exactly what they are doing and I should trust that....I have a need to fix things.

Chodorow (1974, 1978) tells us that when a woman does not develop clear boundaries, she cannot sort out what is her responsibility and what is not. Scarlet concurs: she needs "to take care of everything" and everyone. Contra Chodorow and Scarlet, I suggest, Scarlet's inclusive boundaries in the dream lead to independence: she prefers relying on herself to help others. She criticizes herself for this preference and feels she should defer to Ambulance Man rather than questioning and challenging him.

While autonomy is a major U.S. value, particularly for men (Hsu 1961, Drummond 1996:83, Nuckolls 1998), Americans tend to defer in face of scientific expertise. Medicine represents scientific authority in people's everyday lives. Medical practitioners' message is often: we know best, do what we say, questioning will do no good, "you need to trust me," as Ambulance Man tells Scarlet. In the dream, Ambulance Man presents himself as an authority in the sphere of accidents, "a trained professional," and insists that Scarlet submit to his authority. Yet, Scarlet makes her own decisions: she is highly autonomous. Autonomy is one thing, however, leadership another, and Scarlet is also a leader: she takes responsibility for others in order to "fix things." In Scarlet's dream, taking responsibility for her own car is not a problem: the question is where should her responsibility stop.

I have argued once a model exists, anyone can use it or its constituent schemas. We saw that rescuing is a Supermasculinity schema and fixing is a Supermasculinity motif that enacts problem solving.

Scarlet tries to employ this schema and motif. The result is criticism: Ambulance Man accuses her of overreacting. She expresses an internalized version of this criticism by accusing herself of needing to "take care of everything." By implication, she calls herself, not just caring but compulsive for wanting to rescue the crash victims, just as she did when she told me her about her dedication to exercise. Nonetheless, she went on to side-step Ambulance Man's pronouncement that the crash victims were okay by role-playing them and soliciting their opinions.

> Scarlet: Are you okay?
> Bleeding Child: Yeah, I'm fine just a little blood and it was a pretty scary crash.
> S: Are you sure you aren't hurt? Can you walk? Does anything feel broken?
> B C: No I'm fine I feel a little sore but that's about it.
> S: Who was driving?
> B C: My brother.
> S: Where were you all going?
> B C: We just needed to go out and get some groceries for my mom.
> S: Are those your brother and sister?
> B C: Yeah.
> S: I feel like you are hurt and I need to help....
> B C: ...Scarlet, we're all okay, plus the ambulance is here now and they are taking good care of us. Thank you so much for calling them and helping out but really we will all be fine.

If the crash breaches Bleeding Child's boundaries (along with the car's), he is remarkably self-reliant and intones the same normalizing ("it's all right") message that all the male characters Scarlet role-played did. Yet, Scarlet names him in terms of his injury. Next she role-played the Mexican boy driver:

> Scarlet: So are you okay?
> Other Brother: Yeah, it was just scary, I think I hit something on the road that made me curve off of it and hit those trees. I'm just glad everyone's okay.
> S: Yeah, well aren't you a little young to be driving?
> O B: No, I've been...driving the car for the past 4 years.
> S: How old are you?
> O B: 12
> S: I was really worried there for a while, you all scared me so bad!
> O B: I know you're practically hysterical, I don't understand why...it was just a little crash.

S: Just a little crash? You went into 3 trees!
O B: I know but...no one has any broken bones or other problems.
S: I guess so.
O B: Look I'm not trying to say you didn't help us....But really...you
   don't have to worry.
S: Why am I so worried?
O B: Because you are making this a bigger deal than it really is.

Scarlet wonders through her dream and role-play if males in responsible positions, like Ambulance Man and Other Brother, can be
trusted to care adequately for those in their charge. In defense, they
both invoke the Hysterical Female model. To do so Ambulance Man
must assert that bleeding from head to toe is not a medical problem.
Other Brother tells Scarlet he is twelve and has been driving since
the age of eight. Twelve is too young to drive according to U.S. laws;
eight is too young to see very well over the wheel! These characters
iterate her dilemma: while they dismiss her concerns, they also demonstrate how justified these concerns are.

Bleeding Child's sister is "a white girl," representing Scarlet's
feeling that human beings, of whatever race or ethnicity, are one
family and responsible for one another's well-being. Like George
(Chapter 3), Scarlet has an alternative One-world model of family.
This model makes Scarlet fear that others' suffering is not "okay"
and that authorities cannot be trusted to put things right. Scarlet
next began conversing with the white girl who she named Sister,
again intoning family feeling:

Scarlet: So how are you holding up?
Sister: Oh I'm fine, just my older brother sucks at driving.
Scarlet: Well I wouldn't say it was completely his fault—would you?
Sister: I guess not but I should've been driving.
Scarlet: Why's that?
Sister: Maybe we would not have crashed.
Scarlet: That might be true, but you all look okay—right?
Sister: Yeah...it's just mom is NOT going to be happy he crashed
   the car.
Scarlet: Yeah I bet, but did you want me to come with you to talk
   with your mom?
Sister: Nah, we can do it ourselves, you've helped enough. Thanks
   a lot.

Ambulance Man and Other Brother accuse Scarlet of taking too
much responsibility; Sister accuses herself of taking too little: she

says she should have driven, rather than just riding along. I suspect this is a quandary for many U.S. women. People may still expect them to be dependent/deferential, as Nuckolls (1998) shows, and to allow men to drive, figuratively speaking, yet in face of calamitous events (from car crashes to Mexican boys dying in their attempts to cross the border), they are likely to feel they have wrongly abdicated responsibility.

I am reminded here of Hollan's (2003a:71) client's "Steve." In a dream, Steve is sitting in the backseat of his car. His parents are in the front. His mother drives. Steve wants to stop the car and leans over into the front seat to steer to the curb. His mother appears to cooperate but fails to brake and crashes. Hollan sees this dream as evidence of Steve's inability to construct a bounded sense of self, independent from others. Scarlet is not destructively interfused with others, but she does have a highly developed intersubjective sense of self that drives her to help. The two males she role-plays want her to "leave the driving to us," as U.S. Americans say, and judge her to be acting inappropriately if she demurs.

Scarlet did not relate her need to fix things to gender but to national sentiment, averring that "we as a nation feel it's our right to intervene in other countries problems." She continued:

> Sometimes…we are just making it worse.…If we end up letting those from Mexico in without any sort of pass what will happen? Are we fixing their problems? Are we fixing ours? As Americans we long to fix things. Not just physical things like our cars, houses, or appliances. We long to fix each other. If you look at our society everyone has the answer.

Scarlet's analysis reveals an inner conflict and a counteridentity that may stand behind her fear that she is a compulsive. Scarlet's conscious identity is caring and dedicated, yet her counteridentity, Ambulance Man, dismisses problems as less serious than they appear and as no cause for concern. Counteridentities often represent an underside of a cultural model with which the dreamer has not come to terms, just as one may not follow through the implications of an argument— in this case the underside of a model of self as free, autonomous, and mobile. A part of Scarlet would probably like to dismiss others' problems and leave them to "experts" in authority. The classic Car self-model with its impermeable boundaries serves Scarlet's private interests in a world rife with poverty and suffering. Yet, Scarlet's dream also asks: How can a model of the person as intrinsically separate from others work when we are, as human beings, one family? As Scarlet put it:

> As a result of being born in the United States you are wealthy. You are free, you have the ability to move up in life or stay where you are— you have choices you make on your own. As Americans, we...want to say we fought our way to get where we are and that we deserved it....In most cases we had family, friends, teachers, coaches or others helping us financially, emotionally and mentally along the way. We all believe we deserve every penny of it when really what if you were born in Mexico? Another third-world country? You would not have nearly...the choices.

Scarlet as dreamer deeply wonders what the world's bleeding hearts and bodies mean about the U.S. stand-on-your-own-two-feet Free Individual model and about relations with authority: both immediate authorities like Ambulance Man and, by implication, more remote authorities who tell us everything is as a good as it can be and that we should leave "fixing things" in their hands. Scarlet's answer is spending time in Mexico, building a house for a poor Mexican woman, and developing a family feeling for a boy her age that died crossing the border. That may not be "the answer," but sounds like a place to begin.

Figurative Self-Models and Counteridentities

How can Figurative Analysis supplement a person-centered approach that focuses on the personal life of the dreamer, for example, Hollan's (2003a, 2005) "selfscape" approach? Hollan (2003a:68–69) reports an intriguing dream of a Torajan elder he collected in the early 1980s in which planes fly overhead and a bomb hits the elder who later stands up unhurt. The elder had this dream as a young adult; looking back, he believed it foreshadowed the time when his parents and first wife died. At their funerals, he sacrificed many buffalos and feared financial ruin. For him, his miraculous dream recovery prophesied triumph over these circumstances. Hollan persuasively argues that this elder felt his ritual obligations to be as destructive as aerial bombardment: the dream reflects the high price Torajans generally pay for their investment in family and social networks.

In such a case, Figurative Analysis might add an understanding of changing self-models. At the time that a researcher collected this dream, she would also collect dreams throughout the village, determining if planes were common dream figures. Making a subset of plane dreams, she would look for recurrent features in the set: possibly aerial bombardment, foreigners visiting, or relatives departing and returning. Hollan collected the dream during a fieldwork period between 1981 and 1983 but Grandfather Limbong had this dream during World War II when the Japanese occupied the island. Limbong had worked for the previous government, controlled by the Dutch. During their occupation, Japanese soldiers treated him harshly. Examining plane dreams and their recurrent features when interpreted in relation to major cultural events, such as war, transnationalism, and the encroachment of modernity, could give a fuller sense of how this elder's struggles with his own identity were part of reconfiguring models for being Torajan. Planes may represent a foreign self-model for Torajans but, if this elder is representative, one that they have begun thinking about and making their own in dreams, probably relating it to older forms of travel. As Clifford (1992) remarks, people the world over have histories of travel and, I would add, figures that evoke the transiting-transforming sense of self that derive from these histories.

How does Figurative Analysis compare to a Cultural Consensus approach, which also assesses a large number of respondents across a group to determine salient models? In Cultural Consensus, Dressler and his associates (2007a) first identify "cultural domains": for example, lifestyle, social support, family life, national identity, and food. Through free listing, pile sorts, rating and ranking tasks, focus groups and open-ended interviews, they uncover prototypical beliefs associated with such domains and infer cultural models from these beliefs. Then investigators test individuals to see how well their lives correspond to prototypes. To the extent that subjects' lives are consonant with prototypes, Cultural Consonance researchers have discovered, they experience more well-being and less distress.

Yet, people are often reluctant to admit inconsonance. Cultural models are not norms per se but often indicate deeply internalized norms and ideals to which people aspire. In this chapter, for example, we saw that the Car self-model suggests norms/ideals of freedom, autonomy, and mobility. Those who have internalized this model seldom volunteer that they don't make their own decisions or that they are "going nowhere," as Americans say. When they do, such an admission is tantamount to an expression of distress rather than reflecting simple inconsonance with the model. We also know that internalized norms affect survey responses. Thus, in a meta-analysis of gender studies, Hyde (2005:588–590) found that only in situations of complete anonymity, what researchers call "deindividu-alted" situations, did significant numbers of people report that they did not fit social expectations about gender. Spiro (2003) argues that the same barriers to objective self-reports are present in all but successful long-term therapeutic relationships.

In most dreams, however, like those considered in this chapter, inconsonance with social expectations is rendered symbolically in what Eggan (1952:477–478) calls "a safely cryptic manner," which allows people to share what they would ordinarily be unwilling to admit to others or even to themselves. There is an "I know not of what I speak" quality to dream reports, which permits people to broach anxiety-provoking topics, cultural inconsonance among them. I do not mean that dreams or their accounts disguise latent thoughts, as in the classic Freudian model. Rather, as in Barthes's (1977:54) analysis of the filmic image, people sense that there is an "obtuse" meaning, which provides cover even while it "compels an interrogative reading." Figurative Analysis, like all the forms of analysis offered in this book, takes advantage of this compulsion by supplementing dream reports and journals with projective exercises that can help dreamers reach material incongruent with norms and ideals (Spiro 2003:171).

Cultural Consensus research aims at assessing conscious processes. Figurative Analysis aims at assessing largely unconscious processes and, therefore, may represent an important complement to Cultural Consensus Analysis. If dreams are at least in part about cultural models, as I have argued throughout, and if distress is a measure of cultural inconsonance, then the high incidence of anxiety and negative emotion in REM dreams suggests that they reflect inconsonance. As Garro (2000) points out, Cultural Consensus theory cannot help to understand intracultural variability. Figurative Analysis allows people to identify what models are troubling and why. The Car self-model, for example, putatively means independent movement and progress but to Hester, Reb, and Scarlet it does not have this unequivocal significance. Their dreams, accounts, and projective/analytic work show this discrepancy and redeploy the car as a figure to accommodate their actual experience. Woman's blood in Hester's dream, Woman's death in Reb's, and Bleeding Child's in Scarlet's testify that the kind of autonomy the Car self-model configures is at least potentially injurious.

Dreams point to how a shared model may be a focus of conflict between a dreamer's conscious identity and counteridentities— dream characters that represent dissociated and contrary inner

voices. So, consciously, Hester is afraid of moving on after graduating and would like to cling to the past, just as the wall of flesh clings
to her. Reb expects to find a girlfriend. Scarlet wants to help. Yet,
Hester's Road personifies a part of her that is excited for change;
Reb's Car, his hostility to women; and Scarlet's Ambulance Man her
desire to avoid responsibility. I do not mean that the conscious self
is a ruse or illusion and counteridentities represent dreamers' "real"
feelings. Hester is genuinely afraid; Reb sincerely longs for love;
Scarlet really cares. Tensions between conscious and dissociated
identities generate interior conversations resembling those dreamers play out in this chapter and so characterize the inner world of
the subject. They further suggest that subjectivity, unlike the ego,
is not a coherent whole but inherently multilayered and conflicted.
Counteridentities provide insight into negative and resistive forms
of agency that are more complex than conscious intent and that are
visible in dreams. In dreams, moreover, conscious identities and
counteridentities together constitute dreamers' complex relations to
a model at a certain time and place, tuning us into the "nightly
news" of culture.

Chapter 6

Dreams as Cultural Remembering

I have tried in this volume to contribute to a cultural theory of dreaming. Toward this end, the preceeding chapters advance four related propositions. First dreams must be understood as part of what, in Chapter 2, I called a culture's narrative spectrum: a continuum that runs from very public tales to those more private and disordered narratives we dream. All of these stories concern cultural models but dreams are closest to personal experience and through memory bring it to bear on mastering or adapting models. Contradictions within or among models, or between models and experience, I argued in Chapter 3, stimulate dreaming about a model. Dreamers register contradictions, Chapter 4 proposed, as incomplete figures whose missing pieces evoke memories with the potential to provide a connection or transition useful for resolving those contradictions. Dreamers seek these missing pieces through a process of repetition-with-variation, where successive figures are symbolic kin to their immediate predecessor in the sense that some (but not all) of their meanings are the same. Each new figure offers an original metaphor that summons additional memories to supply what is missing in a model. Major dream figures, recurrent in a large set of dreams, Chapter 5 showed, shed light on typical versions of a salient cultural model along with its probable directions of change.

This chapter forwards one last proposition integral to a cultural theory of the dream. I have demonstrated that dreaming is a way of remembering one's past through socially shared figures that represent models and their attendant problems. It follows that dreaming can be usefully understood as a form of cultural memory.[1] There are what I (2001a) have called two genres of cultural memory: intercultural memory and intracultural memory. Intercultural memories are those likely to be shared between cultural groups. Intracultural memories are those more likely shared among cultural members. In what follows, I do not suggest that these types are essential opposites but rather possible directions that remembering can take.

Grand chronicles and official commentaries that those in authority and those who desire authority incant exemplify *intercultural memory.* Such memories feature cultural models with which groups publicly identify—as Samoans celebrate hospitality and U.S. Americans valorize individual liberty. Intercultural memories employ those tried and true models that shape perduring social sentiments and inspire the confidence that people need to get on with the business of living. They provide something reliable that elders can teach children, be it in grammar school history books or the bush school instruction of boys undergoing initiation.

Through tales that rehearse and celebrate a group's canon of models, intercultural memory seeks to justify or extend social and legal boundaries. U.S. Americans, for example, tell tales that tout freedom and equality before the law as universal human rights, stories that serve as justification for campaigns on billboards and battlefields that seek to extend these rights to people in faraway places. When intercultural memory is weak, models lose their power, boundaries soften and decay, and then a group cannot prevail in disputes with other groups. I think of Clifford's (1988) study of the Mashpee, their social boundaries so diluted by foreign mixings of blood and custom that they lose legal rights to tribal real estate. Indeed, there are so many cases where tidal waves of foreign cultures swamp indigenous ways—ways that people may then abandon, repudiate, or forget (see, for example, Dening 1980, Dureau 2001).

Ambiguous tales that elicit doubt and suggest unsettling complexities exemplify *intracultural memory.* In featuring feelings of failure, subtle or strong, this kind of memory erodes deeply internalized models along with their associated practices and strategies. Dreams are a form intracultural memory. In Chapter 3, for example, Monroe's memories of his girlfriend erode his Supermasculinity model, erosion dramatized by the dream Viking whose jetpack is out of fuel. Dave's memories likewise undermine his masculinity model, depicted in the dream by his dog losing a fight with a supercat. Betsy's difficulty succeeding in college (Chapter 4) challenges her Bad Boy model—a challenge that her crash configures.

Intracultural memories focus on a situation from people's lives when an experience passed through their models as through a sieve. In dreams, an absence first represents this experience. This absence, we saw in Chapter 4, points to what a model is lacking for the dreamer. Bigfoot is precisely what Clark cannot find and his Bigfoot memories (hunting with his dad) point to his problem with the Supermasculinity model: its incompatibility with sustaining a close family. Likewise, Dolly driving with huge Franklin misses the right direction to her destination, which signals her troubles with the Moving on model: this model drives her ever-forward rather than helping her make genuine progress. These absences signify visceral doubts about a model and elicit a preverbal mode of apprehension that Merleau-Ponty's (1962) calls preobjective perception.

Merleau-Ponty (1962) argues that in the prelinguistic period infants have access to perceptions that, while they occur within a culture, are not necessarily limited by the verbal categories of that culture. Dreaming, as an image-based form of thought, bypasses verbal categories and, therefore, can accommodate preobjective perceptions to see around those models with which we normally perceive and process reality. So, Dave's dream visually represents his perception/recognition that pets and dolls and what they signify are not up to the task of making sense of his life and Betsy's that the Car self-model is helping her neither arrive nor escape.

Preobjective perceptions occur in daily situations, although they usually pass beneath conscious awareness or, at any rate, they surpass what we can readily speak of at the time. In dreams, such lingering perceptions elicit memories of similar situations from dreamers' pasts, which the dream distills as figures. These figures, via their resemblance to figures in other tales circulating in the dreamer's culture, combine the dreamer's past with collective pasts to think and feel through problems with a model. Scarlet's dream, for example, responds to distressing and inarticulate apprehensions in her current relationship with Butler (who has heart problems), perceptions that evoke her high school visits to Mexico, which the dream distills in the figure of a bleeding child. This child also combines her memory of a Mexican boy who tried to cross the border lying buried under a cross with Christian "good Samaritan" tales of stopping to aid an injured wayfarer to consider how the Car self-model fails to accommodate her sense of connectedness to others. Her dreaming recognition of resemblances between recent and past memories, as well as between her personal biography and public tales, amounts to realization of a potential fit among them. In fact, these memories/stories don't quite fit. Lack of fit makes for incongruous figures like a mad rush of people racing down a stairwell on bicycles in Dolly's dream. Incongruities further specify a model's deficiencies; these deficiencies lie at the heart of many anxious emotions depicted by dreams, like Madison's anguish at the need to move on in U.S. society before she is ready to move forward symbolized by her frazzled appearance walking down the aisle at her dream wedding.

Because dreams register models' limitations, dreamers seek a broadened spectrum of possible ways of being and acting by allowing potentially threatening others in typecasting them in interior dramas about cultural models. Thus, the Muslim girl impersonates, as it were, Kamil's family values in Marilyn's dream about her Cinderella model. Such others need not be foreign. Our family, friends, and lovers also take the role of the "other," personifying counteridentities at odds with our present identity and the cultural models we use to construct them. So, George's dream mom represents an orientation to family he repudiates in waking life, indeed that seems to contradict his waking affirmation of pluralism in family form, but by acting the part of a teacher she also suggests an education that might include pluralistic understandings and thus expanded possibilities for George's future.

Letting others, along with the ideas and feelings they configure, into the self requires relaxed boundaries. The dream state itself is one of relaxed (inner) boundaries as all our muscles slacken in REM sleep: it is a space where we let go of our defenses. Indeed, soft boundaries correspond to an increase in those intracultural memories rendered visible in dreams. Thus, people with what psychologists call "thin boundaries" dream more, report dreams more, and have more vivid dreams (Blagrove 2007:123–125). Yet, we saw above that permeable boundaries can invite invasions that breach the integrity of one's own cultural or personal territory. In intracultural remembering, therefore, people protect themselves through an elliptical language.

As in a mystery, fragments, like clues, point to meanings beyond our ken, meanings that may be at odds with appearances. Indeed, the mystery is a metaphor for intracultural tales, which perplex us because their meanings lie not on the surface but in an intertext of images, motifs, and figures, which only cultural insiders can read and that even they usually cannot translate into the transparent terms of verbal communication. Thus, Hester's dream enlists a Quaker woman to be her pilgrim—an American icon with perfect historical resonance, but about which Hester showed no conscious knowledge. Often, dreamers experience this opacity not as a shield but as a threat and summons. Retold in many places over coffee or morning firelight, dreams bear an ominous sense of portent. Even where people regard them as mere hunting omens or in other places dismiss them as meaningless biological processes, a vivid dream may elicit overvigorous repudiations or plague waking recollection like a nagging and aggrieved ghost.

Dreaming and Mind

If dreams are a form of remembering, they often feel like a state of memory loss, a state where one thing happens after the other, where we don't know where we're going, where events vanish even as we experience them. There we live in a compelling and disorientating present. In Lacan's (1977b:75) words, the dream consists in "the absence of horizon...and, also, the character of emergence, of contrast, of strain...[I]n the final resort, our position in the dream is profoundly that of someone who does not see." Yet, the dream is primarily a visual experience. Indeed, in many cultures the dream is a source of visions—of illumination. What, then, does Lacan mean?

The ego, in psychoanalytic terms, is that part of the self that uses sequential reasoning and action to solve "real world" problems, which is how many Westerners conceive of agency. But the ego feels blind and ineffectual in dreams. Dreams suggest another form of agency key to understanding indigenous dream theories in many cultures that anthropologists study. People in a host of places believe the person's spirit double acts in dreams in ways that affect waking reality.[2] This double, I believe, is that self who Lacan (1968, 1977a) says little ones discover in the mirror phase: it is this figure they see in the mirror and in others' regard. This imaginal self continues to appear and to act in dreams and is usually the vehicle of our dreaming consciousness, although we often see our dream double as a figure in a drama that we witness and enact at once. Dreaming lends itself to this reflective viewpoint because it is a mode of reflection. In our imaginal thinking, in our dreaming self one might say, we react to cultural models and re-author them in ways that capture our personal experience. People, then, are agents of meaning in dreams. In other words, actions in reality have consequences and in this sense have meanings, but other kinds of meaning are metaphorical in nature and hence proper to the realm of the imagination. Dreams, again, are the place where most of us have the time and attention free for concentrated imaginal thinking—a private theater for acting out and in this way capturing feelings and thoughts that don't fit within our words or worlds. Dreams, then, are a precursor to or even a primary instance of what Holland and her colleagues (1998) call a "space of authoring."

Dreamers re-author meanings through contradictory additional or subtractive marks that differentiate dream figures from their daytime originals. In Clark's dream, he drives a car, a common daily figure but, being miniature, it is *subtractive*, which marks this dream figure as symbolic, in his case of masculinity. Kent dreams about the family dining room, a common daily scene, but a carpet studded with pushpins decorates it. Both the carpet and the ever-multiplying pins are *additions* that contradict his waking experience and comprise a dream figure that is symbolic of Kent's family relations.

Repetition with contradicting marks comprises the modus operandi of dream thinking and dictates the progression of the dream itself: to consider a model, each scene repeats a meaning from the last through a new figure that evokes and opposes its predecessor, along with further memories. George's dream, for example, begins with a figure of convivial bonding, watching TV with Jeff and Thomas, which is repeated in the figure of his mom, who also hung out at home and watched TV with him but who was cold to her Korean relatives. This meaning recurs in the figure of the fridge, which represents his cool and never-stationary dad, the central problem of the dream.

Even when people in their verbal thinking question or reject models like Cinderella or the Pinup or Supermasculinity, intracultural remembering compels them to repeat those figures that represent these models because repeating-with-variation is the way this style of mind operates. The repetition supplies the subject of thought; the variation supplies the commentary; together repetition and variation enact a conversation in metaphor about models and how they work or don't.[3] Meaning-making continues in efforts to recount the dream—to translate its perplexing immediacy into language. Dream meanings, then, are not objectlike, already there, but discovered by an "objective" researcher—an explorer in the realm of the mind who plants his flag on some metaphorical shore. Rather, those who seek to comprehend dream figures and the models they represent repeatedly render them anew. When dreamers change what a model means to them, they inevitably change waking behavior and talk that enlists this model. In this way, a dreamer conveys model transformations to others, who may adopt them as creative solutions to a common malaise. A cultural analysis of dreams, then, can shed light on the psychological roots of social change.

Past Trajectories, Future Directions

Approaches to dreams in academic psychology tend to view them as about the dreamer, her personal relations, and more recently her ability to learn. This book carries forward seminal ideas in Wallace's (1952) and Eggan's (1949) work: dreams concern more than the dreamer's individual waking life. Indeed, in many societies, people see dreams as addressed to the social group rather than about the individual per se.[4] This approach captures a truth that standard academic theories miss, one valuable, not only for fully understanding dreams themselves, but also in our approach to healing. Only by contextualizing personal distress within shared meanings can we fully understand individuals' agitations, anger, angst, and despair.

When neither therapists nor their clients reflect critically on culture, therapy risks perpetuating cultural models that may be at the root of clients' distress (cf. Hare-Mustin 1994). Discerning cultural models and their attendant conflicts through dreams, promises a new direction in therapy and personal growth. Dreams can help people to see problems that seem individual from a cultural viewpoint. Yet, therapists often neglect dreams either because they feel unprepared to work with them or because they fail to see them as a significant source of insight (Pesant and Zadra 2004). *Dreaming Culture* calls for a new look at projective work on dreams as a simple, useful way to address dilemmas that models can pose for individuals. The theories and techniques I offer can help people to comprehend their worries and wishes from a perspective that can strengthen their mindful and original responses to their society. Cultural dream analysis, then, is good medicine for the guilt and shame that too often attends upon a person's anxieties and troubled aspirations—a person who, with or without conscious awareness, may be at odds with his culture.

With therapies that aim at individual adjustment and therapies that aim at more conscious and critical relations between the self and culture, the point is to remedy the person's alienation from others. Resolving alienation is a capacity that Obeyesekere (1981) attributes to "personal symbols." Personal symbols, as he defines them, come from an individual melding her private history, emotional crises, and complexes with public symbols such as those of institutionalized religions. In his groundbreaking work on Sri Lankan ecstatic priestesses, he develops this idea. These women's schizophrengenic personal histories at first precipitate disturbing visions that move them to withdraw from the social world into a state of abjection from which they emerge when a god gives them matted locks. In Sri Lankan religious tradition, matted locks are a public symbol: people generally see them as signs of divine patronage, but also as phallic: as cobralike "buds of flesh" (Obeyesekere 1981:1–12). Through concatenating their private traumas with a canonical religious image, Obeyesekere shows, these women, lacking any social or economic power, come into possession of socially recognized "spiritual" potency. In contrast, Obeyesekere (1981:80, 1990:54–58) argues, dream images are products of "deep motivation"—those compulsions that psychoanalysts attribute to early family relations and view as "biologically based" even if "culturally influenced."

Yet, our deepest motivations also derive, in Vygotsky's (1978:57) terms, from the culturally distinct relationships within which children develop and from the models that these relationships support. These relations and models, moreover, reflect economic and political realities that privilege some, disadvantage others, and change through time. Personal misfortunes alone did not alienate Obeyesekere's priestesses from their society: these women's difficulties with Sri Lankan patriarchal marriage models contributed to their alienation. These difficulties, I suspect, were widespread if not equally acute among other Sri Lankan women. According to Obeyesekere (1981), Sri Lankan women were obligated to serve their husbands and provide them sex without regard to their personal feelings. Possession by a god annulled these obligations and gave them considerable social authority.

In later work, while Obeyesekere (1990:55–57) maintains that "culture is a symbolic order far removed...from dreams," he concedes that, through symbolic substitutions, dreams can produce greater degrees of remove from deep motivation; in this sense, dream transformations of desire resemble what he calls "the work of culture," which blends individual suffering with public symbols to produce personal symbols. The many dreams in this book demonstrate that people make connections between disturbing experiences, often colored by early family relations, and culturally shared metaphors every night. So, Madison's dream of Franklin in a bicycle race connects her private childhood trauma with a U.S. symbol of striving for success.

To the extent that people are alienated from their society by the trials of their existence, as dreamers they do not cease their relentless figurative reflection on how they got there or their attempts to imagine reconnections. Dreams, thus, provide individuals with opportunities to adapt to their social worlds by better mastering shared models and to adapt their cultures by changing these models: they are a two-way street between culture and the self that keeps both vital. Only in extreme cases, like those of Obeyesekere's priestesses, does this bridge between personal and social experience crumble and rip the fabric of daily existence. Then dreaming may erupt into waking and generate visions that at least temporarily sever the person's connection to conventional reality. Dreams are probably the original source of personal symbols in that they endlessly reweave those webs of significance in which our cultures consist.

In a famous essay, Oscar Wilde ([1889]1972) debates with Plato, who asserts that art imitates life. On the contrary, Wilde ([1889]1972:55) declares, art provides models that people later imitate: "a great artist invents a type, and Life tries to copy it, to reproduce it in a popular form, like an enterprising publisher." More likely art constantly reinvents models by manipulating the public symbols that represent them. Yet, surely, we all author cultural change. Prophets, artists, and priestesses do not spring up solitary but rise on a tide of creative imaginings that issues from many individuals' dreams. Their innovations find resonance and support in others because they address problems in meaning that dreamers have already encountered.

Table 8   Models and Schemas Summary*

Meta-models	Major Models	Schemas
Car self-model	Free Individual	Problem-solving
		Detachment (separate/different from others)
		Competing to be Number One
		Risk-taking
		Control
		Extraordinary Power (merit)
		Transiting (transformation)
		Autonomy (singular)
		True Inner Self (unchanging)
		Being Unique
	Intersubjective Person	Caring/Empathy (Attachment)
		Being Recognized (as special & unique)
		Recognizing Another (as special & unique)
		Transiting (transformation)
		Risk-taking
		Control (cooperative)
		Autonomy (inclusive)
		Trouble-sharing
		Giving/getting help
	Moving on	Risk-taking
		Competing/Winning
		Transiting (transformation)
		Busyness

Continued

Table 8 Continued

Meta-models	Major Models	Schemas
	Choice-as-agency	Risk-taking
		Having Options
		Control (over one's life)
Close Family	Devoted Mom	Caring (Attachment)
		Recognizing Another (as special & unique)
		Intimacy (emotional)
	Supportive Dad	Providing (support & transitional space)
		Protecting (Attachment)
		Risk-taking (teaching)
	Good Kid	Caring (Attachment)
		Giving/getting help
		Succeeding (in life)
Dualistic Gender	Supermasculinity	Extraordinary Power
		Dominance/Control
		Competition to be Number One
		Protecting/ Rescuing
		Detachment
		Risk-taking
		Problem-solving
	[Bad Boy Masculinity]	Impulse Gratification
		Devil-may-care
	Cinderella Femininity	Marrying "prince" Perfect Fit (being a perfect romantic other)
		Being Recognized (as "the one")
		Transiting (self-transformation)
Agent/ Object Sexuality	Pinup Sexuality	Perfect Fit (being a perfect sexual object)
		Being Recognized (as desirable)
		Transiting (body transformation)
	Voyeuristic Sexuality	Detachment
		Acting on an object
		Impulse Gratification
		Recognizing Another (as desirable)
Friendship	Boyfriend/ Girlfriend	Caring (Attachment)

Continued

Table 8 Continued

Meta-models	Major Models	Schemas
		Recognizing Another (as special)
		Being Recognized (as special)
		Intimacy (emotional & physical)
		Companionship
	Guyfriends	Companionship
		Loyalty
	Girlfriends	Attachment (Caring)
		Recognizing Another (as special)
		Being Recognized (as special and or desirable)
		Intimacy (emotional and or physical)
	Cliques	Care for insiders (Attachment)
		Detachment from outsiders
		Intimacy (emotional)
		Insiders/Outsiders
	Pets	Companionship
		Loyalty
		Caring (Attachment)
		Intimacy (emotional)
		Recognizing Another (as special)

* Schemas listed in association with models are not ranked.

Appendix A: Dreamers

Because there is a considerable number of people and dreams to keep
in mind, I identify each dreamer here through their major dream
and the chapter in which this dream appears.

Chapter 2

Clark dreams of hunting Bigfoot.
Lois dreams of being at a crossroads.
Kent dreams of his family dining room.

Chapter 3

Marilyn dreams of her boyfriend having a baby with another
    woman.
Betty dreams of a mall and then a lecturer who owns a hotrod.
Monroe dreams of a Viking trying to reach a ship.
Dave dreams of his dog losing a fight with a cat.

Chapter 4

George dreams of his mom showing him their fridge.
Dolly dreams of driving around lost with Franklin.
Madison dreams of being unprepared for her wedding.
Betsy dreams of being chased in her car by an angry man.

Chapter 5

Hester dreams of rescuing a baby.
Reb dreams of dodging a bullet that hits a woman.
Scarlet dreams about witnessing an accident.

Appendix B: Glossary

Counteridentity. An oppositional figure that personifies dissociated thoughts and feelings inconsistent with a dreamer's conscious identity.

Dream image. Any character or object in a dream.

Dream motif. A typical action or action sequence.

Dreamwork. The dream's metaphoric renderings and projective/analytic work that continues this symbolic process.

Figure. An image plus an associated motif.

Foundational schema. A schema that recurs in a number of cultural models and links them together.

Metamodel. A model that provides an organizing framework for a set of tightly linked models.

Model variants. A model that shares most schemas with a major cultural model but includes an additional schema.

Major Models. Models that structure the actions, beliefs, and fantasies of most culture members.

Model. A complex set of ideas about a domain of experience, composed of shared, interrelated schemas.

Schema. A mental representation that one can hold in short-term memory.

Appendix C: Instructions

The Intertextual Method

1. Pick a dream that is imagistically and emotionally vivid and easy to recall. Then name one or more stories (the dream's intertext) that the dream evokes for you from elsewhere in your culture.
2. What personal memories are evoked by the dream's intertext(s). Give yourself time to make these associations; they may not come to mind immediately.
3. Identify salient dream motifs and major images and ask how these relate to the stories and memories evoked by the dream.
4. Guess your dream wish and, then, your dream anxiety.
5. Speculate how this wish and anxiety may link to culturally shared wishes and anxieties.

Narrative Analysis

1. Building on dreams explored through the Intertextual Method, the researcher looks for an emergent topic in the dream data.
2. The researcher contextualizes the emergent topic more broadly in ethnographic data and in other studies of the culture, and considers societal problems with the model indicated by these data and other studies.
3. The researcher then zooms in on individual dreams, considering each subject's insights and autobiographical material.
4. The researcher expands the dreamer's intertext by relating the dream to further stories circulating in the dreamer's culture that share the dreams' images and motifs.
5. The researcher asks how the dream combines motifs and images from the dream's intertexts with incidents from the dreamer's personal history to depict problems with a model *and* with an interrelated model.

6. Last, the researcher asks how image or motif combinations and/ or alterations in each subject's dream or in their dream series comments on or changes models for them.

Dream Play

1. Find a friend to help you act out a dream.
2. Pick any dream character or object to role-play except your own persona.
3. Close your eyes and return to the dream in imagination, zooming in on the image; let this image expand until you blend with it. Then opens your eyes.
4. Acting as this image, tell your friend about yourself and your feelings and respond to any questions the friend may have.
5. Switch to an adjacent chair and to your normal persona and ask the image (which you imagine as sitting in the chair in which you formerly sat) any questions you have about the image or about its actions in the dream.
6. Switch back to your original chair to answer these questions and begin a dialogue with the image and your waking persona. Switch to the appropriate chair (either that of the image or your waking persona), depending which of these characters is speaking. If you role-play alone in fantasy, try placing chairs side-by-side and change chairs when you change roles. Either record this material with a tape player or ask your friend to record it.
7. Repeat steps three and four with at least two other dream images.
8. Guess what "hole" in yourself the dream represents: what unexpressed feelings or unrealized abilities. Guess how this "hole" relates to your current situation and relationships.
9. Guess what "hole" in your culture your dream represents? How does this hole refer to feelings that are hard to express or to abilities that are hard to realize in your culture?
10. Use your guesses to make a dream interpretation—one that relates dream images to current issues in you and in your culture.

Dramatic Analysis

1. Select a number of dreams role-played by dreamers on a common topic, for example girlfriend/boyfriend relationships.

2. Working with ethnographic data on the culture, infer a related model from this material and consider issues surrounding the model evident in the dream set.
3. Using projective exercises and autobiographical material, ask how role-played dialogues reflect the contradictory voices evoked by a model.
4. When possible, consult the dreamer's journal for further insight on those model contradictions that role-play brings into focus.
5. Consider how the dreams and dialogues reflect the dreamer's position in a socioeconomic world and a historical moment.

The Selfscape Method

1. Pick a dream that is imagistically and emotionally vivid and easy to recall. Recount the dream.
2. How does the dream reflect your current life situation? In what sense is the dream a dramatization of your inner life?
3. How does it reflect alterations to your self-esteem and sense of well-being?
4. How does it reflect the current state of your body?
5. How does it reflect your relations to other people and the emotions that go with these relations? In what sense are the characters in your dream internalized representations of other people?
6. Does the dream depict relationships among part-selves, your relative inner wholeness or division?
7. How does it reflect your ideas about yourself?
8. Does the dream reflect ideas shared in your culture (schemas)?
9. How does the dream reflect emotions, anxieties, or experiences that people do not usually talk or think much about in your culture?

Holographic Analysis

1. To make a Holographic Analysis, assemble a set of dreams on a common topic, preferably analyzed by dreamers with a single method and infer a cultural model from this material.
2. Zoom in on individual dreams.
3. In each dream seek a missing or absent part in an opening dream figure.

4. Ask how this missing part relates to memories the figure evokes for the dreamer, both day residues and memories from the dreamer's deep past.
5. How do these memories highlight an inadequacy in the cultural model at issue or in the dreamer's use of the model?
6. How does the next dream figure represent its predecessor: how does it resemble this figure yet enlists new memories with a potential to throw further light on what is wrong with the model or with the dreamer's use of it.
7. Ask these questions of each major dream figure, tracing how the dream raises questions in the form of absences and answers them with memories that address the absence.

Figurative Analysis

1. Gather dreams from members of a cultural group and then review the resulting collection for major figures that are also self-symbols for dreamers.
2. Through ethnographic data along with other studies of the culture, explore what each figure represents for cultural members and how it configures ideas and feelings about the self.
3. Assemble a subset of all dreams where key events happen in or through this figure and delineate the subset's recurrent features, asking how they illustrate alternative versions of the model or current problems with it.
4. Zoom in on individual dreams in the subset that evince recurrent features and work with dreamers to interpret this material, using life history material and, ideally, other dreams from journals.
5. Nest each individual analysis within a broader analysis of the figure in culture, asking how the dream addresses problems with and changes in the model discovered in feature analysis.

Notes

Chapter 1

1. Cognitive anthropologists and psychologists sometimes use schemas and models synonymously. Strauss (1992a:3), for example, defines cultural models as culturally formed schemas. Models, from this viewpoint, are very big, complex schemas.
2. See Strauch and Meier 1996; van de Castle 1994:298; Domhoff and Schneider 2008.
3. The idea that dreams are about emotions and emotion schemas is extremely common in dream studies. See for example Stephen 2003 and States 1993, 2000.
4. On divorce rates, see further "Highlights of a New Report from the National Center for Health Statistics (nchs): Advance Report of Final Divorce Statistics" (http://www.cdc.gov/nchs/pressroom/95facts/fs _439s.htm) and the Centers for Disease Control statistics provided by Infoplease at http://www.infoplease.com/ipa/A0005044.html. In *Habits of the Heart* (1985), Bellah et al. argue that there is a contradiction between U.S. traditional views of marriage as about lastingness and a contemporary view of marriage as about personal fulfillment. Quinn (1996) disagrees, contending rather that cultural models exist to *resolve* contradictions, among other problems, and this is no doubt true. Marriage models include well-wrought resolutions to an apparent contradiction between lastingness and fulfillment that Quinn traces back to earlier times in U.S. history. Yet, this historical view implies that the resolutions that models provide evolve over time. It is unlikely that all models would evolve at the same pace.
5. See also Cartwright 1991, Greenberg et al. 1992, Fosshage 1997, and Ogden 2004.
6. Winnicott (1951) always looked for dream elements that symbolized transitional phenomena. See also Khan 1974. Grolnick (1978) argues that dreams are transitional phenomena in the sense that they provide an emotional bridge like transitional objects (Linus's blanket in the comic-strip *Peanuts* for example) in face of separation anxiety and castration anxiety.
7. Shore distinguishes between models as "publicly available forms" and models as "mental constructs" (1996:45). Dreams are an extreme example of the latter. Mental models, he says, are more idiosyncratic

than public models because people interpret them in terms of their personal experience.

8. See, for example, Eggan 1952; French and Fromm 1964; Noy 1969, 1979; Tedlock 1987; Hollan 1989; Stephen 1989, 199; Fosshage 1997; Mageo 2003; Lohmann 2003a; Grenell 2008.

9. I thank my research assistant, Kristine Cantin, for making and assessing this sample. Depressed subjects who report more negative dreams at the beginning of the night and fewer at the end are more likely to recover within the following year than those with few negative dreams at the beginning of the night and more at the end (Cartwright et al. 1998).

10. See, for example, French and Fromm 1964; Kohut 1971; Basso 1987; Hollan 1989, 2003a, 2003b, 2005; Stephen 1989, 1995, 1997, 2003; Globus 1989; Cartwright 1991; Greenberg et al. 1992; Foulkes 1993,1999; Fosshage 1987, 1997; Kokkou and Leman 1993; Mageo 2001a, 2001b, 2003, 2006, 2007, 2010; Reiser 2001; Ogden 2004; Grenell 2008.

11. For examples see Wallace 1952; Crapanzano 1975; Tedlock 1992; Arrington and Bitton 1992; Dilley 1992; Irwin 1994; Stephen 1995, 1997; Fixico 2003; Lohmann 2003a.

12. On this point, see also Kohut 1971, Cartwright 1977:131–133, Fosshage 1997:434.

13. For examples, see Holland and Quinn 1987, D'Andrade and Strauss 1992a, Strauss and Quinn 1997, Holland et al. 1998, Mageo 1998, 2002a, Quinn 2005.

14. See for example Romney, Weller, and Batchelder 1986; Garro 2000; Atran, Medin, and Ross 2005; Dressler et al. 2007a, 2007b.

15. For examples, see Damasio 1994 and Sacks 1996. Desjarlais (1991) documents an example of a cultural system of dream diagnosis.

16. For examples see Foulkes 1985; Hunt 1989; Kilroe 2000; States 1993, 2000; Grenell 2008; Fosshage 1997, 1987:299–318.

17. Subjectification is the reverse of objectification for Obeyesekere: public symbols are used to "justify the introduction of innovative acts and meanings" (1891:123). Dreamers require no such justifications, although they do use public symbols as a basis for improvisation. Fosshage (1987:301) also sees dreams' constituents as imagistic elements connected by themes and believes that the resulting "configurations" represent ways dreamers think about and solve their personal problems.

18. Cognitive anthropologists discuss narrative models (Casson 1983), by which they mean how people in various cultures tell stories. My interest is in stories as *conveying* cultural models and in their movement on what, in Chapter 2, I call a culture's "narrative spectrum." Hill (2005) finds cultural models in narratives' inferential gaps.

19. See further Kimmel 1996 on the U.S. male role as breadwinner.

20. During the 1990s, many evolutionary social scientists saw this gender model as biologically based. See, for example, Buss 1994; Lancaster 1997; Ellis and Symons 1997. For a critique of this view see Small 1993, Mageo and Stone 2005, and McKinnon 2005.
21. On this point, see further, Kracke 2003:211, Bulkeley 2001a: 369–372, Damasio 1994.
22. Turning in a dream journal was a course requirement, but I did not grade these journals. In 2005 and 2006, when students asked me how many dreams they needed for their journal, I told them five: one for each of the three in-semester papers and two for their final papers. I encouraged them to record more dreams; they could possibly select a more promising dream for analysis. Van de Castle (1994:319–320) reports that females typically report more dreams than males.

Chapter 2

1. Lohmann (2003a:206) argues that there is a "transfer of schemas among forms of consciousness," such as normal waking awareness, daydreaming, dreaming, trance, and so forth. He shows this transfer between dreams and religious schemas. I am arguing for a transfer of models and schemas via images, motifs, and figures among forms of narrative.
2. See for example Bruner 1986; Fernandez 1991; Horton and Finnegan 1973; Lévi-Strauss 1970; Neisser 1967; Price-Williams 1999; Stephen 1989, 1995, 2003; Werner 1973.
3. Tedlock describes a folk approach to dreams that she calls intertextual (1981:319–320, 327–329). In this approach, an interpreter takes the dream as prophetic and compares it to other forms of prophesy. Romans read birds' entrails, for example, to confirm a dream interpretation. In contrast, Narrative Analysis compares the dream *only* to stories in cultural circulation during the dreamer's lifetime.
4. Schema theorists also hold that there are higher- and lower-order schemas (D'Andrade 1995:122–149).
5. While in the early 1980s, the number of kids who did not have *any* contact with dads two to three years after a divorce was 50 percent, by the late 1990s the number had decreased to between 18 percent and 26 percent (Kelly 2006). On divorce rates, see Kreider and Fields 2002:18.
6. See also Ritchie and Ritchie (1979, 1989) on contact between mothers and toddlers in traditional Polynesian cultures. Where Devoted-mother models exist, they vary greatly. In Korea, for example, while mothers are supposed to nurture an achievement orientation in children and serve them selflessly in their educational endeavors, people do not expect mothers to create a capacity for close interpersonal relating in their offspring (Jung 2008).

7. See further Kimmel 1996 and Holt and Thompson 2004 on U.S. men's role as breadwinners. These days Dads and Moms sometimes switch roles, Moms providing financial support and Dads attending to the child's immediate needs, or, more often, parents share both roles. My data does not document how well these All-purpose Parent models work, but Betsy's dreams (Chapter 4) gives some insight.

8. Holt and Thompson (2004) call this model the "man-of-action hero."

9. See further, http://www.bigfootencounters.com/classics/walker.htm. Retrieved on June 10, 2011.

10. Studies indicate that recurrent dream themes illustrate cultural schemas. See for example Ewing 2003, Hollan 2003a, Mageo 2002b, 2003:3–42, Stephen 2003, Shulman and Stroumsa 1999.

11. Euro-American Knight tales, King Arthur's and Lancelot's for example, are about (male) ancestors: like myths in many cultures, they feature historical actors who generate the present order of society, or who restore it, like the lawmen of movie Westerns. The most famous Euro-American fairytales (Snow White, Rapunzel, and so forth) feature young woman whose accomplishments are more personal and psychological than historic.

12. There are cultures, like Bali, where witch stories are more salient than father-son and fraternal tales. See Mead 1942b; Bateson 1972:107–127, Covarrubias 1972; Favret-Saada 1980.

13. See for example, Leacock 1981, Shore 1981, Mageo 1998, Schoeffel 1979, Ackerman 2003, McKinnon 2005.

14. Laura is very "cool." Never ruffled in face of any threat, when police show up to find her estate in shambles after international criminals have tried to kill her and her associates, she calmly tells them she has had a wild party.

15. Holt and Thompson (2004:427-428) discuss the U.S. rebel model and see "bad boys" as an instance of the rebel.

16. Sanday describes menstrual pollution beliefs and associated purification rituals in U.S. fraternities (1990:156–173).

Chapter 3

1. In cultures characterized by a machismo ethos, in contrast, men's control of their women's sexuality is an explicit part of masculinity models. See, for example, Suarez-Orozco 1993. In machismo cultures, male-to-male interactions are the dominant context of male gender identity development. See, for example, Linger 1992.

2. Hall and van de Castle hypothesize that this gender difference in dreaming is universal (van de Castle 1994:320). While this difference is extremely common across cultures, their own data does not support its universality (ibid.).

3. Typically, U.S. males strive to become "number one" through competition. Yet, competitions with other males, sports being a key example, often involve teams and teamwork, which may require members to submerge their individuality. The U.S. football player, Drummond (1842:83) says, is "virtually faceless," his individuality consumed by his function.

4. This schema is not a part of the Cinderella story in all cultures where it occurs. In the Samoan story, Scabby Oven Cover (Chapter 1), for example, no item of clothing reveals the heroine's beauty or identifies her as small. In old Samoa, no one wore shoes and big was beautiful for both sexes. Yet, it was also true that women could be socially as large as men: women held the highest titles even though males held these titles more frequently (Mageo 1998).

5. On Gaze theory see Mulvey 1992.

Chapter 4

1. See for example Bion [1959]1992; Palombo 1978; Hunt 1989; Foulkes 1993; Hartman 1998; Stickgold et al. 2001; Stephen 2003; Stickgold and Walker 2004; Barrett and McNamara 2007.

2. I have changed the store and location.

3. Another of Madison's dreams indicates ambivalence about children. "I was babysitting a bunch of infants and toddlers and feeling overwhelmed by the amount of children that one by one they kept slipping into the couch cushions.... They were getting lost left and right."

4. Cliques may also have a Care schema among group members. The more detached-dominating the clique is vis-à-vis outsiders, like a gang (a male-identified group model), the less its members need to act out attachment among themselves. Conversely, the less the clique distances and denigrates others, the more clique members tend to act like girlfriends, practicing fond attachments to one another. Cliques can achieve cohesion by either method.

Chapter 5

1. See for example, Hollan 2003a, 2005; Fosshage 1997; Damasio 1994, 1999; Kohut 1971, 1977; Noy 1969, 1979; Fairbairn 1952.

2. Van de Castle (1983) was also interested in the symbolic nature of dream content and conducted a major study of dreams with animal figures. While he noted different relations to animals in different cultural groups, he did not let specific animals emerge from his data, as one would do in a Figurative Analysis. Dogs and cats, for example, frequently appear in my U.S. collection. In hunter/gatherer cultures, the

Parintintin for example (Kracke 2003), game animals more frequently appear in dreams.

3. Based on a random 250-dream sample from my collection, my research assistant, Kristina Cantin, found that other salient dream figures include: friends-roommates/supporting (20 percent), boyfriends-girlfriends/providing intimacy (20 percent), homes/sheltering (19 percent), and parents/providing security (12 percent).

4. D'Andrade (2008) found that a quantitative approach failed to reveal statistically significant value differences between U.S. Americans, Japanese, and Vietnamese. D'Andrade addresses the problem by focusing his analysis only on values most highly rated by his respondents.

5. Lohmann (2003b) takes traveling to be a uniting theme in Pacific Island dreams.

6. Hall and Van de Castle found that in U.S. adult dreams generally males instigated physical aggression two-thirds of the time (Van de Castle 1994:322–323). Schredl and Pallmer (1998) studied dream aggressors in the dreams of children and adolescents. Male strangers were the most likely aggressors in all dreams; male familiars were the second most likely aggressors, followed by female familiars in both girls' and boys' dreams. Female strangers were the least likely aggressors, and never committed aggression in boys' dreams. Van de Castle (1983, 1994:306–309) found that the presence of animal figures in U.S. dreams correlated with heightened levels of aggression for all dreamers; 73 percent reported that the animals were male. This frequency does not reflect actual aggressive animal behavior. Female lions and tigers, for example, hunt and kill more frequently than males to supply cubs with food. Males of many species, however, are more likely to engage in interspecies aggression.

7. See further www.onlinelawyersource.com/criminal_law/statisics.html. Retrieved on June 15, 2011.

8. In male and female dreams, being locked-out of a car represented a heightened vulnerability to aggression. Remember Marilyn (Chapter 3) who runs from a lion and arrives at her car without keys. A man, who described himself as "not a fighter," fumbles with car keys as another man attacks him.

9. Brenneis (1970) found that boundaries between the dreamer and others tended to be "fixed" in male dreams, whereas female dreams tended to revolve around issues of intimacy.

10. The same problem arose in another woman's dream who saw an upside-down van on fire. She ran toward the male driver who screamed for help, noticed a paramedic was already there, and then went on to draw a homeless man away from the van, which was about to explode.

Chapter 6

1. On socially shared metaphors that bespeak shared memories see also Garro 2000, Halbwachs 1992.
2. See for example Tedlock 1987, Dalton 2001, Kracke 2003, Lohmann 2003a, Groark 2009, 2010.
3. For another example of repeating-with-variation as a conversation about conventions, rather than just their reiteration, see McClintock's work on Arthur J. Munby and Hannah Culwick (1995:132–180).
4. For examples, see Graham 1995; Tedlock 1987, 2001; Shulman and Stroumsa 1999; Bourguignon 2003; Ewing 2003; Lohmann 2003a.

References Cited

Ackerman, Lillian. 2003. *A Necessary Balance: Gender and Power among Indians of the Columbia Plateau*. Norman: University of Oklahoma.

Ahnert, L., M. R. Gunnar, M. E. Lamb, and M Berthel. 2004. "Transition to Care." *Child Development* 75:639–650.

Ainsworth, Mary D. Salter. 1973. "The Development of Infant-Mother Attachment." In *Review of Child Development Research*. Vol. 3 (Bettye M. Caldwell and Henry N. Ricciuti, eds.), pp. 1–94. Chicago: University of Chicago Press.

Allison, Anne. 2002. "Playing with Power." In *Power and the Self* (Jeannette Mageo, ed.), pp. 71–93. Cambridge, UK: Cambridge University Press.

Antze, Paul and Michael Lambek. 1996. *Tense Past: Cultural Essays in Trauma and Memory*. New York: Routledge.

Aries, Philippe. 1962. *Centuries of Childhood*. New York: Random House.

Arrington, Leonard J. and Davis Bitton. 1992. *The Mormon Experience*. Urbana: University of Illinois Press.

Atran, Scott and Douglas Medin. 2008. *The Native Mind and the Cultural Construction of Nature*. Cambridge, MA: MIT Press.

Atran, Scott, Douglas L. Medin, and Norbert O. Ross. 2005. "The Cultural Mind: Environmental Decision Making and Cultural Modeling within and across Populations." *Psychological Review* 112(4):744–776.

Atwood, Margaret. 1986. *The Handmaid's Tale*. Boston: Houghton Mifflin.

Bailey, Beth L. 1988. *From Front Porch to Back Seat: Courtship in Twentieth Century America*. Baltimore, MD: The John Hopkins University Press.

Bakhtin, Mikhail M. [1975] 1981. *The Dialogic Imagination: Four Essays by M. M. Bakhtin* (M. E. Holmquist, ed.; Caryl Emerson and Michael Holquist, trans.). Austin: University of Texas Press.

Barrett, Deirdre and Patrick McNamara. 2007. *The New Science of Dreaming*. Vols. 1–3. Westport Connecticut: Praeger.

Barthes, Roland. 1977. *Image-Music-Text* (S. Heath, trans.). New York: Hill and Wong.

Bartky, Sandra Lee. 1997. "Foucault, Femininity, and the Modernization of Patriarchal Power." In *Writing on the Body* (Katie Conboy, Nadia Medina, and Sarah Stanbury, eds.), pp. 129–153. New York: Columbia University Press.

Basso, E. Barbara. 1987. "The Implications of a Progressive Theory of Dreaming." In *Dreaming* (Barbara Tedlock, ed.), pp. 86–104. Santa Fe: School of American Research.

Bateson, Gregory. 1972. "Bali: The Value System of a Steady State." In *Steps to an Ecology of Mind*, pp. 107–127. San Francisco: Chandler.

Baudrillard, Jean. 1988. *Jean Baudrillard: Selected Writings* (Mark Poster, ed.). Stanford: Stanford University Press.

Bean, Susan S. 1976. "Soap Operas: Sagas of American Kinship." In *The American Dimension* (W. Arens and Susan P. Montague, eds.), pp. 80–98. Port Washington, DC: Alfred Publishing.

Beeman, William O. 1986. "Freedom to Choose: Symbols and Values in American Advertising." In *Symbolizing America* (Hervé Varenne, ed.), pp. 52–65. Omaha, NE: University of Nebraska Press.

Bellah, Robert, Richard N. Madsen, William M. Sullivan, Ann Swindler, and Steven M. Tipton. 1985. *Habits of the Heart: Individualism and Commitment in American Life*. New York: Harper and Row.

Benjamin, Jessica. 1988. *The Bonds of Love: Psychoanalysis, Feminism, and the Problem of Domination*. New York: Pantheon Books.

Berg, Charles. 1951. *The Unconscious Significance of Hair*. London: Allen and Unwin.

Berger, John. 1972. *Ways of Seeing*. New York: British Broadcasting Corporation and Penguin.

Berne, Eric. 1968. *A Layman's Guide to Psychiatry and Psychoanalysis*. New York: Simon and Schuster.

Bettelheim, Bruno. 1976. *The Uses of Enchantment*. New York: Alfred A. Knopf.

Betzig, Laura. 1997. "Introduction." In *Human Nature* (Laura Betzig, ed.), pp. 1–17. New York: Oxford University Press.

Bion, Wilfred R. [1959] 1992. *Cogitations* (Francesca Bion, ed.). London: Karnac Books.

Blagrove, M. 2007. "Dreaming and Personality." In *The New Science of Dreaming* (Deirdre Barrett and Patrick McNamara, eds.). Vol. 2, pp. 115–158. Westport, CT: Praeger.

Bonime, Walter and Florence Bonime. 1987. "Culturalist Approach." In *Dream Interpretation* (J. L. Fosshage and C. A. Loew, eds.), pp. 79–124. New York: PMA Publishing.

Bordo, Susan. 1997. "The Body and the Reproduction of Femininity." In *Writing on the Body: Female Embodiment and Feminist Theory* (Katie Conboy, Nadia Medina, and Sarah Stanbury, eds.), pp. 90–110. New York: Columbia University Press.

Bourdieu, Pierre. 1992. *Outline of a Theory of Practice* (Richard Nice, trans.). Cambridge, UK: Cambridge University Press.

Bourguignon, Erika. 2003. "Dreams that Speak." In *Dreaming and the Self* (Jeannette Mageo, ed.), pp. 133–154. Albany: State University of New York Press.

Brenneis, C. B. 1970. "Male and Female Ego Modalities in Manifest Dream Context." *Journal of Abnormal Psychology* 76:434–442.

Bright, Brenda. 1998. "Heart like Car: Hispano/Chicano Culture in Northern New Mexico." *American Ethnologist* 25:583–609.

Brown, Lyn M. and Carol Gilligan. 1993. *Meeting at the Crossroads.* New York: Ballantine.

Bruner, Jerome. 1986. *Actual Minds, Possible Worlds.* Cambridge, MA: Harvard University Press.

Bruner, Jerome, Jacqueline Goodnow, and George Austin. 1956. *A Study of Thinking.* New York: John Wiley.

Bucci, Wilma. 1997. *Psychoanalysis and Cognitive Science.* New York: Guildford Press.

Bulkeley, Kelly, ed. 2001a. *Dreams: A Reader on the Religious, Cultural, and Psychological Dimensions of Dreaming.* New York: Palgrave Macmillan.

Bulkeley, Kelly, ed. 2001b. "Penelope as Dreamer: The Perils of Interpretation." In *Dreams: A Reader on the Religious, Cultural, and Psychological Dimensions of Dreaming* (Kelly Bulkeley, ed.), pp. 223–232. New York: Palgrave Macmillan.

Buss, David M. 1994. *The Evolution of Desire.* New York: Basic Books.

Butler, Judith. 1990. *Gender Trouble.* New York: Routledge.

Cage, John. 1967. *A Year from Monday: New Lectures and Writings.* Middletown, CT: Wesleyan University Press.

———. 1983. *X: Writings '79–'82.* Middletown, CT : Wesleyan University Press.

Cairns, Robert B. and Beverly D. Cairns. 1989. "Growth and Aggression: 1. Childhood to Early Adolescence." *Developmental Psychology* 25:941–951.

Canaan, Joyce. E. 1990. "Passing Notes and Telling Jokes." In *Uncertain Terms: Negotiating Gender in American Culture* (Faye Ginsburg and Anna Lowenhaupt Tsing, eds.), pp. 215–231. Boston: Beacon.

Cartwright, R. D., M. A. Young, P. Mercer, and E. Bears. 1998. "Role of the rem Sleep and Dream Variables in the Prediction of Remission from Depression." *Psychiatry Research* 80:249–255.

Cartwright, Rosalind D. 1977. *Night Life: Explorations in Dreaming.* Englewood Cliffs, NJ: Prentice-Hall.

———. 1981. "The Contribution of Research on Memory and Dreaming to a 24-Hour Model of Cognitive Behavior." In *Sleep, Dreams and Memory.* Advances in Sleep Research. Vol. 6 (William Fishbein, ed.), pp. 239–247. New York: Spectrum.

———. 1991. "Dreams That Work: The Relation of Dream Incorporation to Adaptation to Stressful Events." *Dreaming* 1:3–9.

Cashdan, E. 1996. "Women's Mating Strategies." *Evolutionary Anthropology* 5(4):134–143.

Cassidy, Judy and Phillip R. Shaver. 1999. *Handbook of Attachment.* New York: Guilford.

Casson, Ronald. 1983. "Schemata in Cognitive Anthropology." *Annual Review of Anthropology* 12:429–462.

Chesler, Phyllis. 1972. *Women and Madness*. Garden City, NY: Doubleday.

Chodorow, Nancy. 1974. "Family Structure and Feminine Personality." In *Women, Culture and Society* (Michelle Aimbalist Rosaldo and Louise Lamphere, eds.), pp. 42–66. Stanford: Stanford University Press.

———. 1978. *The Reproduction of Mothering*. Berkeley: University of California Press.

Clifford, James. 1992. "Traveling Cultures." In *Cultural Studies* (L. Grossberg, C. Nelson, and P. A. Treichler, eds.), pp. 96–111. New York: Routledge.

———. 1988. "Identity in Mashpee." In *The Predicament of Culture*, pp. 277–348. Cambridge MA: Harvard University Press.

Comaroff, Jean and John Comaroff. 2001. *Millennial Capitalism and the Culture of Neoliberalism*. Durham: Duke University Press.

Covarrubias, Miguel. 1972. *Island of Bali*. Oxford: Oxford University Press.

Crapanzano, Vincent. 1975. "Saints, Jnun, and Dreams: An Essay in Moroccan Ethnopsychiatry." *Psychiatry* 38:145–159.

———. 1981. "Text, Transference, and Indexicality." *Ethos* 9:122–148.

———. 1992. "Kevin: On the Transfer of Emotion." *American Anthropologist* 96(4):866–885.

———. 2003. *Concluding Reflections*. In *Dreaming and the Self* (Jeannette Mageo, ed.), pp. 175–198. Albany: State University of New York Press.

Csordas, Thomas J. 1990. "Embodiment as a Paradigm for Anthropology." *Ethos* 18:5–47.

Dallet, Janet. 1982. "Active Imagination Practice." In *Jungian Analysis* (M. Stein, ed.), pp. 173–191. La Salle, IL: Open Court.

Damasio, Antonio R. 1994. *Descartes' Error: Emotion, Reason, and the Human Brain*. New York: Avon Books.

———. 1999. *The Feeling of What Happens: Body and Emotion in the Making of Consciousness*. New York: Harcourt Brace.

D'Andrade, Roy G. 1984. "Cultural Meaning Systems." In *Culture Theory: Essays on Mind, Self, and Emotion* (Richard A. Shweder and Robert A. LeVine, eds.), pp. 88–119. Cambridge, UK: Cambridge University Press.

———. 1995. *The Development of Cognitive Anthropology*. Cambridge, UK: Cambridge University Press.

———. 2008. *A Study of Personal and Cultural Values, American, Japanese, and Vietnamese*. New York: Palgrave Macmillan.

D'Andrade, Roy and Claudia Strauss, eds. 1992. *Human Motives and Cultural Models*. Cambridge, UK: Cambridge University Press.

Dalton, Douglas. 2001. "Memory, Power, and Loss in Rawa Discourse." In *Cultural Memory: Reconfiguring History and Identity in the Pacific* (Jeannette Mageo, ed.), pp. 105–129. Honolulu: University of Hawai'i Press.

Davidoff, Leonore and Catherine Hall. 1987. *Family Fortunes: Men and Women of the English Middle Class, 1780–1850*. Chicago: University of Chicago Press.

Davidson, Julian M. and Richard J. Davidson, eds. 1980. *The Psychobiology of Consciousness*. New York: Plenum Press.

Degarrod, L. N. 1989. "Dream Interpretation among the Mapuche Indians of Chile." Ph.D. Dissertation. University of California at Los Angeles.

Degler, Carl N. 1988. *At Odds: Women and the Family in America from the Revolution to the Present*. Oxford: Oxford University Press.

Dening, Greg. 1980. *Islands and Beaches: Discourse on a Silent Land, Marquesas 1774–1880*. Honolulu: University of Hawai'i Press.

Derrida, Jacques. 1978. *Writing and Difference* (A. Bass trans.). Chicago: Chicago University Press.

Desjarlais, Robert. 1991. Samsars Sadness: Sherpa Shamanism and the "Calling of Lost Souls." Ph.D. Dissertation. University of California at Los Angeles.

Dilley, Roy. 1992. "Dreams, Inspiration, and Craftwork among Tukolor Weavers." In *Dreaming, Religion, and Society in Africa* (M.C. Jedrej and R. Shaw, eds.), pp. 71–85. Leiden: Brill.

Domhoff, G. William. 1993. "The Repetition of Dream and Dream Elements: A Possible Clue to a Function of Dreams." In *The Functions of Dreaming* (Alan Moffitt, Milton Kramer, and Robert Hoffmann, eds.), pp. 293–320. Albany: State University of New York Press.

———. 1996. *The Meaning of Dreams: A Quantitative Analysis*. New York: Plenum Press.

———. 2001. "Using Content Analysis to Study Dreams." In *Dreams* (Kelly Bulkeley, ed.), pp. 307–320. New York: Palgrave Macmillan.

———. 2007. "Realistic Simulations and Bizarreness in Dream Content." In *The New Science of Dreaming* (Deirdre Barrett and Patrick McNamara, eds.). Vol. 2, pp. 1–28. Westport, CT: Praeger.

Domhoff, G. William and Adam Schneider. 2008. "Similarities and Differences in Dream Content at the Cross-cultural, Gender, and Individual Levels." *Consciousness and Cognition* 17: 1257–1265.

Dressler, William W., Mauro C. Balieiro, Rosane P. Ribeiro, and Jose E. dos Santos. 2007a. A Prospective Study of Cultural Consonance and Depressive Symptoms in Urban Brazil. *Social Science and Medicine* 65(10):2058–2069.

———. 2007b. Cultural Consonance and Psychological Distress: Examining the Associations in Multiple Cultural Domains. *Culture, Medicine, and Psychiatry* 31(2):195–224.

Dreyfus, Hubert L. 1984. "What Expert Systems Can't Do." *Raritan* 3(4):22–36.

Drummond, George. 1842. October 26 letter to London Missionary Society Headquarters from Savai'i. Council of World Mission Archives (box 15/folder 5/jacket D). School for Oriental and African Studies. University of London.

Drummond, L. 1996. *American Primitive*. Lanham, MD: Littlefield Adams.

Dunn, Mary Maples. 1979. "Women of Light." In *Women of America: A History* (Carol Ruth Berkin and Mary Beth Norton, eds.), pp. 114–136. Boston, MA: Houghton Mifflin.

Dureau, Christine. 2001. "The Coming of the 'Ship People': Recounting and Remembering 'First Contact' on Simbo, Western Solomon Islands." In *Cultural Memory: Reconfiguring History and Identity in the Pacific* (Jeannette Mageo, ed.), pp. 130–162. Honolulu: University of Hawai'i Press.

Edgar, Iain R. 2004. *Guide to Imagework: Imagination-based Research Methods*. London: Routledge.

Eggan, Dorothy. 1949. "The Significance of Dreams for Anthropological Research." *American Anthropologist* 51:177–198.

———. 1952. "The Manifest Content of Dreams: A Challenge to Social Science." *American Anthropologist* 54:469–485.

Ellis, B. J. and Symons, D. 1997. "Sex Differences in Sexual Fantasy." In *Human Nature* (L Betzig, ed.), pp. 194–212. New York: Oxford University Press.

Erikson, Erik. 1963. *Childhood and Society*. New York: Norton.

Evans, Sara M. 1997. *Born for liberty: A History of Women in America*. New York: Free Press.

Ewing, Katherine Pratt. 2002. "Consciousness of the State and the Experience of Self: the Runaway Daughter of a Turkish Guest Worker." In *Power and the Self* (Jeannette Mageo, ed.), pp. 93–113. Albany: State University of New York Press.

———. 2003. "Diasporic Dreaming, Identity, and Self-Construction." In *Dreaming and the Self* (Jeannette Mageo, ed.), pp. 43–60. Albany, NY: State University of New York Press.

Fairbairn, W. Ronald D. 1952. "Endopsychic Structure Considered in Terms of Object-Relationships." In *Psychoanalytic Studies of the Personality* (W. Ronald D. Fairbairn, ed.), pp. 82–136. London: Tavistock Publications.

Favret-Saada, Jeanne. 1980. *Deadly Words: Witchcraft in the Bocage*. Cambridge: Cambridge University Press.

Fernandez, James W. 1991. *Beyond Metaphor: The Theory of Tropes in Anthropology*. Stanford: Stanford University Press.

Fields, Jason and Lynne M. Casper. 2001. "American Families and Living Arrangements, 2000." *Current Population Reports* June 2001, pp. 20–537. Washington, DC: United States Census Bureau.

Fischer, Calude S. 2009. "Self-Fashioning Across American History." A paper delivered at the meetings of the Society for Psychological Anthropology, Asilomar, CA.

Fixico, Donald Lee. 2003. *The American Indian Mind in a Linear World: American Indian Studies and Traditional Knowledge*. New York: Routledge.

Fosse, Magdalena J., Roar Fosse, J. Allan Hobson, and Robert J. Stickgold. 2003. "Dreaming and Episodic Memory: A Functional Dissociation?" *Journal of Cognitive Neuroscience* 15(1):1–9.

Fosshage, James L. 1987. "A Revised Psychoanalytic Approach." In *Dream Interpretation* (J. L. Fosshage,. and Clemens A. Loew, eds.), pp. 299–318. New York: PMA Publishing.

———.1997. "The Organizing Functions of Dream Mentation." *Contemporary Psychoanalysis* 33:429–458.

Fosshage, James L. and Clemens A. Loew, eds. 1987. *Dream Interpretation*. New York: PMA Publishing.

Foucault, Michel. 1977. *Language, Counter-Memory, Practice* (Donald F. Bouchard and Sherry Simon, trans.). Ithaca, NY: Cornell University Press.

———. 1979. *Discipline and Punish*. New York: Vintage.

———. 1982. "The Subject and Power." In *Michel Foucault* (P. Rabinow and H. Dreyfus, eds.), pp. 208–226. Chicago: University of Chicago Press.

———. 1986. *The Care of the Self* (Robert Hurley, trans.). Vol. 3. New York: Pantheon.

———. 1988. "Technologies of the Self." In *Technologies of the Self* (Luther H. Martin, Huck Gutman, and Patrick H. Hutton, eds.), pp. 16–49. Amherst: University of Massachusetts Press.

———. 1990. *The History of Sexuality, Vol. 1: An Introduction* (Robert Hurley, trans.). New York: Random House.

Foucault, Michel and Ludwig Binswanger. 1994. *Dream and Experience*. Atlantic Highlands, NJ: Humanities Press.

Foulkes, D. 1985. *Dreaming: A Cognitive-psychological Analysis*. Hillsdale, NJ: Lawrence Erlbaum.

———. 1993. "Data Constraints on Theorizing about Dream Function." In *The Functions of Dreaming* (Alan Moffitt, Milton Kramer, and Robert Hoffmann, eds.), pp. 11–20. Albany: State University of New York.

———. 1999. *Children's Dreaming and the Development of Consciousness*. Cambridge, MA: Harvard University Press.

French, Thomas M. and Erika Fromm. 1986. *Dream Interpretation*. New York: International Universities Press.

Freud, Sigmund. [1900] 1964. "Interpretation of Dreams." In *The Standard Edition of the Complete Psychological Works of Sigmund Freud* (J. Strachey, trans. in collaboration with A. Freud, assisted by Alix Strachey and Alan Tyson). Vols. 4 and 5. London: Hogarth.

———. [1916] 1963. "Dreams." In *The Standard Edition* 15:83–242.

———. [1920] 1964. "Beyond the Pleasure Principle." In *The Standard Edition* 18:1–64.

———. [1913] 1962. "Totem and Taboo." In *The Standard Edition* 13:1–161.

———. [1930] 1964. "Civilization and Its Discontents." In *The Standard Edition* 21:57–146.

Freud, Sigmund. [1931] 1964. "Female Sexuality." In *The Standard Edition* 21: 221–246.

———. 1963. *Introductory Lectures on Psycho-Analysis.* Vol. XV. Part II:83–242.

Garro, Linda C. 2000. "Remembering What One Knows and the Construction of the Past: A Comparison of Cultural Consensus Theory and Cultural Schema Theory." *Ethos* 28(3):275–319.

Geertz, Clifford. 1984. *Interpretations of Culture.* New York: Basic Books.

Giddens, Anthony. 1991. *Modernity and Self-identity.* Stanford: Stanford University Press.

Gilligan, Carol. 1982. *In a Different Voice.* Cambridge, MA: Harvard University Press.

Globus, Gordon G. 1989. "Connectionism and the Dreaming Mind." *Journal of Mind and Behavior* 10(2):179–195.

Gone, Joseph P. 2008. "Dialogue 2008 Introduction: Mental Health Discourse as Western Cultural Proselytization." *Ethos* 36(3):310–315.

Gone, J. P., P. J. Miller, and J. Rappaport. 1999. "Conceptual Self as Normatively Oriented." *Culture and Psychology* 5:371–398.

Goodwin, Marjorie Harness. 2006. *The Hidden Life of Girls: Games of Stance, Status, and Exclusion.* Oxford: Blackwell.

Graham, Laura. 1995. *Performing Dreams.* Austin: University of Texas Press.

Grall, Timothy S. 2007. *Custodial Mothers and Fathers and Their Child Support: 2005.* Washington DC, Bureau of the Census.

Greenberg, Ramon. 1981. "Dreams and REM Sleep—An Integrative Approach." In *Sleep, Dreams and Memory.* Advances in Sleep Research. Vol. 6. (William Fishbein, ed.), pp. 125–133. New York: Spectrum.

Greenberg, Ramon, Howard Katz, Wynn Schwartz, and Chester Pearlman. 1992. "A Research-based Reconsideration of the Psychoanalytic Theory of Dreaming." *Journal of the American Psychoanalytic Association* 40:531–550.

Gremillion, Helen. 2003. *Feeding Anorexia: Gender and Power at a Treatment Center.* Durham: Duke University Press.

Groark, Kevin P. 2009. "Discourses of the Soul: The Negotiation of Personal Agency in Tzotzil Maya Dream Narrative." *American Ethnologist* 36(4):705–721.

———. 2010. "Willful Souls: Dreaming and the Dialectics of Self-Experience among the Highland Maya of Chiapas, Mexico." In *Toward an Anthropology of the Will* (Keith M. Murphy and C. Jason Throop, eds.), pp. 101–122. Stanford, CA: Stanford University Press.

Grolnick, Simon A. 1978. "Dreams and Dreaming as Transitional Phenomena." *Between Reality and Fantasy* (S. A. Grolnick, L. Barkin, and Muensterberger, eds.), pp. 211–233. New York: Jason Aronson.

Grenell, Gary. 2008. "Affect Integration in Dreams and Dreaming." *Journal of the American Psychoanalytic Association* 56(1):223–251.

Grimm, Jakob and Willhelm. [1819] 1977. *Grimm's Tales for Young and Old* (Ralph Manheim trans.). Garden City, NY: Doubleday.

Halbwachs, Maurice. 1992. *On Collective Memory*. (L.A. Coser, ed. and trans.). Chicago: Chicago University Press.

Hall, Calvin. 1966. *The Meaning of Dreams*. New York: McGraw Hill.

Hall, Calvin S. and Robert Van de Castle. 1966. *The Content Analysis of Dreams*. New York: Appleton-Century-Crofts.

Hall, Stuart. 1996. "Introduction." In *Questions of Cultural Identity* (Stuart Hall and Paul DuGuy, eds.), pp. 1–17. London: Sage.

Hallpike, C. R. 1969. "Social hair." *Man* (n.s.) 4:254–264.

Haraway, Donna J. 1991. *Simians, Cyborgs, and Women: The Reinvention of Nature*. New York: Routledge.

Hare-Mustin, Rachel T. 1994. "Discourses in the Mirrored Room: A Postmodern Analysis of Therapy." *Family Process* 33:19–35.

Hartman, Ernest. 1981. "The Functions of Sleep and Memory Processing." In *Sleep, Dreams and Memory*. Advances in Sleep Research. Vol. 6. (William Fishbein, ed.), pp. 111–124. New York: Spectrum.

———. 1998. *Dreams and Nightmares*. New York: Plenum.

Hays, Sharon. 1996. *The Cultural Contradictions of Motherhood*. New Haven, CT: Yale University Press.

Hazlewood, Lee. 1966. *These Boots Are Made for Walking*. Burbank, CA: Reprise Records.

Heim, Pat. 1995. *Power Dead Even Rule*. Buffalo Grove, IL: Core Vision Media.

Heine, Steven J. and Darrin R. Lehman. 2004. "Move the Body, Change the Self: Acculturative Effects on the Self-Concept." In *The Psychological Foundations of Culture* (M. Schaller and C. S. Crandall, eds.), pp. 305–331. Mahwah, NJ: Lawrence Earlbaum Associates.

Hemingway, Ernest. 1940. *For Whom the Bell Tolls*. New York: Scribner.

Herdt, Gilbert H. 1987. *The Sambia*. New York: Holt, Rinehart and Winston.

Hill, Jane. 2005. "Finding Culture in Narratives." In *Finding Culture in Talk* (Naomi Quinn, ed.), pp. 157–202. New York: Palgrave Macmillan.

Hiltebeitel, Alf and Barbara D. Miller, eds. 1998. *Hair: Its Power and Meaning in Asian Cultures*. Albany: State University of New York Press.

Hjarnø, Jan. 1979/1980. *Social Reproduction*. Folk 21–22:72–123.

Hollan, Douglas. 1989. "The Personal Use of Dream Beliefs in the Toraja Highlands." *Ethos* 17:166–186.

———. 2000. "Constructivist Models of Mind, Contemporary Psychoanalysis, and the Development of Culture Theory." *American Anthropologist* 102:538–550.

———. 2003a. "Selfscape Dreams." In *Dreaming and the Self* (Jeannette Mageo, ed.), pp. 61–74. Albany: State University of New York Press.

———. 2003b "The Intersubjective Context of Dream Remembrance and Reporting: Dreams, Aging, and the Life Cycle in Toraja, Indonesia." In *Dream Travelers of the Western Pacific: Sleep Experiences and Culture in Australian Aboriginal, Melanesian, and Indonesian Societies* (Roger I. Lohmann, ed.), pp. 169–188. New York: Palgrave Macmillan.

Hollan, Douglas. 2005. "Dreaming in a Global World." In *A Companion to Psychological Anthropology* (C. Casey and R. B. Edgerton, eds.), pp. 90–102. Oxford: Blackwell Publishing.

Holland, Dorothy and Naomi Quinn. 1987. *Cultural Models in Language and Thought.* Cambridge, UK: Cambridge University Press.

Holland, Dorothy C. and Margaret A. Eisenhart. 1990. *Educated in Romance: Women, Achievement, and College Culture.* Chicago: University of Chicago Press.

Holland, Dorothy, William Lachicotte Jr., Debra Skinner, and Carole Cain. 1998. *Identity and Agency in Cultural Worlds.* Cambridge, MA: Harvard University Press.

Holt, D. and Thompson, C. J. 2004. "Man-of-Action Heroes: The Pursuit of Heroic Masculinity in Everyday Consumption." In *The Journal of Consumer Research* 31:425–440.

Horton, R. and R. Finnegan. 1973. *Modes of Thought: Essays on Thinking in Western and Non-Western Societies.* London: Faber and Faber.

Howard, Alan and Jeannette Mageo. 1996. "Introduction." In *Spirits in Culture, History, and Mind* (Jeannette Mageo and Alan Howard, eds.), pp. 1–10. New York: Routledge.

Hrdy, Sarah. 2009. *Mothers and Others: The Evolutionary Origins of Mutual Understanding.* Cambridge, MA: Harvard University Press.

Hsu, Francis L. K. 1961. "American Core Value and National Character." In *Psychological Anthropology: Approaches to Culture and Personality* (Francis L. K. Hsu, ed.), pp. 209–230. Homewood, IL: Dorsey.

Hunt, Harry T. 1989. *The Multiplicity of Dreams: Memory, Imagination and Consciousness.* New Haven, CT: Yale University Press.

Hyde, Janet S. 2005. "The Gender Similarity Hypothesis." *American Psychologist* 60:581–592.

Ingham, John M. 2007. "Matricidal Madness and Foucault's Anthropology: The Pierre Riviere Seminar." *Ethos* 35:130–158.

Irwin, Lee. 1994. *Dream Seekers: Native American Visionary Traditions of the Great Plains.* Norman: University of Oklahoma Press.

James, Karen. 1968. *The Endless Cycle: Migrant Life in the Yakima Valley, 1967.* Seattle: The Bureau of Community Development at University of Washington.

Jameson, Frederic. 1991. *Postmodernism, or the Cultural Logic of Late Capitalism.* Durham: Duke University Press.

Jennings, Jan, ed. 1990. *Roadside America.* Ames: Iowa State University Press.

Josephs, I. E. 1998. "Constructing One's Self in the City of the Silent: Dialogue, Symbols and the Role of 'as-if' in Self-development." *Human Development* 41:180–195.

Jung, Carl G. 1967. "Alchemical Studies." In *The Collected Works* (R. F. C. Hull, trans.). Vol. 13. Bollingen Series. Princeton: Princeton University Press.

———. 1966. "Two Essays on Analytical Psychology." In *The Collected Works*. Vol. 7.

———. 1968. "The Archetypes and the Collective Unconscious." In *The Collected Works*. Vol. 9.1.

———. 1970. "Mysterium Coniunctionis." In *The Collected Works*. Vol. 14.

———. 1972. "The Structure and Dynamics of the Psyche." In *The Collected Works*. Vol. 8.

———. 1976. *The Vision Seminars*. Vol. 2. Zurich: Spring.

Jung, Jae. 2008. "Contested Motherhood: Self and Modernity in South Korean Home-schooling." Ph.D. Dissertation. Washington State University.

Kahn, D. and J. A. Hobson. 1993. "Self-organization Theory of Dreaming." *Dreaming* 3:151–178.

Keller, Janet. 1992. "Schemes for Schemata." *New Directions in Psychological Anthropology* (Theodore Schwartz, Geoffrey M. White, and Catherine A. Lutz, eds.), pp. 59–67. Cambridge, UK: Cambridge University Press.

Kelly, Joan B. 2006. "Children's Living Arrangements Following Separation and Divorce: Insights from Empirical and Clinical Research." *Family Process* 46(1):35–52.

Kessler, Suzanne J. 1998. *Lessons from the Intersexed*. New Brunswick, NJ: Rutgers University Press.

Khan, M. R. 1974. "The Use and Abuse of a Dream." In *The Privacy of the Self*. London: Hogarth Press.

Kimmel, Michael. 1996. *Manhood in America: A Cultural History*. New York: The Free Press.

Kinnvall, Catarina. 2004. "Globalization and Religious Nationalism: Self, Identity, and the Search for Ontological Security." *Political Psychology* 25(5):741–767.

Kilroe, P. 2000. "The Dream as Text, the Dream as Narrative." *Dreaming* 10(3):125–137.

Klein, Melanie. 1988. *Love, Guilt and Reparation: and Other Works 1921–1945*. London: Virago Press.

Kleinberg, S. J. 1999. *Women in the United States, 1830–1945*. New Brunswick, NJ: Rutgers University Press.

Kluckhohn, Clyde and William Morgan. 1951. "Some Notes on Navaho Dreams." In *Essays in Honor of Géza Róheim* (Wilbur and Muensterger, eds.), pp. 120–131. New York: International Universities Press.

Kluger, Richard. 1977. *Simple Justice*. New York: Random House.

Kohut, Heinz. 1971. *The Analysis of the Self*. New York: International Universities Press.

———. 1977. *The Restoration of the Self*. Madison, CT: International Universities Press.

Kokkou, Martha and Dietrich Lehman. 1993. "a Model of Dreaming and Its Functional Significance: The State-Shift Hypothesis." In *The Functions of Dreaming* (A. Moffitt, M. Kramer, and R. Hoffman, eds.), pp. 139–196. Albany: State University of New York Press.

Kondo, Dorinne K. 1990. *Crafting Selves*. Chicago: University of Chicago Press.

Kracke, Waud H. 1987. "Myths in Dreams, Thoughts in Images: An Amazonian Contribution to the Psychoanalytic Theory of Primary Process." In *Dreaming: Anthropological and Psychological Perspectives* (Barbara Tedlock, ed.), pp. 31–54. Cambridge, UK: Cambridge University Press.

———. 2003. "Dream Ghost of a Tiger, a System of Human Words." In *Dreaming and the Self* (Jeannette Mageo, ed.), pp. 155–164. Albany, NY: State University of New York Press.

Kreider, Rose M. and Jason M. Fields. 2002. "Number, Timing, and Duration of Marriages and Divorces." In *Current Population Reports,* pp. 70–80. U.S. Census Bureau Current Population Reports: Washington, D.C.

Kristeva, Julia. 1986. *The Kristeva Reader* (L. S. Roudiez, trans.). Oxford: Basil Blackwell.

Kusserow, Adrie. 2004. *American Individualisms: Child-rearing and Social Class in Three Neighborhoods*. New York: Palgrave Macmillan.

Lacan, Jacques. 1968. "The Mirror Phase." *New Left Review* 51:70–79.

———. 1977a. *Écrits: A Selection* (Alan Sheridan trans.). New York: W. W. Norton.

———. 1977b. *The Four Fundamental Concepts of Psycho-Analysis* (Alan Sheridan, trans.). New York: W. W. Norton.

Lacquer, Thomas. 1990. *Making Sex*. Cambridge, MA: Harvard University Press.

Lakoff, Andrew. 1996. "Sorry, I'm Not Myself Today." In *Spaces, Worlds and Grammar* (Gilles Fauconnier and Eve Sweetser eds.), pp. 91–123. Chicago: Chicago University Press.

———. 2001. "How Metaphor Structures Dreams." In *Dreams* (Kelly Bulkeley, ed.), pp. 265–284. New York: Palgrave Macmillan.

Lancaster, J. B. 1997. "The Evolutionary History of Human Parental Investment in Relation to Population Growth and Social Stratification." In *Feminism and Evolutionary Biology* (P. A. Gotway, ed.), pp. 466–488. New York: Chapman and Hall.

Leach, Edmund R. 1958. "Magical Hair." *Journal of the Royal Anthropological Institute* 88:147–164.

Leacock, Eleanor. 1981. *Myths of Male Dominance*. New York: Monthly Review Press.

Lévi-Strauss, C. 1966. *The Savage Mind*. London: Weidenfeld and Nicholson.

————. 1970. *The Raw and the Cooked* (J. and D. Weightnor, trans.). New York: Harper and Row.

Levy, Robert I. 1973. *Tahitians: Mind and Experience in the Society Islands*. Chicago: Chicago University Press.

————. 1974. "Tahiti, Sin, and the Question of Integration between Personality and Sociocultural Systems." In *Culture and Personality* (Robert A. LeVine, ed.), pp. 287–306. New York: Aldine.

————. 1984. "Emotion, Knowing, and Culture." In *Culture Theory* (Richard A. Shweder and Robert LeVine, eds.), pp. 214–237. Cambridge, UK: Cambridge University Press.

Lincoln, Jackson S. 1935. *The Dream in Primitive Cultures*. Baltimore: Williams and Wilkins.

Linger, Daniel T. 1992. *Dangerous Encounters*. Stanford, CA.: Stanford University Press.

Lohmann, Roger I. 2003a. "Supernatural Encounters of Asabano in Two Traditions and Three States of Consciousness." In *Dream Travelers of the Western Pacific* (Roger I. Lohmann, ed.), pp. 189–210. New York: Palgrave Macmillan.

Lohmann, Roger I, ed.. 2003b. *Dream Travelers of the Western Pacific*. New York: Palgrave Macmillan.

Lutz, Catherine. 1990. "Engendered Emotions." In *Language and the Politics of Emotion* (C. Lutz and L. Abu-Lughod, eds.), pp. 69–91. Cambridge, UK: Cambridge University Press.

Mageo, Jeannette. 1992. "Male Transvestism and Culture Change in Samoa." *American Ethnologist* 19:443–459.

————. 1994. "Hairdos and Don'ts." *Man* 29:407–432.

————. 1995. "The Reconfiguring Self." *American Anthropologist*. 97(2):282–296.

————. 1996. "Samoa, on the Wilde Side: Male Transvestism, Oscar Wilde, and Liminality in Making Gender." *Ethos* 24:588–627.

————. 1998. *Theorizing Self in Samoa: Emotions, Genders, and Sexualities*. Ann Arbor: Michigan University Press.

————. 2001a. "Dream Play and Discovering Cultural Psychology." *Ethos* 29:187–217.

————. 2001b. "On Memory Genres." In *Cultural Memory: Reconfiguring History and Identity in the Pacific* (Jeannette Mageo ed.), pp. 11–36. Honolulu: University of Hawai'i Press.

————. 2002a. "Self-models and Sexual Agency." In *Power and the Self* (Jeannette Mageo, ed.), pp. 141–176. Cambridge, UK: Cambridge University Press.

————. 2002b. "Intertextual Interpretation, Fantasy, and Samoan Dreams." *Culture and Psychology* 8:417–448.

————. 2002c. "Towards a Multidimensional Model of the Self." *The Journal of Anthropological Research* 58:339–365.

————. 2003. "Theorizing Dreaming and the Self." In *Dreaming and the Self* (J. Mageo, ed.), pp. 3–22. Albany, NY: State University of New York Press.

Mageo, Jeannette. 2005. "Male Gender Instability and War." *Peace Review* 17(1):73–80.

———. 2006. "Figurative Dream Analysis and U.S. Traveling Identities." *Ethos* 13(4):456–487.

———. 2007. "Dream Stages: Stress/Success Models in US." Paper presented at the 10th biennial meetings of the Society for Psychological Anthropology, Manhattan Beach, CA.

———. 2008a. "Zones of Ambiguity and Identity Politics in Samoa." *Journal of the Royal Anthropological Institute* 14:61–78.

———. 2008b. "Transgender Issues." In *The Encyclopedia of the Modern World*. Oxford University Press.

———. 2010. "Internalization and the Dream: The U.S. Cinderella Model of Sexuality and Agency." *Anthropological Theory* 10(3):229–247.

———. 2011. "Empathy and 'As-if' Attachment in Samoa." In *The Anthropology of Empathy: Experiencing the Lives of Others* (D. Hollan and J. Throop, eds.), New York: Berghahn.

Mageo, Jeannette and Bruce M. Knauft. 2002. "Theorizing Power and the Self, Jeannette Mageo and Bruce M. Knauft." In *Power and the Self* (Jeannette Mageo, ed.), pp. 1–29. Cambridge, UK: Cambridge University Press.

Mageo, Jeannette and Linda Stone. 2005. "Screen Images in Science and Social Science." *Studies in Gender and Sexuality* 6:77–104.

Malinowski, Bronislav. 2001. *Sex and Repression in Savage Society.* London: Routledge.

Marcus, Steven. 1966. *The Other Victorians.* New York: Basic Books.

Marcuse, Herbert. 1955. *Eros and Civilization.* Boston: Beacon.

Markus, Hazel R. and Shinobu Kitayama. 1991. "Culture and the Self: Implications for Cognition, Emotion and Motivation." *Psychological Review* 98:224–253.

Masters, W. and V. Johnson. 1965a. "The Sexual Response Cycle of the Human Female. Vol. I. Gross Anatomical Considerations." In *Sex Research* (J. Money, ed.), pp. 53–89. New York: Holt, Rinehart, and Winston.

———. 1965b. "The Sexual Response Cycle of the Human Female." Vol. I. The Clitoris. In *Sex Research* (J. Money, ed.), pp. 90–104. New York: Holt, Rinehart, and Winston.

———. 1966. *Human Sexual Response.* Boston: Little, Brown.

Maugham, W. Somerset. 1915. *Of Human Bondage.* New York: G. H. Doran.

McClintock, Anne. 1995. *Imperial Leather.* New York: Routledge.

McKee, Nancy and Linda Stone. 2007. "Gender and Culture in America." Cornwall-on-Hudson, NY: Sloan.

McKinnon, Susan. 2005. *Neo-liberal Genetics: The Myths and Moral Tales of Evolutionary Psychology.* Chicago: Prickly Paradigm, University of Chicago Press.

McLean, Kate C., Monisha Pasupathi, and Jennifer L. Pals. 2007. "Selves Creating Stories Creating Selves: A Process Model of Self-Development." *Personality and Social Psychology Review* 11(3):262–278.

Mead, Margaret. 1942a. *And Keep Your Powder Dry: An Anthropologist Looks at America.* New York: W. Morrow.

———. 1942b. "Balinese Character." In *Balinese Character.* (Coauthored with Gregory Bateson), pp. 1–48. New York: The New York Academy of Sciences.

———. 1961 *Coming of Age in Samoa.* New York: Morrow Quill.

Meigs, Anna. 1984. *Food, Sex, and Pollution.* New Brunswick: Rutgers University Press.

Merleau-Ponty, Maurice. 1962. *Phenomenology of Perception* (Colin Smith, trans.). London: Routledge and Kegan Paul.

Miller, Peggy J. 1994. "Narrative Practices: Their Role in Socialization and Self-construction." In *The Remembering Self: Construction and Accuracy in Self-narrative* (U. Neisser and R. Fivush, eds.), pp. 158–179. Cambridge, UK: Cambridge University Press.

Miller, Peggy J., Heidi Fung, and Judith Mintz. 1996. "Self-Construction through Narrative Practices." *Ethos* 24(2):237–280.

Minsky, Jean M. 1975. *Stories, Scripts, and Scenes: Aspects of Schema Theory.* Hillsdale, NJ: Lawrence Erlbaum.

Montgomery, Laura M. 1997. "'It's Just What I Like': Explaining Persistent Patterns of Gender Stratification in the Life Choices of College Students." Paper presented at the annual meeting of the American Anthropological Association, Washington, DC, November 1997.

Morris, William. 1979. *The American Heritage Dictionary of the English Language.* Boston: Houghton Mifflin.

Moyle, Robert. 1981. *Fagogo.* Oxford: Oxford University Press for Auckland University Press.

Muller, Heidi. 1989. "Good Roads." In *Matters of the Heart.* CD. Twisp, WA: Cascadia Music.

Mulvey, Laura. 1992. "Visual Pleasure and Narrative Cinema." In *The Sexual Subject: A Screen Reader in Sexuality* (M. Merck, ed.), pp. 22–34. London: Routledge.

Murray, David J. 1995. *Gestalt Psychology and the Cognitive Revolution.* New York: Harvester Wheatsheaf.

Neisser, Ulric. 1967. *Cognitive Psychology.* New York: Appleton-Century-Crofts.

Nishida, Masaki, Jori Pearsall, Randy L. Buckner, and Matthew P. Walker. 2009. "REM Sleep, Prefrontal Theta, and the Consolidation of Human Emotional Memory." *Cerebral Cortex* 19(5):1158–1166.

Nordstrom, Alison Devine. 1995. "Photography of Samoa." In *Picturing Paradise: Colonial Photography of Samoa, 1875 to 1925* (C. Blanton, ed.), pp. 11–40, 75. Daytona Beach, Florida and Cologne, Germany: Southeast Museum of Photography and Rautenstrauch-Joest-Museum of Ethnology.

Noy, Pinchas. 1969. "A Revision of the Psychoanalytic Theory of the Primary Process." *International Journal of Psychoanalysis* 50:155–178.

Noy, Pinchas. 1979. "The Psychoanalytic Theory of Cognitive Development." *The Psychoanalytic Study of the Child* 34:169–216.

Nuckolls, Charles W. 1998. *Culture: A Problem that Cannot be Solved.* Madison, WI: University of Wisconsin Press.

Obeyesekere, Gananath. 1981. *Medusa's Hair.* Chicago: Chicago University Press.

———. 1984. *The Cult of the Goddess Pattini.* Chicago: University of Chicago Press.

———. 1990. "Symbolic Remove and the Work of Culture." In *The Work of Culture: Symbolic Transformations in Psychoanalysis and Anthropology.* pp. 51–70. Chicago: University of Chicago Press.

Ochs, Elinor. 1982. "Talking to Children in Western Samoa." *Language in Society* 11:77–104.

Ogden, Thomas H.. 2004. "On Holding and Containing, Being, and Dreaming." *International Journal of Psychoanalysis* 85(6):1349–1364.

Orenstein, Peggy. 2011. *Cinderella Ate My Daughter: Dispatches from the Front Lines of the New Girlie-Girl Culture.* New York: HarperCollins.

Ortner, Sherry B. 2003. *New Jersey Dreaming: Capital, Culture, and the Class of '58.* Durham: Duke University Press.

Palombo, Stanley, R. 1978. *Dreaming and Memory: A New Information-Processing Model.* New York: Basic Books.

Peacock, James L. 1984. "Religion and Life History: An Exploration in Cultural Psychology." In *Text, Play, and Story* (E. M. Brumer, ed.), pp. 19–55. Washington, DC: American Technological Society.

Perls, Frederick S. 1971. *Gestalt Therapy Verbatim.* New York: Bantam.

Pesant, Nicholas and Antonio Zadra. 2004. "Working with Dreams in Therapy: What Do We Know and What Should We Do?" *Clinical Psychology Review* 24(5):489–512.

Petermann, Bruno. 1932. *The Gestalt Theory and the Problem of Configuration* (M. Fortes, trans.). New York: Harcourt Brace.

Piaget, Jean. 1985. *The Equilibration of Cognitive Structures.* Chicago: University of Chicago Press.

Price-Williams, Douglas. 1999. "In Search of Mythopoetic Thought." *Ethos* 27:25–32.

Proust, Marcel. 1956. *La Recherché Du Temps Perdu* (C. K. Scott Moncrieff and Terence Kiolmartin, trans.) New York: Random House.

Quinn, Naomi. 1987. "Convergent Evidence for a Cultural Model of American Marriage." In *Cultural Models in Language and Thought* (D. Holland and N. Quinn, eds.), pp. 173–192 Cambridge, UK: Cambridge University Press.

———. 1996. "Culture and Contradiction: The Case of Americans Reasoning about Marriage." *Ethos* 24(3):391–425.

———, ed. 2005. *Finding Culture in Talk.* New York: Palgrave Macmillan.

Reiser, Morton F.. 2001. "The Dream in Contemporary Psychiatry." *American Journal of Psychiatry* 158:351–359.

Ricoeur, Paul. 1981. *Hermeneutics and the Human Sciences* (J. B. Thompson, trans.). Cambridge, UK: Cambridge University Press.

Ritchie, James and Jane Ritchie. 1979. *Growing up in Polynesia*. Sydney: George Allen and Unwin.

———. 1989. "Socialization and Character Development." In *Developments in Polynesian Ethnology* (Alan Howard and Robert Borofsky, eds.), pp. 95–135. Honolulu: University of Hawai'i Press.

Robinson, William. [1962] 1988. "Smoking." In *Rise Up Singing* (Peter Blood-Patterson, ed.). Bethlehem, PA: Sing Out Corporation.

Romney, A. K., Susan C. Weller, and William C. Batchelder. 1986. "Culture as Consensus: A Theory of Culture and Informant Accuracy." *American Anthropologist* 88(2):313–338.

Ross, Norbert. 2004. *Culture and Cognition: Implications for Theory and Method*. Thousand Oaks, CA: Sage Publications.

Rotenberg, Vadim S. 2004. "The Psychophysiology of REM Sleep in Relation to Mechanisms of Psychiatric Disorders." In *Sleep Psychiatry* (A.Z. Golbin, H.M. Kravitz, and L.G. Keith, eds.), pp. 35–63. London: Taylor and Francis.

Sacks, Oliver. 1996. "Neurological Dreams." In *Trauma and Dreams* (Deirdre Barrett, ed.), pp. 212–216. Cambridge, MA: Harvard University Press.

Sanday, Peggy R. 1990. *Fraternity Gang Rape*. New York: New York University Press.

Schneider, David M. 1968. *American Kinship: A Cultural Account*. Chicago: University of Chicago Press.

Schoeffel, Penelope. 1979. "The Ladies Row of Thatch: Women and Rural Development in Western Samoa." *Pacific Perspective* 8(2):1–11.

Schredl, M. and R. Palmer. 1998. "Geschlechtsunterschiede in Angstträumen von Schüler-Innen." *Praxis der Kinderpsychologie und Kinderpsychiatrie*. 47:463–476.

Schultz, E. [(1911] n.d. "Samoan Laws Concerning the Family, Real Estate and Succession." (Rev. E Bellward and R.C. Hisaioa, trans.). University of Hawai'i Pacific Collection.

Shaw, T.A. 1994. "The Semiotic Mediation of Identity." *Ethos* 22:83–119.

Shore, Bradd. 1981. "Sexuality and Gender in Samoa." In *Sexual Meanings* (S. B. Ortner and H. Whitehead, eds.), pp. 192–215. New York: Cambridge University Press.

———. 1996. *Culture in Mind*. New York: Oxford University Press.

Shulman, David and Guy G. Stroumsa. 1999. *Dream Cultures*. New York: Oxford University Press.

Shweder, Richard A. 1991. *Thinking through Culture*. Cambridge, MA: Harvard University Press.

Slater, Philip. 1968. *The Glory of Hera*. Boston: Beacon.

Small, Meredith. 1993. *Female Choices*. Ithaca, NY: Cornell University Press.

Somer, M.R. 1994. "The Narrative Construction of Identity: A Relational and Network Approach." *Theory and Society* 23:605–649.

Spiro, Melford E. 1987. "Religious Systems as Culturally Constituted Defense Mechanisms." In *Culture and Human Nature: Theoretical Papers of Melford e. Spiro* (Benjamin Kilborne and L.L. Langness, eds.), pp. 145–160. Chicago: University of Chicago Press, 1987.

———— 2003. "The Anthropological Import of Blocked Access to Dream Associations." In *Dreaming and the Self* (Jeannette Mageo, ed.), pp. 165–174. Albany, NY: State University of New York Press.

States, Bert O. 1993. *Dreaming and Storytelling.* Ithaca: Cornell University Press.

————. 2000. "Inner Speech and Thought and Bizarreness in Dreams." *Dreaming* 10(4):179–192.

————. 2001. "Dreams: The Royal Road to Metaphor." *Substance* 94/95:104–118.

Stephen, Michele. 1989. "Self, the Sacred Other, and Autonomous Imagination." In *The Religious Imagination in New Guinea* (Gilbert Herdt and Michele Stephen, eds.), pp. 41–64. New Brunswick: Rutgers University Press.

————. 1995. "Dreaming and the Hidden Self." In *A'aisa's Gifts*, pp. 111–173. Berkeley: University of California Press.

————. 1997. "Cargo Cults, Cultural Creativity and Autonomous Imagination." *Ethos* 25:333–358.

————. 2003. "Memory, Emotion and the Imaginal Mind." In *Dreaming and the Self* (Jeannette Mageo, ed.), pp. 97–132 Albany, NY: State University of New York Press.

Stern, W. (1938). *General Psychology from the Personal Standpoint.* New York: Macmillan.

Stewart, Kilton. 1951. "Dream Theory in Malaya." *Complex* 6:21–33.

Stickgold, Robert and Matthew Walker. 2004. "To Sleep, Perchance to Gain Creative Insight." *Trends in Cognitive Science* 8(5):191–192.

Stickgold, Robert, J. Allen Hobson, Roar Fosse, and Magdalena Fosse. 2001. "Sleep, Learning and Dreams: Off-Line Memory Reprocessing." *Science* 294(5544):1052–1057.

Stone, Linda. 2004. :Has the World Turned? Kinship and Family in Contemporary American Soap Opera." In *Kinship and Family: An Anthropological Reader* (Robert Parker and Linda Stone, eds.), pp. 395–407. Madeleine, MA: Blackwell.

Strauch, Inge and Barbara Meier. 1996. *In Search of Dreams.* Albany: State University of New York Press.

Strauss, Claudia. 1992a. "Models and Motives." In *Human Motives and Cultural Models* (Roy R. D'Andrade and Claudius Strauss eds.), pp. 1–20. Cambridge, UK: Cambridge University Press.

————. 1992b. "What Makes Tony Run? Schemas as Motives Reconsidered." In *Human Motives and Cultural Models* (Roy R.

D'Andrade and Claudius Strauss eds.), pp.191–225. Cambridge, UK: Cambridge University Press.

Strauss, Claudia and Naomi Quinn. 1997. *A Cognitive Theory of Cultural Meaning.* Cambridge, UK: Cambridge University Press.

Suarez-Orozco, Marcelo. 1993. "A Psychoanalytic Study of Argentine Soccer." *The Psychoanalytic Study of Society* 18:211–234.

Tannen, Deborah. 1990. *You Just Don't Understand.* New York: Balllantine.

———. 2001. *He Said, She Said.* Video. Los Angeles: Into the Classroom Media.

Tavris, Carol. 1992. *The Mismeasure of Women.* New York: Simon and Schuster.

Tedlock, Barbara. 1981. "Quiché Maya Dream Interpretation." *Ethos* 9(4):313–330.

———. 1987. *Dreaming: Anthropological and Psychological Interpretations* (Barbara Tedlock, ed.). Cambridge, UK: Cambridge University Press.

———. 1991. "The New Anthropology of Dreaming." *Dreaming* 1(2):161–178.

———. 1992. "The Role of Dreams and Visionary Narratives in Mayan Cultural Survival." *Ethos* 20:453–476.

———. 2001. "The New Anthropology of the Dreaming." In *Dreams* (Kelly Bulkeley, ed.), pp.249–264. New York: Palgrave Macmillan.

Turner, Victor. 1977. *The Ritual Process: Structure and Anti-Structure.* Chicago: Adline.

Tylor, E. B. 1873. *Primitive Culture.* 2 Vols. London: John Murray.

Urban, Greg. 1992. "The 'I' of Discourse." In *Semiotics of Self and Society* (Benjamin Lee and Greg Urban, eds.), pp.27–51. Berlin: Mouton de Gruyter.

Valsiner, Jaan. 1989. *Human Development and Culture.* Lexington, MA: Lexington Books.

Van de Castle, Robert. 1983. "Animal Figures in Fantasy and Dreams." In *New Perspectives on Our Lives with Companion Animals* (A. Kacher and A. Beck, eds.), pp.148—173. Philadelphia: University of Pennsylvania Press.

———. 1994. *Our Dreaming Mind.* New York: Ballantine.

Von Grunebaum, G. E. and Roger Caillois, eds. 1966. *The Dream and Human Societies.* Berkeley: University of California Press.

Vygotsky, L. S. 1962. *Thought and Language* (E. Hanfmann and G. Vakar, trans.). New York: John Wiley and Sons.

———. 1978. "Internalization of Higher Psychological Functions." In *Mind in Society* (Michael Cole, ed.), pp.52–57. Cambridge, MA: Harvard University Press.

Wagner, Roy. 2001. *An Anthropology of the Subject.* Berkeley: University of California Press.

Walker, Matthew P. 2005. "A Refined Model of Sleep and the Time Course of Memory Foundation." *Behavioral and Brain Sciences* 28(1):51–104.

Wallace, Anthony. 1952. "Handsome Lake and the Great Revival in the West." *American Quarterly* Summer:149–165.

Werner, Heinz. [1948]1961. *Comparative Psychology of Mental Development*. New York: Science Editions.

Westen,. D. 1994. "Toward an Integrative Model of Affect-regulation." *Journal of Perosnality* 62:641–667.

Whiting, Beatrice. 1978. "The Dependency Hang-up and Experiments in Alternative Lifestyles." In *Major Social Issues* (J. Milton Yinger and Stephen J. Cutler, eds.), pp. 217–228. New York: Macmillan.

Whiting, John W. M. 1961. "Socialization Process and Personality." In *Psychological Anthropology: Approaches to Culture and Personality* (Francis L. K. Hsu, ed.), pp. 355–380. Homewood, IL: Dorsey.

Wilde, Oscar. [1889] 1972. "The Decay of Lying." In *Essays by Oscar Wilde* (H. Pearson, ed.), pp. 33–72. Freeport, NY: Books for Libraries Press. [Reprint from 1950 ed.].

Winnicott, Donald W. 1967. *Playing and Reality*. London: Tavistock.

Index

absent fathers, 26–28, 56, 76, 100
  divorce, 31, 44
  emotional absence, 102–103
  fails to foster risk-taking for
    daughter, 108, 112–114, 121
  in Tomb Raider, 45–46
  in Viva la Bam, 49
  see also Close Family metamodel;
    Supportive Dad model
acceptance, 60, 69–71, 73–76, 84,
  90, 107
Active Imagination, 63
Agent/Object Sexuality metamodel,
  75–76, 78
  see also metamodels; Pinup
    Sexuality model; Voyeuristic
    Sexuality
Attachment schema, 66, 85, 88,
  89, 101
  and Car self-model, 144
  studies of, 53
  see also Care schema;
    Foundational schemas, Care
    schema
Autonomy schema
  and Car self-model, 127, 132
  confusion about, 129
  and independence, 150–152,
    155, 158, 185n4
  singular versus inclusive 132–144
  see also Free Individual model

Bad Boy Masculinity model, 29
  and cars, 77–78, 115–119,
    135, 162
  as rebel, 184n15
  in Viva la Bam, 48–49, 51
  see also Supermasculinity model

Baudrillard, Jean, 48, 61, 72, 74, 110
Benjamin, Jessica, 44, 113, 133
Bettelheim, Bruno, 71
biopower, 79, 84, 90
  see also Foucault, Michel
bizarreness, 4–5, 94, 99
boundaries
  confused (eroded), 42–43,
    46–47, 139, 143, 150–153
  porous (inclusive), 128, 132, 135,
    137, 145, 150–152
  sacred, 34, 132, 141, 150, 155
  see also Car self-model; mother-
    child over-involvement; witch
Boyfriend/Girlfriend model, 2, 46,
  60–91, 150–151
  see also Girlfriend model; major
    models, Girlfriend model
Bruner, Jerome, 2
Busyness schema, 102, 107, 109, 121
  see also Moving on model
Butler, Judith, 70

Car self-model, 33–34, 103–107,
  126–159
  and Bad Boy Masculinity, 77–78,
    115–120
  and transiting schema, 70
  see also Free Individual model;
    Intersubjective Person model;
    metamodels; Traveling Self
    metamodel
Care schema, 52–55, 78,
  86–87, 140
  boyfriend/girlfriend, 119
  and cliques, 185n4
  and fixing, 152, 153, 155
  and God, 142

Care schema—*Continued*
    lack of, 117–118, 121
    self-care, 77, 90
    see also Attachment schema;
        Devoted Mom model;
        Foundational schemas;
        Girlfriend model; Help schema
Choice-as-Agency model, 43–47,
    59–91, 112–114, 156
    see also Free Individual model;
        major models; Risk-taking
        schema
Cinderella Femininity model, 66,
    76–77, 89, 90, 164, 166, 185n4
    and cliques, 54
    as default model, 119
    and feet, 51
    Hypergamy, 9–10, 68
    men in Cinderella position, 74,
        82, 86–87
    today, 70–71
    weddings, 110
    see also Dualistic Gender
        metamodel; major models;
        Perfect Fit schema
cliffhanger (thriller), 40, 43–44,
    77, 138–139, 142, 145
Clifford, James, 13, 16, 157, 162
Clique model, 54, 117, 121, 132,
    185n4
    see also Attachment schema;
        Insiders/Outsider schema
Close Family metamodel, 26–58,
    100–106, 120, 150, 162–163
    see also Devoted Mom model;
        Good Kid model; metamodels;
        Supportive Dad model
Companionship schema, 48,
    99–100, 117
    see also Foundational schemas;
        Guyfriends model
Competition schema, 107–109,
    134, 149, 185n3
    see also Foundational schemas;
        Free Individual model;
        Supermasculinity model

Content Analysis, 124
Control schema, 46, 129
    and dominance, 85, 88, 90
    and fixing, 82–84
    losing, 137, 145
    over girlfriend, 60, 88, 89
    over one's body, 60, 74, 150
    seeking indirectly, 146–149, 150
    sexual, 70
    see also Car self-model;
        Foundational schemas; Free
        Individual model
counteridentities, 53, 147,
    155–159, 164
Cultural Consensus theory, 6,
    157–158

Damsel in Distress tales, 39–40,
    145–148
    see also Supermasculinity model
D'Andrade, Roy, 60, 97, 186n4
Detachment schema, 37, 89, 117, 139
    and Bad Boy masculinity, 53
    and cliques, 185n4
    dream frame, 55
    and fixing, 90
    and risk-taking, 44–46, 85, 108
    and Supermasculinity model,
        80–83, 118
    see also Foundational schemas;
        Free Individual model
Devil-may-care schema, 53, 78,
    116, 135
    see also Bad Boy masculinity
        model; Impulse Gratification
        schema
Devoted Mom model, 27–28, 41,
    44, 78, 97, 183n6
    and surveillance, 52–54
    see also Care schema; Close
        Family metamodel; major
        models
dolls, 85–89, 110–112, 163
    and cliques, 185n4
Dominance schema, 117, 149
    position, 80

struggle for, 90
and Supermasculinity, 84–89
dreamwork, 56, 79, 142–144,
150, 175
dressing up, 61, 70, 72,
109–111, 150
see also Cinderella Femininity
model; Perfect Fit schema
Dressler, William W., 157
see also Cultural Consensus
theory
Dreyfus, Hubert L., 95, 121–122
Dualistic Gender metamodel,
34–35, 170
see also Cinderella Femininity
model; metamodels;
Supermasculinity model

eating disorders, 43, 150
Electra, 42, 116
empathy, 151–156
Extraordinary Powers schema, 31,
33, 38, 48, 80, 88
see also Supermasculinity
model; Television shows,
Superman

feet, 9, 28–40, 47, 56, 70, 73
fixing, 130
others, 15–16, 150, 152,
155–156
as problem-solving, 35–36, 38
and Supermasculinity model, 50,
79–84, 90
Foucault, Michel, 76–77, 91
see also biopower
Foundational schemas, 46, 54,
169–171, 175
Attachment schema, 66, 85, 88,
89, 101
Autonomy schema, 150–152,
155, 158, 185n4
Care schema, 52–55, 78,
86–87, 140
Companionship schema, 48,
99–100, 117

Competition schema, 107–109,
134, 149, 185n3
Control schema, 46, 129
Detachment schema, 37, 89,
117, 139
Perfect Fit schema, 70, 72–77,
82, 110–111, 151
Problem-solving schema, 35, 37,
38, 82, 152
Protecting schema, 54, 138, 142,
145, 147
Recognition schema, 66, 133, 140
Risk-taking schema, 116, 129
Transiting schema, 16, 70, 127,
137, 139, 144
fraternal tales, 39, 86–88
Free Individual model, 2, 27–29,
49, 65–66, 84
and Car self-model, 126–127,
129, 132, 139, 151, 155–156
and Choice-as-Agency model, 112
in Tomb Raider, 46–47
see also major models
Freud, Sigmund, 7, 39, 41, 56, 83,
94, 120, 133, 134
Friendship, 98–100, 113, 116–117
see also Boyfriend/Girlfriend
model; Clique model;
Girlfriend model; Guyfriends
model

Games, 80–81, 85, 88, 95, 107–108,
121, 163, 168
Gestalt psychology, 94
Gestalt Therapy, 63
Giddens, Anthony, 3, 16, 69, 138
Gilligan, Carol, 78, 132, 134
Girlfriend model, 54–55, 78, 117,
145, 185n4
see also Attachment schema;
Boyfriend/Girlfriend model;
Clique model; major models
Good Kid model, 36, 50–55, 124
see also Close Family
metamodel; Help schema;
major models

Guyfriends model, 48, 54, 99
　see also Companionship schema;
　　major models

hair, 32, 35, 51, 71, 106,
　109–110, 141
Hall, Calvin, 124, 184n2, 186n6
happiness, 68, 72–73
Help schema (giving/getting), 50,
　128, 139, 151, 153–155
　see also Care schema; Good Kid
　　model; Intersubjective Person
　　model
Hollan, Douglas, 95
　see also selfscape dreams
Holland, Dorothy C. and Margaret
　A. Eisenhart, 8, 22, 109
Holland, Dorothy C. et. al., 165
hunting, 30, 32–40, 56, 102
hypergamy, 8–10, 65–71
　see also Cinderella Femininity
　　model
hypocognition, 2, 62, 96
Hysterical Female model, 152–153

Impulse Gratification schema,
　48–49, 52, 78, 116, 135
　see also Bad Boy Masculinity
　　model
Insiders/Outsider schema, 54,
　117–118
　see also Clique model
Intersubjective Person model,
　133–134, 137–149
　see also Benjamin, Jessica; Car
　　self-model; Traveling Self
　　metamodel
intertextuality, 25–55
　see also Kristeva, Julia

Jung, Carl G., 13, 59, 63, 122, 147

Klein, Melanie, 42–43
Knight (tales), 39, 54, 145, 184n11
　see also Supermasculinity model

Kristeva, Julia, 23, 25
Kusserow, Adrie, 28

Lacan, Jacques, 5, 24, 32, 39, 53,
　64, 77, 94
Levy, Robert I., 2, 62, 96, 132–133
　see also hypocognition
Lohmann, Roger, 57, 183n1, 186n5

major models, 14, 169–171
　Boyfriend/Girlfriend model, 2,
　　46, 60–91, 150–151
　Choice-as-Agency model, 43–47,
　　59–91, 112–114, 156
　Cinderella Femininity model,
　　66, 76–77, 89, 90, 164, 166,
　　185n4
　Devoted Mom, 27–28, 41, 44,
　　78, 97, 183n6
　Free Individual model, 2, 27–29,
　　49, 65–66, 84
　Girlfriend model, 54–55, 78,
　　117, 145, 185n4
　Good Kid model, 36, 50–55, 124
　Guyfriends model, 48, 54, 99
　Intersubjective Person model,
　　133–134, 137–149
　Moving on model, 97–121,
　　149, 163
　Pets model, 84–89
　Pinup Sexuality model, 75–76,
　　78, 119, 166
　Supermasculinity model, 31,
　　79–82
　Supportive Dad model, 26–28,
　　32, 44–46, 97, 112–114, 116
　Voyeuristic Sexuality model,
　　75–76, 85, 89
Marcuse, Herbert, 2, 49
　see also performance principles
marrying, see weddings
Mead, Margaret, 51, 66
metamodels, 26, 133, 134,
　169–171, 175
　Agent/Object Sexuality, 75–76, 78

Car self-model (Traveling Self),
33–34, 70, 77–78, 103–107
Close Family, 26–58, 100–106,
120, 150, 162–163
Dualistic Gender, 34–35, 170
Friendship, 98–100, 113,
116–117
mnemonic meanings, 56–57
mother-child over-involvement, 37,
42–43, 46, 53, 54, 143, 150
see also boundaries, confused
(eroded)
Movies, 84, 88, 89, 138
Cinderella (Walt Disney's), 29
*Guess Who's Coming to
Dinner*, 68
Harry and the Hendersons, 29,
30, 32
How to Marry a Millionaire,
9–10
The Littlest Mermaid (Walt
Disney's), 42
Oceans 11, 39
Pretty Woman, 9–10
Sasquatch Mountain, 29, 30,
33, 38
Saving Private Ryan, 39
Sex and the City, 10
Sleeping Beauty (Walt Disney's),
40–43
*Snow White and the Seven
Dwarfs* (Walt Disney's), 42
Superman, 31, 37
Tomb Raider, 45–46, 184n14
When Harry met Sally, 60
Moving on model, 97–121, 149, 163
see also Car self-model; Free
Individual model; major
models; Traveling Self
metamodel

Nuckolls, Charles W., 155

Obeyesekere, Gananath, 7, 137,
167–168, 182

Oedipus, 13, 26, 37, 39, 42, 50–55,
59, 85
post-Oedipal, 49
Options, *see* Choice-as-Agency
model

Perfect Fit schema, 70, 72–77, 82,
110–111, 151
see also Cinderella Femininity
model; Foundational schemas;
Pinup Sexuality model
performance principles, 2, 49, 62,
99, 102, 119
see also Marcuse, Herbert
Perls, Fritz, 63
Pet model, 84–89, 163, 185n2
see also Care schema; major
models
Piaget, Jean, 32
Pinup Sexuality model, 75–76, 78,
119, 166
see also Agent/Object Sexuality
metamodel; major models;
Perfect Fit schema; Voyeuristic
Sexuality
Problem-solving schema, 35, 37,
38, 82, 152
see also fixing; Foundational
schemas; Free Individual
model; Supermasculinity
model
Protecting schema, 54, 138, 142,
145, 147
see also Supermasculinity model;
Supportive Dad model

Quinn, Naomi, 3, 4, 19

Recognition schema, 66, 133, 140
see also Boyfriend/Girlfriend
model; Devoted Mom
model; Foundational
schemas; Girlfriend model;
Intersubjective Person model
REM dreams, 2–6, 164

Rescuing schema
    failure to, 145–147, 149–156
    and inclusive autonomy, 139,
        141, 142–143, 150–156
    and Supermasculinity model, 31,
        35, 54
    see also Help schema; Protecting
        schema
Risk-taking schema, 116, 129
    and detachment, 85
    fear of, 53
    and modernity, 28, 138–139
    and problem-solving, 37
    and transitional space, 28, 44,
        46, 97, 113, 121
    see also Foundational schemas;
        Free Individual model; Moving
        on model
    roads, 36, 104–105, 118, 127, 129,
        135, 136, 138–144

Samoa, Samoans, 124, 132, 133,
        162, 185n4
    George's ancestry, 100,
        102, 103
    and hypergamy, 7–8
selfscape dreams, 95–97
shoes, 10, 51–54, 74
shopping, 71–76, 110–111, 130
Shore, Bradd, 46, 181n7
Spiro, Melford E., 12, 158
States, Bert O., 4, 7, 23, 94–95
Strauss, Claudia, 3, 8, 181n1
Supermasculinity model, 31, 79–82
    associated schemas, 60–61
    in Car dreams, 128, 144–147
    and Car self-model, 34–35
    failure of, 84–89
    and listening, 118
    and Pinup model, 76–77
    and protection, 54
    and rescuing, 152–153
    in stories, 184n10
    versions, 31, 48–49

see also Bad Boy Masculinity
        model; Dualistic Gender
        metamodel; major models
Supportive Dad model, 26–28, 32,
        44–46, 97, 112–114, 116
    see also major models; Risk-
        taking schema; transitional
        space

Tannen, Deborah, 134, 148
Television shows (TV), 85, 87,
        99–100, 110–111, 120, 166
    Arrested Development,
        99–100, 103
    Father Knows Best, 47
    Leave it to Beaver, 47–55
    Pepe LePue, 37
    Smallville, 31
    Superman, 31, 77
    Viva la Bam, 29, 47–55
therapy, 63, 91, 167–168
thriller (cliffhanger), 40, 43–44,
        77, 138–139, 142, 145
transference, 12, 79, 119
transformation (self), 70, 72
    see also Transiting schema
Transiting schema, 16, 70, 127,
        137, 139, 144
    see also Car self-model;
        Foundational schemas;
        Moving on model; Traveling
        Self metamodel
transitional space (realm), 3–4, 28,
        44, 46, 97, 108, 181n6
    and play, 113, 116
    and Supportive Dad model, 121
    and U.S. adulthood,
        139, 144
    see also Risk-taking schema;
        Winnicott, D. W.
Traveling Self metamodel, 36,
        104–107, 114–120
    and Car self-model, 33–34, 70,
        77–78, 126–160

see also Free Individual model;
Moving on model
trouble-sharing, 54

Van de Castle, Robert, 124, 184n2,
185n2, 186n6
see also Content Analysis; Hall,
Calvin
Voyeuristic Sexuality, 75–76, 85–89
see also major models; Pinup
Sexuality model

Vygotsky, L. S., 23–24, 168

weddings, 109–114, 121, 163
Whiting, Beatrice, 27–28
Winnicott, D. W., 3, 133,
181n6
see also transitional space
witch, 40–43, 184n12
see also boundaries, confused
(eroded); Klein, Melanie;
mother-child over-involvement